J. S. Campion

On the Frontier

Reminiscences of Wild Sports, Personal Adventures and Strange Scenes

J. S. Campion

On the Frontier

Reminiscences of Wild Sports, Personal Adventures and Strange Scenes

ISBN/EAN: 9783337146092

Printed in Europe, USA, Canada, Australia, Japan

Cover: Foto ©Andreas Hilbeck / pixelio.de

More available books at **www.hansebooks.com**

ON THE FRONTIER.

REMINISCENCES OF WILD SPORTS, PERSONAL ADVENTURE, AND STRANGE SCENES.

By J. S. CAMPION,

LATE MAJOR, STAFF, FIRST BR. C.N.G. (U.S.A.)

WITH EIGHT ILLUSTRATIONS.

SECOND EDITION.

LONDON:
CHAPMAN AND HALL, 193, PICCADILLY.
1878.

[*All rights reserved.*]

TO THE AUTHOR'S FIRST, OLDEST, AND BEST FRIEND,

HIS FATHER,

This Work is Inscribed,

IN TESTIMONY OF RESPECT, ESTEEM, AND AFFECTION.

PREFACE.

IF the following pages prove but a tithe part as interesting to the reading public as did the experience from which is drawn the matter of them to the Author, he will feel not only amply repaid for venturing himself in print, but glad that he has done so.

That while writing these reminiscences he has not wandered into fiction, nor been guilty of exaggeration, can be honestly averred; and if he has erred by a too free use of Westernisms and local expressions, it has been from the wish to give a dash of true tone and colour to the pictures he has aimed to place before the mental vision of the reader.

Nor are the illustrations fancy work. They are by the hand of a conscientious, observing artist—the " comrade and companion staunch and true " mentioned in this book; who, for his pleasure and as *souvenirs*, made sketches as he went—and are reproductions of the few drawings that, out of some hundreds, escaped the vicissitudes of frontier life.

Trusting his work may prove a source of pleasure to many, and of offence to none, the Author places it before an indulgent public in hopeful confidence.

CONTENTS.

	PAGE
PREFACE	vii

CHAPTER I.

Opinion *versus* Experience—Seeking Advice—"Jack"—Our Outfit—The Stove—Captain John Connor—His Views regarding Wives—The Start—The Grand Prairie—Coffee and how to make it—Camping out 1

CHAPTER II.

An unwelcome Visitor and a warm Reception—St. Mary's Mission—A genial old Soul—Chicken White Soup—The Big Blue—We seek Advice again—Very contradictory—A System of Rejections—The last Settlement 11

CHAPTER III.

The Republican river—Valley Bluffs and their Formation—"Buffaloes at Last!"—Our nightly Concert—Buffalo Wolves—Camp Gibraltar—Getting in Hay—Disappointed—Whisky-poker—A mysterious Noise—The Herd—Danger—A Fire—Safe 19

CHAPTER IV.

Tightening Girths—The upland Plain—"The Cattle upon a thousand Hills"—Stalking—A Rogue Bull—The Chase—Missed—The Boys pot a Buffalo—A Post-mortem—Antelope—Beaver . . . 29

CHAPTER V.

Lost—Where is the Camp?—We tighten our Waistbelts—Wet, cold, hungry, and forlorn—A Cropper—Which River?—A Light—The Recall—Safe—Jerking Meat 38

CONTENTS.

CHAPTER VI.

Skinning a Buffalo—A Panorama of Life and Motion—Another Rogue Bull—An Escape—A good Shot—Trying to turn him over—The Virtues of a Pipe—"Catch him by the Hind-leg and throw him over"—How to get at the Tongue 47

CHAPTER VII.

A solitary Elk—A careless Sentinel—Preparations for Departure—A phantom Horseman—A striking Picture—A narrow Escape—A Consultation—Our Chances—A new Sensation—Precautions—The Vedettes—Safe at Fort Riley 56

CHAPTER VIII.

We make a Sensation—Indian Hostilities—A kind Offer—Our new Camp Ground—Our Visitors—Frontiersmen and Frontiersmen—An Attempt to give Advice—My Rebuff—A good Laugh—What would be said 66

CHAPTER IX.

The Pottowattomic Country—An Indian Camp—Old Acquaintances—Captain Connor's Adventures—His Speech—The Surprise Party—The Design—Night Attacks—Captain Connor's Success—The Festivities—"Let it alone" . . . , . . . 77

CHAPTER X.

Quarter-racing—Old Double S.—The Wager—The Colt—The Race—Denver City—The Murder 91

CHAPTER XI.

More Denver—The Indian Scare—Preparations—My Camp—The Effects of Fear—Panama—The Railroad Journey to Colon—A Fright—The Sensitive Plant—A Pointer 99

CHAPTER XII.

The Bar-room—My Bargain—A Momentous Question—Tragic Fate of the Bar-keeper—Indian Massacres—"A high-toned Sport"—J. P.'s Visit—The Sale of "Grouse"—J. P. goes under . . . 109

CHAPTER XIII.

"The best Dog in the World"—Nip and Tug—Joe and Laughfy—Their Peculiarities—The Outfit—Traps—Description of Wet-mountain Valley—Sangre de Cristo Pass—The Mósca Pass . . . 117

CONTENTS. xi

CHAPTER XIV.

The Scenery—Our Winter Quarters—A Lean-to—The Country—White Tails—Black Tails—Spruce Deer—Ashlata, or Bighorn—Antelopes—Bears—Wolves—Foxes—Pumas—Lynx and other Game—The Snow-storm—An empty Larder 127

CHAPTER XV.

A Drove of Turkeys—A fat Buck—Coming to grief—Cold Work—The Turkeys again—Skyed—The flowing Bowl—The big Buck "gone for"—Our Bill of Fare complete—How it all happened—Our Christmas Dinner 136

CHAPTER XVI.

The Beaver—Trappers and Ex-trappers—Captain John Connor—Beaver-houses: their Construction and Position—Breeding in-and-in—Food—Aquatic Romps—Attempt to "outsmart" a Beaver—Beaver-dams: how built—Traps—Beaver Medicine: its Manipulation—The "Setting Ground"—Beaver Trapping—How he is Caught—Disappointment—The Pursuit of the Beaver as a Sport—Frost . 147

CHAPTER XVII.

A white World—The Animals gone—A Gale—Snowed-up—A Chance of Starvation—Disagreeable Alternatives—The Party determines to divide—A Substitute for Starvation—Adieu—Nip and Tug "strike a Lead"—Wild Cat as Food—A Fairy Godmother—Go after her with a Rifle—Joe on the Watch—Death of the Doe—The missing Stock come into View 166

CHAPTER XVIII.

Gray Mountain Wolves—The Traps again—Caught—A Trap missing—On a Wolf-trail—Sagacious rather !—A Jump for Life—Fagged-out—An unearthly Scene—A Night's Rest—Nip and Tug take the Track—The Wolf before us—The Fight—A Pause—Death of the Wolf—Joe and the Ashlata—A happy Return 177

CHAPTER XIX.

The Start—Unsatisfactory Travelling—The Camping Ground—A wakeful Night—Fagged-out and Short Commons—The Mósca Pass in Sight—An Ocean of Air—The Gap—Danger—A cold Camp—The Fuel lost 195

CHAPTER XX.

A Table-land—A dreary View—Breaking the Way—The San Luis Valley — Rio Grande-del-Norté —*Facilis descensus Averno*—"Away down Souf"—The Third Night—The Weak Point—A Stone Rabbit—A Rest—Mexican Hospitality—The Zazal's Music—Arrival at the Fort—Captain B.—A Road Party—Return to Camp 203

CHAPTER XXI.

The Utés—A Deer Hunt—Nip and the Indian—Peace—"My Name is Norval"—A Visit from Uté Warriors—A Pow-wow—A Surprise—Diplomacy—"All do some Swap"—The Indians take their Departure 216

CHAPTER XXII.

A Return Visit—Indian Dogs—Uté Coquettes—Their " Get-up "—The Children—Indian Bucks—Trading—Glimpses of Indian Social Life—Married Women 224

CHAPTER XXIII.

Game Drives—Old Silver Medal—A Uté Diana—Turkey-roosting—A strange Scene by Moonlight—A bold Puma—A Robbery . . 232

CHAPTER XXIV.

A Desert View—Salt Grass— The Caves—A Desert Valley—An improbable Tradition—Soda Lake—A medicinal Spring—Beelzebubs—Snipe 239

CHAPTER XXV.

The Pinch of the Journey—Marl Springs—The Pied Quail—Rock Springs—Silver Mine—Pah-Uté Hill—The Great Moss Lode—The Colorado—An extensive View—A Mountaineer's Opinion . 249

CHAPTER XXVI.

The Colorado Bottoms—Coal—Climate—Gum—The Mojave Indians—A thoroughbred Look—Their Diet—Mojave Costumes—" Fixed to Kill "—Chá-cha—Divinity of the Human Form . . . 259

CONTENTS. xiii

CHAPTER XXVII.

A Fight—Irrataba—A Case of Possession—The Body Guard—The Harvest Full-Moon Dance—Mescal—Wild Orgies 269

CHAPTER XXVIII.

Acapulco — The Bay — The Women — The Fandango — Beauty and Ugliness—La Maripósa—Lozada—My little Speech—The Appointment—Good Advice—How I keep the Assignation—Throwing Light on a Dark Scene—The Confessor 281

CHAPTER XXIX.

Mojave M.D.'s—Three Mistakes—Polyandry—A Westernised Yankee— The Tin Pot—" A Gentleman and a Scholard" . . 293

CHAPTER XXX.

Indian Campaigning—Apache-Yumayas—The General gives his Views —" Eminently practical but desperately dangerous "—We make a Start—Tunás—The Lava Beds—The Programme—Indian Trick . 300

CHAPTER XXXI.

Face to Face—Pah-Squal—A joint Breakfast—Wood-rats—On the *Qui vive*—An Ancient—The Terms—An unwelcome Invitation— Winchester's Improved Henry's—A good Shot—A Chat with Pah-Squal 311

CHAPTER XXXII.

The three Ranchéros—The two W.'s—Our Arrangements—A military Picnic—Preparations to receive the Apaches—The Indians arrive —A War Party—X.'s Speech—Pah-Squal's Reply—A Feast . . 322

CHAPTER XXXIII.

A Council—The big White War Chief—A Challenge—Muncho Bravo, muncho Sabó—Departure—Precautions—The three Chiefs—An Indian Wag 331

CHAPTER XXXIV.

The Lone Oak—A Surprise—We open the Ball—A Panic—The Chase —A dead Chieftain—The Spoils of War—A sad Tale—A big Fire— Al fresco Toilette—We excite Attention 340

CONTENTS.

CHAPTER XXXV.

Apachedom—Is Truth stranger than Fiction ?—What Trappers say of the Apaches—What the Philanthropists—Apache Notions of Generosity—The mental Differences between Races—Impossibility of Civilising the Apaches—Their consequent natural Extinction—The Mexican of To-day 351

CHAPTER XXXVI.

Caution of the Apaches—Their Bands—The Rancho—A Government Contract—An Attack—The Storm—A Solitary Apache—The Stampede—A fruitless Chase 358

CHAPTER XXXVII.

Pi-Nolé turns his Toes up—A sad Scene—A Privilege of Chiefship—Indian Impulses—" Hold, enough !"—The End 368

LIST OF ILLUSTRATIONS.

		PAGE
1.	PORTRAIT OF THE AUTHOR .	*Frontispiece*
2.	SITE OF CAMP GIBRALTAR ON THE REPUBLICAN RIVER, GRAND PRAIRIE	24
3.	ROAD STATION IN WET-MOUNTAIN VALLEY, AND THE SIERRA VÉRDE	124
4.	FORT GARLAND, IN THE ROCKY MOUNTAINS, AND THE DIVIDE BETWEEN THE SAN LUIS AND WET-MOUNTAIN VALLEYS	214
5.	SODA LAKE (IN THE WET SEASON)	214
6.	BLACK CANON IN THE LAVA BEDS	306
7.	PORTRAIT OF PAH-SQUAL, WAR CHIEF OF THE APACHE-YUMAYAS	336
8.	DISTRICT HEAD-QUARTERS, ARIZONA	360

ON THE FRONTIER.

CHAPTER I.

Opinion *v.* Experience—Seeking Advice—"Jack"—Our Outfit—The Stove—Captain John Connor—His views regarding Wives—The Start—The Grand Prairie—Coffee and how to make it—Camping out.

WHEN quite a small boy, I was for a short period much in company with Mr. George Catlin, the American traveller, then on a short visit to my father. I listened with delighted attention to his anecdotes of Western life, and spent hours poring over his folio of drawings; amongst these, certain sketches of buffalo hunts (the finished paintings from which, by the way, now hang in the Ethnological Room at the Luxembourg) most strongly impressed my imagination. It seemed to the ardent young mind of a born sportsman, that to become a buffalo hunter was a wild and glorious, if most unattainable ambition. Catlin and buffaloes were, however, soon supplanted in my childhood's reveries by other youthful vagaries, and for many years I thought neither of him nor them.

There is an Arabic saying: "All things happen to him who waits." In my case, in this instance, the proverb fulfilled itself, for the course of events brought about that the day came when both the time and the occasion served; then the old glamour came back, the temptation was irresistible, and conjointly with one who has been the comrade and companion staunch and true of many a wild adventure, it was determined to organise a hunting party forthwith. We would turn our backs to the Missouri river and civilisation, and try the practically unknown to us pleasures and dangers of "The Plains." Nor in the matter were we diffident of ourselves. Had we not shot, fished, and hunted, ridden races, broken dogs, read all authorities on sporting matters? Had not England, France, and Albania furnished us with sporting fields? —Canada, too, and the Far West, to the Missouri river, been our familiar hunting grounds? Did we not consider ourselves most knowing hands at chase and venery— *chasseurs consommés*—the last modern improvements on old Nimrod. Ah! when then I called him "*only* a hunting *savage*," I indeed proved myself to be but a "silk-velvet sportsman."

Since that earlier time I have become familiar with savages and savage wiles, with Nimrod's modern representative, perhaps direct descendant—the Red Indian. He has taught me due respect for his grand old prototype, "the mighty hunter."

Having had no prairie experience beyond "chicken" shooting, we sought advice from all and sundry claiming to be "posted." Some said: "Do not go. In the present state of the frontier you will be killed;" others: "What is the use of your going? your trip will never pay," and so on. But the majority of our advisers, chiefly young fellows, who, as we subsequently discovered, had been no farther West than we, were quite enthusiastic. Might they join us? In fact, at one time, there seemed a probability the projected expedition would more resemble an invading column than be the small hunting party intended. But when preparations had to be commenced in earnest, when the time for departure drew near, great was the falling off.

The number that really did start was but five: ourselves; our two "hired men," both regular backwoodsmen, "clear grit" and "lively" with axe and rifle, but decidedly babes *out of* the wood, having never been on the prairies before; and lastly, but not least in importance, Jack A. Now Jack was a clever, well-educated ne'er-do-weel, who had run away from his good home in the East. He longed for the adventure of the trip, but having no money, knew not how he could equip himself; so, on the strength of having once, when driven by necessity, served as a cook for saw-mill hands, he offered himself for the post of what he inelegantly called, "chief cook and bottle-washer to the outfit," undertaking to discharge the high and important duties of that exalted position gratuitously and admirably if we would only take him along with us.

The "outfit" consisted of a light concord waggon, having a tilt or cover, four good Missouri mules, two Delaware ponies—both trained buffalo runners, and splendid fellows. We might have been—we were—green enough, but we mounted ourselves well; a small tent, a good watch-dog and a portable stove. Oh that stove! It was one of those camp miracles that are *so* nice. It smoked the tent; it smoked everything. It burned the bread. It scorched the meat. It let the coffee-pot drop through into the coals. It was the first—if I remain sane, it is the last—camp-stove I will ever travel in company with. And we had a large camp-kettle to render down buffalo tallow, and two barrels, well stuffed with necessaries, but to be emptied and filled with buffalo tongues, pickled.

We were made much sport of on the strength of those barrels for tongues. It was pleasantly suggested the Indians would pickle *us* in them; that they would make excellent coffins; that their staves would not stave off starvation, when, having lost our way, our mules, our horses, we should be in danger of death from hunger. Thus did our festive friends give us words of advice and encouragement.

We could have got sound counsel from our friend and neighbour, Captain John Connor, the head chief of the Delaware Indians, but he had been gone some time with a little band of braves on his annual hunt; and to have awaited his return would have detained us past the buffalo season.

Old Connor was a very good friend to me, and as he was unquestionably the first hunter, trapper, and mountaineer of his day, the best civilised Indian I have ever seen, and a reliable and upright man, I will sketch his history before going further, for such specimens are scarce.

Captain John Connor was born in Texas; the Delaware band to which his parents belonged being then there. Of course his father's name was not Connor, for the Captain was thoroughbred. What his father's name was I do not know. Likely enough it was "Whistling Rattlesnake," "Howling Washpot," or some other such poetic (?) and descriptive Indian appellation. But, when John was a very little savage, his father being converted to Methodism, Johnnie was sent to the nearest missionary day-school, and received, literally in his case, his christian name; to wit, John Connor. There he obtained the foundation of a good education, and in his leisure hours acquired the savage accomplishments of his relatives. Young hopeful showing talent and aptitude in his studies, the idea of his being qualified to become a preacher was entertained with such "acceptance" that he was sent to a leading Methodist seminary to complete his studies. There he remained some years, but when he approached manhood, "the devil having strengthened himself in him," his Indian blood showed itself, and he left college by invitation. The Seminole war being then going on, our ex-missionary-apparent collected around him some braves, went to Florida, and offered his and their services to the United States Government against the Seminoles. In that war Connor so distinguished himself, as to receive a commission, and with the quick imitativeness of his race, soon acquired the manners and tone of an officer and a gentleman. When, some years after, the Texan War of Independence broke out, Captain Connor raised a considerable body of Delawares, Lepans, and renegade Comanches; and, as commander of what was known as the Indian Contingent, rendered such service that at the successful termination of the war he was publicly thanked by the President of the then Republic of Texas, and presented with a considerable grant of land on the Red river.

On the death of the head chief of the Delawares, Captain Connor was elected to the vacant office, and with the entire tribe removed to "The Delaware Reserve," a tract of land set apart for their use for ever by the Government, and where, when I knew him, he was living.

The Captain resided in a good house on his own farm, a very fine one, which was worked for him on shares by a smart Yankee, who was married to one of his nieces. Old "Uncle John" had numerous nieces, and it was a standing joke to get the old chief over a glass of grog and tangle him up trying to explain how it was he had so many of them.

Besides his farm, "Uncle John" enjoyed an annuity from government, had plenty of horses and cattle on the neighbouring prairie, and, better than all, the respect and obedience of his tribe, over whom he reigned like a king; neither writ ran, nor sheriff had jurisdiction, in *his* reserve; Delaware law and a Delaware executive were supreme.

In practice, the old chief was a monogamist, having only one wife, though four is the tribal allowance. He considered that being a professed Methodist it would not be quite the correct thing to be married to more than one woman. But he often wondered why the whites, who were so smart about everything, should "have made such a great social mistake as to set their faces against polygamy." He considered the advantages of having a plurality of wives were most manifest, arguing thus: "If a man's one wife is quarrelsome, contradictious, or aggravating—my experience is, some women are so—why, she quarrels with, contradicts, and aggravates her husband—there is no one else for it; while, if he has two or more wives, they can have it out each with the other, to their mutual satisfaction and content, and leave him in peace and comfort. Besides, where there is more wives than one, there always is more or less jealousy, which works very well. Each wife wants to be the favourite, get the best dresses, and so on ; and of course to do so has to make herself agreeable, so that there is a contest of amiability always going on, to the great gain in comfort to all parties." But *this* was a subject he never entered upon in the presence of Mrs. Connor.

This Indian chief, though getting into years, was still a fine specimen of a man. Over six feet high, broad shouldered, deep chested, and straight as an arrow, but getting very corpulent, weighing something near eighteen stone. Every inch an Indian when his blood was up, he ordinarily displayed a dignified mien and quiet manners, affected the dress of a middle-aged swell, was very particular about his linen, his thin French kid boots, his gloves, his hat; wore his hair, then beginning to be streaked with white, cut close to his head, *en militaire*, and sported a small black moustache.

As I said before, advice, unfortunately, could not be got from Captain Connor, so we determined to "run our luck" and "play our own hand."

From our starting-point a waggon trail led to Fort Riley, a little more than one hundred miles off; thence, two to five days' travel farther west, would probably bring us where buffaloes were to be found. Our route to Fort Riley lay through the land of the Pottowattomies, a partly-civilised tribe, and then across a portion of the country claimed by the Pawnees. These latter were "wild," and, though "treaty Indians," had a well-deserved reputation of being the most expert horse-thieves of the Plains. Then after leaving Riley we should be in a region roamed over by bands of Sioux, Cheyennes, and Kiowas—Indians nominally at peace with the whites, but known to be disaffected; three tribes of evil repute, and no respecters of treaties when fortune gives them a temporary advantage. As I sit here writing, and look back calmly and dispassionately to that trip, with my since-acquired knowledge on the subject, and therefore able to form a correct estimate of the dangers we then ran, it seems to me impossible we could ever have been such hare-brained enthusiasts as to have started out, five young and inexperienced men, into what was then an unsettled wilderness, infested with wandering bands of remorseless savages; and still more impossible that we should have returned therefrom unharmed and unmolested.

Though a long time ago, I vividly recollect our start. It was on a lovely August day, the sky was without a cloud, blue, clear, and brilliant as a sapphire.

Around us was a rolling prairie, with an horizon like the ocean's, and a balmy, invigorating, almost intoxicating air blew over it into our faces, coming untainted and unpoisoned by the breaths, smells, and smoke of cities, from the Rocky Mountains, seven hundred miles off. An undulating, ever-moving sea of waving grass and flowers, the ground seemed a mosaic of many hues, a boundless expanse of brilliant green, spangled with the myriad fragments of shattered rainbows. And in the distance, long dark winding lines and clumps indicated the course of one of the numerous streams that water the eastern edge of the Grand Prairie, the one on whose bank we were to pass our first night out.

As day after day the apparently unattainable roll of ground whose edge met the sky in front of us seemed still to keep its distance, a new-born appreciation of what was meant by space seemed to reveal itself to us. Nature's immensity became a tangible fact.

The regular routine was to turn out of our blankets at the first streak of dawn, the last on watch having lit the fire in "that awful stove," set the kettle on, and aroused all hands.

Coffee, hot, strong, and plenty, was, as always on the Plains, the main feature of our breakfast. And here let me give, for the benefit of all whom it may concern, my views on coffee-making. The berry should be *lightly* roasted, as near the time of using as possible, and ground very coarse, say to about the size of half a grain of rice, which is quite small enough to enable boiling water to extract everything except the tannin and woody flavour. And who wants to subject the coats of his stomach to a hot solution of tan, or to imbibe wood broth? When the water boils, throw the crushed berries into it, let all boil for a few seconds, pour a little cold water into it *from a height*, and your coffee is made. It will be settled, clear and bright as a cut cairngorm, and have a flavour and aroma unattainable by any other process.

Breakfast despatched, mules were caught, unhobbled, and

harnessed; horses saddled, bridled, and tied behind the waggon; pipes lit, and away we went, each happy as the proverbial sand-boy.

After going ten to fifteen miles—as the case might be—our noon halts were made, when possible, where the three camp requisites, wood, water, and grass, were to be had; dinner cooked, and the animals grazed, watered, and rested for four hours; then we drove to our halting-place for the night, hobbled, and turned out the mules, and gave the horses a small feed of grain—we were not able to carry enough corn to give large ones, but as they had many a hard gallop before them, some was necessary; supped, chatted, smoked, and rolling ourselves in our blankets, slept soundly in our *big room*. The tent was only for wet weather—of which we had none while *en route*—and for permanent camps.

A night guard was regularly mounted, each one taking by rotation a two hours' watch; the chief amusement while standing guard being star-gazing, with the very useful result that ere long any of us knew by them the time to a quarter of an hour at any period of the night.

We were a well "healed" party, the armament being two good double-barrels, five rifles—twelve balls to the pound gauge every one of them, not toys—and to each man a brace of six-shooters, a bowie and a tomahawk.

Any of us was ready to shoot "against creation" and to "all eternity" for a dollar a shot.

We were full of health, strength, and confidence, and voted civilised life to be a nuisance and a bore.

CHAPTER II.

An unwelcome Visitor and a warm Reception—St. Mary's Mission—A Genial old Soul—Chicken white Soup—The Big Blue—We seek Advice again—Very contradictory—A System of Rejections—The last Settlement.

OUR first adventure befell us but a few days after starting; and almost immediately upon entering the country of the Pottowattomies.

We had arrived at our camp-ground unusually late; the sun was already down, the moon not risen, and it was quite a dark night. Supper was being prepared, and the blaze, from what our *chef de cuisine* coarsely but forcibly designated as "that portable h——" made the surrounding darkness appear almost solid, and brought into ruddy relief Jack's flannel shirted, buckskin-breeched figure, as he stooped over the portable aforesaid to bake what he called a "pome"—that is to say, he had achieved a lump of dough, grease, and sceleratus, half as thick as a brick, twice as large, and about as digestible, which aid to suicide he was placing, by means of a shovel extemporised out of the top of a candle-box, into a large bed of red-hot wood-coals—when, to our amazement, suddenly, and with a fearful yell, there dashed out of the darkness into the circle of light a horrid and fantastic figure—a Pottowattomie brave. He seemed all paint, feathers, and loose ends; and, as he drew up, almost threw on his haunches the fine gray horse that bore him. There stood the gallant steed, his nostrils dilating, his eyes flashing, his whole frame quivering, his tail tucked, and his long mane and gaudy trappings streaming out on the wind. The rider was drunk—very drunk. His drawn hunting-knife was in his hand, and, flourishing it over his head, he expressed aloud most unfavourable opinions of whites in general, and ourselves in particular, ending with an emphatic declaration of instant hostilities.

Instinctively our hands sought our revolvers; but Jack cried out: "Don't shoot, for goodness' sake! I'll settle him." And settle him he did. Down on the ground went the "pome;" into the bed of charcoal went the shovel; right into the Indian's face Jack let him have it. The hot ashes blinded the Pottowattomie's eyes, filled his open mouth, and started his greasy locks into a blaze. He dropped the reins to rub the coals and dust out of his eyes, and, his horse driven frantic by burns, dashed into the darkness; and that Indian's face we saw no more.

The day following the Pottowattomie's unceremonious visit we arrived at St. Mary's Mission, the oldest mission in the West. St. Mary's is an establishment of French Catholic ecclesiastics, and there is quite a settlement of converts and their descendants round it. We found before us the brightest, neatest, most charming little picture of the kind we had ever seen. The quaint chapel, the long, low schoolhouse, the priest's quarters, and Mission-Indians' huts, were all nicely whitewashed, and surrounded with little gardens of flowers and vegetables, through which a clear stream of water, abounding with cresses, and fringed with cotton-woods, willows, and butternuts, rippled and gurgled along—a little vision of Arcadia, set like a gem in the green expanse of the all-surrounding prairie. In the porch of one of the huts was an old Indian, decently clothed in homespun, his gray hair carefully combed, his face guileless of paint, and he sat there busy shucking pop-corn, presenting a remarkable contrast to the drunken savage we had so lately seen.

The holy fathers received us most kindly, and appeared to be quite glad to entertain strangers who could talk with them in their mother-tongue, and had lived long enough in their native country to converse intelligently with them about it. With evident pride they showed us over their entire establishment, and gave a most interesting history of the mission. They appeared well satisfied with its progress and prosperity, and seemed confident of its ultimate success in Christianising the entire Pottowattomie nation. Certainly their predecessors had achieved much. The chapel services had an attendance of nearly one hundred and fifty Indians, and their school of about twice as many.

One of the missionaries was a fat, jolly-looking, genial old soul, and he and I got quite friendly before night—so much so that I was tempted to say to him I had that day noticed a remarkable confirmation of the theory of the correlation of mind and matter. It had appeared to me among the younger children—those who had been born after their parents had been converted—that many looked appreciably different from wild Indian children. Their parents' minds had been doubtlessly imbued with the ideas and notions of the whites, French influences had been brought to bear on their intellects, and, lo and behold! some of the little ones were almost as fair as the holy fathers, and had quite a French cast of face. His reverence regarded me with an austere countenance. His mouth was very solemn, but there was an irrepressible twinkle in his eyes. He called me "*un malin*," and said that, having long since abandoned philosophy for theology, he could not throw any light on the question. We spent a day at St. Mary's most pleasantly. Though heretics, we were blessed at our departure, and contributed our little mite towards assisting "the children of Mary." We left the mission with our best wishes for its success, and with a feeling of hearty respect for the devoted men who were willing, in the discharge of duty, to spend their lives far away from La Belle France they loved so well, trying to make a set of lazy, lying, thieving, murdering, savages into good Christians and respectable citizens—no easy task, as experience well attests.

In due course we arrived at what was then a very small settlement close to Fort Riley, and near it for the first time pitched our tent, intending to remain there a day or two, in order to obtain such information as we could to guide our future movements, rest and recruit the animals, and renew our stock of provisions and grain.

Up to that time we had not seen any of the larger

kinds of game, except a few distant bands of antelopes; but grouse (prairie chickens), quails, hares, and rabbits had been numerous. The shot-guns had kept the mess well supplied with fresh meat, and given our *chef* a fair chance to show off his "saw-mill cookery." Jack did not neglect his opportunities, and when we were at St. Mary's covered himself with glory by his chicken white soup. The young grouse were then only just able to fly, and their flesh was white and tender as frog-meat. A dozen of them were skinned, dissected, and placed with their giblets in a pot, a lump of lard and some of the lean of a ham chopped very fine added, and the mixture judiciously seasoned; the pot was filled up with milk, procured from the missionaries, and set on to cook; the soup allowed to come just to the boil and skimmed, then simmered down to about half its original quantity, served steaming hot, and eaten with gusto.

Jack was no longer, in the words of his favourite song, "Chief-cook and bottle-washer," &c. &c. No; he was *artiste consommé—cordon bleu.*

The morning after encamping near Riley we enjoyed the luxury of a swim in the river on whose banks we had stopped—The Big Blue; and a beautiful little prairie river it is, about the size and depth of the Thames at Richmond, with water bright, clear, and sparkling, but which, when viewed *en masse*, is of a deep-blue colour, whence, I suppose, the river's name.

Breakfast over, we put on decent apparel, and sallied forth to make our inquiries—one going to the Fort, the other to the little settlement, and both meeting at dinner to compare notes. The intelligence and advice we severally received could not, by the wildest stretch of the imagination, be considered encouraging, excepting that, as it was quite contradictory, it might be all unreliable.

To give the service due precedence—firstly, the word from the Fort. I had there been told, should we strike north-west to the Republican fork of the Kaw river, we would find a few deer and some turkeys, and, if the buffalo were working that way, there would be plenty of them in a week or two, though none were then there, nor, did my informants think, any Indians; but such route was in the track of the Indian hunting-parties from the north, and, should one of them discover us, if we were a smaller party than thirty to forty, they might "gobble us up," for the peace was already broken. News had just come in that the Santa Fé train had been attacked on the Arkansas route, captured, and the teamsters scalped by, it was believed, a band of united Sioux and Cheyennes, who were moving towards the Salinas river; and for us to go in *that* direction would be simply to court destruction.

My comrade had seen the "storekeeper" of the settlement, and some men who were loafing at his bar. Their united statements amounted to this: It was no use going to the Republican to hunt buffaloes, or anything else; the Indians were too thick there, and had driven all the game to the Salinas river. That was the place to go to! The officers at the Fort were trying to get up a scare about an Indian war. It was all stuff; they did it to make themselves important; they—the speakers—were, any one of them, willing to go alone to the Salinas, and hunt there all the season. No danger of Indians pestering hunters.

But the best thing for us to do was to move our camp down into the "city." A party would soon be in from "down there," and *they* would be able to "post us up" on the subject; in the meantime, we could look around—maybe we might conclude to settle. "The city" was growing "fine," and town lots would never be so cheap again. How would we swop an "animile" or two against a "corner lot?"

When the different statements were compared, it became a rather difficult question what should be done. Clearly the most sensible, in fact the proper, thing was to go back. I thought so; I have no doubt that the others thought so; but none of us said so; nor, I am certain, would any of us have gone back of his own free will and accord. We tried a system of rejections. We would not move camp to the settlement; we did not want town lots in that swindling little bilk of a "city;" we did not believe in the existence of "the party" that was soon to arrive from "down there." The animus of landlord and loafers was *too* plain. Their bright idea was, evidently, "First catch your hare, then skin it." A few days spent amongst them, gossiping, drinking, and standing drinks at the bar; a horse trade or two; a bill run up at the store; and perhaps a few little games at "draw-poker" or "monté;" and then we might be killed by the Indians or not. *That* was our "circus," not theirs.

Should we wait where we were until we could get some reliable information? No; certainly not! How could we tell whether or not any information was reliable? Nobody was responsible for the consequences of what they told us;

and the less any one of our informants had known, the more positive he had been in his statements. We determined to have all our preparations finished by sunset of the next day, and the following daybreak should see our start for the Republican. If we found no signs of buffalo there, we would turn south-west and try the Salinas. We were in for it, and, Indians or no Indians, we would see it through. We were like the miner, who, as he started his shaft down, declared it was a case of "gold, China, or bust."

We had the feet of our mules attended to by the Government blacksmith, the shoes taken off our horses and replaced by "running plates;" a further supply laid in of bacon and flour, beans and coffee, sugar and salt, grain for our hunters, and whisky for ourselves; and, at the appointed time, bid adieu to the Big Blue and the last settlement.

CHAPTER III.

The Republican river—Valley Bluffs and their Formation—"Buffaloes at Last!"—Our nightly Concert—Buffalo Wolves—Camp Gibraltar—Getting in Hay—Disappointed—Whisky-poker—A mysterious Noise—The Herd—Danger—A Fire—Safe.

Two days' travel passed barren of adventure, and on the following one we made our first camp on the bank of the Republican.

We first struck the river about forty miles above where it joins the Kaw, and over four hundred below its sources, and, though at its lowest stage, found it to be a much more considerable stream than the one we had left. It was meandering a most winding course in the "bottom" down which it flowed, with a sharpish current of two and a half miles an hour. The central portion of every curve it made was fringed and clustered with strips and groups of cottonwood trees, fifty or sixty feet high, and averaging two feet six inches through at their butts, and with large willows, osiers, and wild plums. The bottom varied in width between its bluffs from a half mile to five miles, and looked as level as a billiard-table; but such was only a deceptive general appearance, it was in reality full of depressions known as "buffalo wallows," and seamed with deep narrow gullies, "wash-outs" of rain storms, and covered with a carpet of coarse "bottom grass," nearly waist-high in many places.

This bottom had bluffs varying in height from a few feet to a couple of hundred, and was of an ever varying width. Coincident with the river from its source to its mouth, it might have been called with propriety "The Valley of the Republican."

The formation of the ground seemed to be bottomless sand, and the banks of the river were always perpendicular at one side of it, and sloped gently on its other; the perpendicular wall and the slope regularly alternating from side to side with the change of direction of the river's course; the banks being perpendicular and timbered when salient, and where the river made a re-entering bend, sloping and grassy.

Where we were, the bottom had so many prairie-dog towns scattered over it as to make galloping quite dangerous; and the inhabitants of them, prairie-dogs, owls, rattlesnakes, and rabbits, seemed to be the original and only settlers in the country.

The succeeding day we journeyed up the valley, keeping the general course of the stream, but taking the chord of its numerous arcs. On the second day's travel along it, on coming to where the river swung round ahead of us in an unusually large bend—making an elbow, in fact—it was thought best to attempt a cut off, so we then left the river valley, ascending the bluff to the general level of the country.

FORMATION OF VALLEY BLUFFS.

The valley bluffs of all the prairie streams seem to have been the original banks of rivers once entirely occupying what is now valley, and doubtless then extending in depth to where the permanent formation of which the bluffs are composed now underlie both streams and valleys; and which, filling up gradually in the lapse of ages to their present level by deposit of the sand washed down and carried in suspension by the waters from the upper country, have become the bottoms through which the present streams —remnants of those mighty rivers—now wind their devious courses. To this, as to all theories, there is a stumbling-block; there *are* localities where the valleys of these rivers temporarily lose their continuity by there being a bluff on only one side of them; on the other, the rise to the general level of the country being so gradual as not to be perceptible to the eye. These expanses would therefore have been immense river back-waters; places where drift of all kinds would accumulate, and an aquatic vegetation flourish; possibly some of the coal-fields were once such.

An old and well-worn buffalo trail of about twenty feet in width, beaten hard by many a year's annual migration, gave us easy access up the face of the bluff to the level ground above; and, on attaining it, we took the course we judged would bring us to the valley again in ten or fifteen miles. Our direction and conjecture as to distance proved correct, and after about twelve miles' travelling we again arrived at the edge of the general level, but at a place where descent was impossible, the bluff being there perpendicular, and over two hundred feet in height.

The river was flowing below us, now hiding behind the

dark green clumps and clusters of the trees upon its banks, anon showing flashes of sparkling water. But where was the valley? The bluffs we had expected to see opposite to us were vanished. From the further edge of the river a grassy plain extended to the far horizon. We were looking west, and the sinking August sun, shining full in our faces, threw a gorgeous flood of colour to our very feet, tinging the grass with purple and gold, throwing a halo of glory round the tree-tops, and a blaze of crimson on the water.

But what were those few dark specks in the middle ground, the small masses farther off, that dark line on the horizon? Each man's hand was to his forehead shading his eyes as he took a close scrutiny. With one accord, and with a wild "hurrah!" every hat was flung into the air.

"Buffaloes at last! and heading straight to us."

But it was no time for fooling, for we had to be down off that bluff before dark, or stop there all night with no water to drink or cook supper with, which meant nothing to eat; so two horsemen started, one right and another left, to discover a practicable descent. An old buffalo pass was found a couple of miles off, and we reached the Republican river again without misadventure.

When darkness fell the regular concert we had nightly been enjoying for some time received a most important addition; new and distinguished performers were at hand. We had early become accustomed to the cheering nightly howls of the sportive coyoté; then to an obligato accompaniment thereto by the burrowing owls, who tooted with great impartiality in every hour of the night; latterly the fox with his sharp yap-yap, the wild cat with her Scotch bagpipes run mad, and the plaintive whip-poor-wills had joined in and done "their level best" to make night hideous. But these had only been the orchestra; the "chief musicianers" had at length arrived, and when the overture had been played, and the moon shone forth, the grand chorus broke on our startled ears.

The light cavalry, who hang in squadrons round the main army of the buffaloes, cutting off stragglers, devouring the defenceless and the weak, making a prey of the unwary, the gray-coated uhlans of the Plains—the buffalo-wolves—were upon us. Wolf answered to wolf, pack answered to pack. Pandemonium had been a quiet tea-party to it. Fortunately the din was soon over, and the remainder of the night was much quieter than any we had experienced since we started out. The cunning fox and sly coyoté knew well their masters had arrived, and kept most discreet silence. The midnight cat was scared. The nightingale of the plains tooted only at long intervals, and the whip-poor-will's low cry hardly disturbed the ear.

Morning brought excitement and bustle. Our intended quarry were still far away, but permanent camp and all necessary preparations for action had to be made. The first thing to do was to choose a site, and of course the idea of taking a good defensive position presented itself. It was an absurd idea. What could five men avail against a band of Indians? Still, one of us was a soldier by profession. We were in an enemy's country, a strategic position was *de rigueur*.

We found an excellent place for our purpose. A more than usually sharp curve of the river washed close round a triangular point of land, whose precipitous banks were forty feet high, and which was covered with heavy timber and thick brushwood. The trees would render the smoke of our fire invisible at a distance, as it would be dissipated in going through the thick overhanging boughs. The thickets would mask our tent. The steep banks would make two sides of our position inaccessible. The base of the triangle, the edge of the timber, would be only a hundred yards wide from edge to edge of the river's bank, and in front of it the level grass land reached out to the valley's bluff, a mile off, without a bush to cover an advance. The situation seemed made to order.

A place opposite the middle of our position, and advanced in the open some twenty yards beyond the edge of the timber, was pitched upon for an outpost. There our solitary night-watch was to keep his guard. It is well understood that, when watching against Indian surprise, a sentinel never walks, never stands; if he did either, his wily foe might snake up to him in the grass, and the well-directed silent arrow would place a sleeping camp at the mercy of its assailants. No. The guard who understands his business lies on the ground on his chest, his elbows far apart, his wrists brought together, his chin supported on his hands, his ears open, and his eyes everywhere; that is to say, he keeps as much in such attitude as he can, for of course he cannot maintain it for two hours without change. This is the best position to "sky" any object approaching a night-guard, and should anything be moving near him in the grass, its waving tops would give him indication and warning. Besides, with the ear near the

ground, sounds can be distinctly heard that, standing up, would be inaudible.

A few large stones, a sage-brush or two, placed so as to look as natural as possible, a hole in the ground, made a fair rifle-pit.

The highest tree in the grove was utilised as a look-out station, sufficient foot and hand holes were soon made in the trunk to enable a climber to reach its branches. From these the top of the tree was easily accessible, and the lopping off of a few boughs permitted the eye to have a clear view to the horizon. No more could be done. The festive tin cup was passed round. "Camp Gibraltar" received its christening.

After dinner all hands turned out with sharpened hunting knives, to work till night cutting and stacking the long grass: thenceforth the animals were to be securely tied up every night in the thicket, and would require to have hay.

An observation, taken at sunset from our look-out, revealed the fact that the buffaloes were drawing nearer, and we lay down for the night in a fever of expectation. Sleep, except in broken snatches, was an impossibility. The peep of dawn found a watcher in the tree, but disappointment was his lot. The main herd seemed to have moved diagonally to our left, and to be really no nearer than when last seen, and so we had to employ and amuse ourselves, and wile away the time as well as we could. More grass was cut, wood was chopped, collected, and piled up for future use. Arms were examined and cleaned. Cards brought out; seven-up, mountain-jack, and euchre had each their turn, and whisky-poker, a harmless, non-gambling game, in which the winner gets a drink and the losers a smell at the cork of the bottle, was tried.

Fifty times in the day some one or other climbed the look-out tree. Gradually it became certain that the main herd of buffaloes was approaching us. The outside fringes of bulls were becoming more and more defined, the dark patches behind them were resolving themselves into distinct groups, the dusky streak on the horizon was widening and widening, spreading and spreading, it was covering the ground by square miles. The excitement became intense, but night again fell, and the buffaloes were still far off.

About ten o'clock, camp was aroused by the watchman. He had heard a sound which he could not make out. We all listened with breathless attention. The light western breeze brought at intervals a low distant murmur, like that from a far-off sea. What could it be? Anon it became more and more distinct, then died away, then came louder than before. Ere long it sounded like the roll of distant thunder, the hum of a busy city, the surf breaking over sunken reefs.

Was it the roar of a prairie fire? No. There was no glow in the sky, and the grass was too green to burn. Was it the rush of waters, had there been a storm to westward, was a flood coming down the river? The idea took away our breath. We were camped on sand, and a big head of water would ground-sluice our foundations from beneath us. Could the sound be made by the distant herd? The wind was coming directly from them.

It was the noise of the herd. They *were* coming. By-and-by, however, we ceased to hear them. The day-wind, which had been dying out, no longer blew. The night-breeze had set in from the opposite direction, and its sigh through the tree-tops, the hoot of the owl, and the ripple of the stream were the only audible sounds—and soon all were fast asleep again. I have reason to believe the guard slept, worn out with excitement and expectancy.

Suddenly everyone jumped to his feet. A terrific row smote upon our ears. The air shivered with noise; the earth trembled under our feet. The main herd was crossing the river close to camp. The roar of the bulls, the lowing of the cows, the tramp of thousands of feet, the splash of water as the huge mass of animals plunged and struggled through it, the crumbling fall of the bank as the buffaloes forced their way up its steep face—all were blended in one mighty tumult.

We stood spell-bound for an instant, then a thought of terror forced itself upon us. What if the herd should come our way? What if they should stampede over the camp? Nothing could save us. We should be crushed into the earth, ground into powder. There would not be a "grease spot left of us." We might climb a tree, true; but we should be left without transport, without food, without ammunition, out in the wilderness on foot. Better to be killed at once. There was but one safeguard—fire!

True it would be a beacon to any Indians who might be near, but that was only a possible, a contingent danger, while an immediate one stared us in the face. A pile of wood, grass, leaves, anything, everything, was raked together, the contents of the grease-pot poured over it, a double-handful of powder scattered on, a match applied, and a column of fire shot up towards the sky. We were in safety so long as our blaze lasted.

We stood watching and waiting, hour after hour, as that seemingly interminable multitude surged by, the ground trembling, and the din ceasing not. Since that night I have gone through many strange adventures, witnessed many striking scenes. The din of conflict, the terrors of an earthquake, the conflagration of a Western city. I have stood on the deck of a ship a-flame in mid-Atlantic. The murderous midnight rush of moccasined savages upon a surprised camp has found me *there*. I have been startled from deep sleep by the sharp firing of rifle balls, the quick zip-zip of flying arrows, the death-scream of a slaughtered sentinel, and the war-whoop of the Red Indian. But none of those scenes recall themselves more forcibly to me than does that midnight crossing of the Republican river by that mighty host of buffaloes in thousands.

CHAPTER IV.

Tightening Girths—The upland Plain—"The Cattle upon a thousand Hills"—Stalking—A Rogue Bull—The Chase—Missed—The Boys pot a Buffalo—A Post-mortem—Antelope—Beaver.

THE next day broke bright and clear—the long-looked for day when our first buffalo was to die. The time had come when salt bacon at the rate of twenty-one times a week was to be a thing of the past; the juicy steak, the tender hump, the appetising tongue, were at hand, waiting for us to go and get them. What were butchers' bills to us? Yet but for the hoof-prints in the sand, the last night's spectacle might have been a dream. The last straggling bull had disappeared. Doubtless the buffaloes were feeding on the short, sweet, grama grass growing on the upland.

The morning's bacon was eaten with contempt. Our "buffalo-runners" were saddled; our arms and accoutrements adjusted; and about nine o'clock we waived our hands to "the boys," and telling them to get hungry for buffalo steak, rode forth to slay.

A quiet walk across the valley to the foot of the bluff gave time and opportunity for a smoke, for the saddles to warm to the horses' backs, and for the horses to get in galloping order. Then a halt and dismount. Girths were tightened, loose ends made fast, rifles unslung, and waist-belts taken up a hole, for our game might be but just beyond the edge of the bluff.

Slowly and cautiously we "raised" the summit and gazed across the table-land.

What a sight was there! The rolling prairie looked as though it might have been a tumultuous sea of monstrous waves, suddenly transmuted into solid ground, and covered with a brilliant carpet of green grass. It was an interminable repetition of little undulating hills when viewed in detail. In its totality it was a vast upland plain. And there, spread all over it, were the buffaloes; the nearest, within a mile; the farthest—who could tell how far away! The whole country was alive with them. They were there in troops; in squadrons, in divisions, in armies!

The herds of the Lord! "The cattle upon a thousand hills!" We stood entranced. But we did not stand entranced long—"not much." There was more hunt than poetry about us that morning; so we noticed the wind, observed the lay of the ground, picked out a small herd to be "rushed"; got into the nearest hollow and dismounted.

With bridle in one hand and rifle in the other, we carefully advanced, and a very winding advance it was. To give any of the buffaloes our wind, was to ensure, not only *their* making off immediately, but all the neighbouring animals doing so too. To show ourselves suddenly when crossing any of the ridges was to produce a like result. We knew the great weight and strength of buffaloes would render the broken ground more favourable to them than it would be to our horses. We had never tried our steeds against such animals. We were most anxious to get as near to them as possible, so that when the chase began they would have but little start of us. Therefore, whenever the crossing of an eminence was unavoidable, one of us remained in the hollow holding the horses, and the other reconnoitred. As the scout approached a summit, he first crawled on his hands and knees, then, snaked along on his chest, and when he arrived there, peeped cautiously through some tuft of grass, to survey the route, note the position of the buffaloes in sight and lay out the further line of progress.

The buffaloes being continually on the move, we had to make many long detours, and a couple of hours were soon spent in stalking. At last, patience being exhausted, and the game being pronounced as near as we were likely to get to them unperceived, we made final preparations, and dashed over the intervening ridge.

To our disgust, something had alarmed the buffaloes, and all of them that had been near us were in rapid retreat. We reined in with expressions of chagrin. As we did so, a huge old bull came lumbering round a corner to our left, scarcely two hudred yards off. Evidently he was a "rogue": that is to say, a cantankerous old patriarch buffalo, who, for his sins, had been turned out of his herd by younger and more active rivals, and thereafter had to hang sulkily on its flanks, or in its rear. A rogue bull is tough as shoe-leather, vicious as tough, and only his tongue and a portion of his hump eatable. But that one insulted us; he stopped, pawed the ground, lashed his tail, and finally bellowed at us; there was no standing that. Giving our mustangs a taste of the steel, we dashed at him. Instead of standing his ground like the brave defiant monster he tried to look, he incontinently turned tail and fled; going with long powerful bounds, that plainly showed no sudden rush would directly close on him. A waiting race had to be made to win; so, getting our weight well forward, and taking a steady pull on the snaffle reins, we settled down into a long swinging canter.

A mile or two, perhaps more—we were not then taking much notice of time or distance—was soon ridden, though we had not increased our pace, for we were waiting for a stretch of level ground over which to do so. Suddenly the bull changed his course to the right; either he had caught a glimpse of some of the herd in that direction, and expected to find safety with numbers—something in his immediate front had alarmed him—or possibly, he had winded danger from his left; but to the right he turned his flight. My side that. First turn for me. Now for first blood! A fine chance for a cut off presents itself. The ground is tolerably good. I settle well down in the saddle for the contest, gather my nag together, and force the running.

Old bull instantly notices my change of pace, appreciates the disadvantage to him of my having the cut off; but, bull like, being determined to go the way he wanted, tears along on it at full tilt. It is a Derby finish. My gallant hunter closes rapidly on the buffalo; as I gain his off flank, the reins are gathered in my left hand, my right grasps my rifle just behind the guard, its barrel is thrown across my left arm, and, dashing past him, I deliver my fire. Simultaneously the bull whirls half round, pivoting on his hind legs; with tail in air, head lowered, and eyes glaring, he charges me, and I am only saved from overthrow by the trained agility of my buffalo-runner. A quick glance at the old rogue as he flashes past satisfies me he has been clean missed; but, as I pull myself and steed together, I hear the crack of my comrade's rifle, and the unmistakable thud of its ball as it strikes. But the bull is only wounded, and still presses onward at a rolling gallop, so losing no time to load, pistols are drawn, and we again close on him—one on each quarter. Excited by the novelty of the chase, the size of the game, and the pace we are going at, we empty our revolvers with more rapidity than judgment; and, though the bull's sides are streaked with gore, his mane flecked with bloody foam, his tongue hanging out, and his gait a staggering roll, he still pounds along. We pull up to load, but our horses are quite pumped out, and the pursuit is abandoned. The wolves will have a feast to-night. The gray-coated marauders will capture a prey.

We stripped the nags, hobbled them, rubbed them with wisps of grass, spread the saddle blankets in the sun to dry, lit the pipe of consolation, and sat down to rest. It was quite evident we had yet to learn *where* to hit a buffalo, and by practice acquire ability to strike him there. Certainly, had our horses not known more about buffalo hunting than we did, one of us would have come to grief in that day's chase.

Slowly we returned to camp. We were by no means a triumphant procession: we were more like a funeral one; but, alas! without the corpse. The intended corpse had escaped.

In due time we arrived at the brow of the bluff, and looked in the direction of our camp. On the plain, about half a mile from it, lay a dark object, round which some smaller ones were moving busily about. What did it mean? One of the specks was presently made out to be a horse, the two others, men, but the biggest one puzzled us. It was stationary, did not seem to have any shape; the men kept going from it to the horse and back again; by-and-by they started off, leading the horse; evidently it was carrying something, or one of them would be riding it. Was the object lying on the plain—could it be—a dead buffalo? Had we boasted and bragged, schemed and crawled, galloped our good horses to a stand-still, turned our bullets loose in vain, like lunatics? and were we to go back with a tale of sound and fury signifying nothing, to find, that while we had been "cavorting" around to no earthly purpose, the boys in camp had "potted" a buffalo, and supplied our larder with meat we had failed to get? But such we found had been the case. A small band had come to the river to drink, had been cleverly ambushed on their return by our artist in soup, one of them killed in his tracks by a well-directed bullet. Verily the laugh was against us! But there was attendant consolation : buffalo steaks for dinner, and marrow-bones! Marrow-bones with a little pepper and salt in them, a cloth tied over their ends to keep the marrow in, boiled in a pot—a large pot, and full! And there was also a fine chance to go in the pursuit of useful information, with a certainty of obtaining the desired knowledge. We started after the useful, &c., and on dissecting the subject, found it.

A single shot having killed the buffalo whose body lay in the valley, evidently one shot in the right place was sufficient to kill—but where was that spot? We sat down on the body and held a post-mortem. Verdict: Death by a gun-shot wound through the butt of the lights, causing stoppage of the beat of the heart by drowning it in blood. Not scientific, perhaps, but eminently satisfactory; because the lights of a buffalo are as big as your hat, and, being situated where there is least motion when its owner is galloping, they afford a comparatively easy target; while the only place in his head where a ball would stop him is so small, and from the shape of his skull, and its up and down motion when the animal is going, so difficult to hit, as to render a shot thereat as uncertain as one at his heart would be; which, lying low down, and far forward, is a most risky mark, especially as it does not give a section larger than the palm of the hand.

All which facts we discovered by that interesting post-mortem, as also the different angles at which the fatal shot could be made; and before many days the killing of two or three buffaloes to the "run" became a matter of course.

The main herd seemed to have settled to their feeding ground, and as we were careful only to disturb the small outlying bunches of cattle, we had a continuation of excellent sport, and yet did not drive the buffaloes off the range.

A small flock of antelope frequented the bottom, and some of them were killed by careful stalking and flagging. A chase after them on horseback was also attempted, and the fact revealed that they completely had the heels of us. A large and densely-wooded island was also discovered some ten miles up the river, and found to be the head-quarters of a numerous drove of turkeys, whose lives were conspired against on many a night, but which conspiracies all ended in smoke (tobacco). We had killed turkeys before, it was a long way to go, buffaloes were what we were after, so the turkeys remained unmolested.

There was one thing bothered us. During the daytime someone was always in camp, of course, and though he had his attention more or less constantly directed to the river, he never saw a fish rise, and yet the guard at night constantly heard the splash of fish rising, and large fish. It could be nothing else, the noise was unmistakable.

Now, we had never heard of fish of purely nocturnal habits. We knew there were such things as cat-fish—we had eaten them—but cat-fish do not rise to the fly; besides, "what's in a name?" A cat-fish is not obliged to hunt for its food at night because a cat does, any more than he is obliged to catch mice and drink milk. That clearly was not "how the cat jumped." So one bright night, near the full of the moon, a concealed spy was set to watch the river. He discovered the truth. The Republican was full of beavers, who nightly enjoyed their aquatic gambols, and it was the splash of their big broad tails on the surface of the water, as a preliminary to a dive, that had deceived us. Had we taken beaver traps along, and known how to use them then, roast legs, boiled feet and tail, fried liver—supplied by them—would have made welcome *entrées* after our rounds of wild beef. As it was, they swam, dived, and amused themselves in peace.

CHAPTER V.

Lost—Where is the Camp?—We tighten our Waistbelts—Wet, cold, hungry, and forlorn—A Cropper—Which River?—A Light—The Recall—Safe—Jerking Meat.

WE had not been long at Camp Gibraltar before my comrade and I had a most unpleasant adventure. We lost ourselves. No. We did not lose ourselves. We lost camp. We knew where we were quite well, too well to be altogether comfortable. What we wanted to know was—where was our camp? This was how it happened: We started out after an early breakfast; and, expecting to return before dinner, took no luncheon with us. Our game was unusually far off that morning. We were also getting quite particular as to what we killed. It had to be a fat cow, a very young and tender bull, or a well-grown calf. No more bull-beef for us, and we had plenty of trophies of the Monarch of the Plains. Each had a splendid cushion to sit upon—the hairy scalp from the matted forehead of an ancient buffalo—moccasins made from the skin off their hocks, Indian whips from their tails, and tobacco pouches, while our barrels were full of their tongue, pickling. No, we did not want any more old bulls. So we had had to manœuvre round and through the outlying bands of them, and get to where we could pick and choose from out the main bodies. That day we charged into a mass of animals, cut out a fine cow and calf, and after a short and sharp run finished them off, and the choice pieces were "fleeced" from the carcasses and packed on our horses.

When we left camp, the weather was bright and cloudless, with a light breeze from the west. But a change had occurred; the air had become still, perfectly still; the blue above had changed to a dull gray; a small rain had begun to fall, kept falling, thicker, and in larger drops; every minute our horizon got smaller and smaller; one monotonous jumble of prairie rolls, hillocks and hollows surrounded us: not a gleam from the sun showed where *he* was; the ground was covered with short grama grass, and no friendly "compass-weed" was there to give us our direction.

Where was camp?

We tried taking the heel of our track; no go. It had been crossed and recrossed innumerable times by the buffaloes whose flanks we had turned in the morning's stalk; it had been utterly obliterated. We had stalked our game with many a twist and curve, cut them out at right angles from their herd, followed them in their many turns and doubles. We could not tell where we—I mean where camp was. Each asked the other why the—— mischief he had not got his pocket compass with him!

A bright idea! The natural sagacity of our horses would bring us out all right. Nothing like the instincts of nature.

We therefore mounted, threw our reins on the horses' backs, lit our pipes, and proceeded slowly and confidingly along.

Now philosophers are known to have differences of opinion; must horses be unanimous? Certainly our steeds soon showed a determination to go different ways; then, to go all ways; to go any way. What was camp to them? they were not thirsty, the rain—then coming down in a steady pour—had cooled them off and refreshed them; if they were hungry, grass was all around them. Upon mature reflection I believe they were hungry, certainly the object of every turn they took was some extra large bunch of grass. I know we were hungry—very. We had plenty of meat, but, it was raw: and our education had been neglected in our early youth in the matter of eating raw meat. To make a fire out in the grassy prairie in the pouring rain was simply an impossibility. Clearly the only luncheon we could take was—tightening our waistbelts to the last hole. We did not say grace to *that* meal.

Evidently we were in a most anomalous position; nothing in sight but grass! grass! grass! and yet most decidedly "up a tree."

It would not do to stop where we were. It would not do to wander about like babes in the—prairie.

To begin with: what did we *know* of our position? That we were north of the general course of the Republican river not less than ten miles, perhaps as many as fifteen; that said river so wound and turned about that even if we had known the points of the compass we should not have known whether to go east, south, or west to strike its nearest point; that we were twenty to thirty miles south of the upper waters of the Big Blue, and that *it* twisted and snaked more, if possible, than did the Republican—and that was about all.

One thing was quite clear: the water that fell between those rivers sooner or later found its way into one or the other of them. The natural drainage systems would not cross; therefore, if we followed the first gully we came to, and always went with its fall, we should eventually arrive at the bank of one river or the other, according to the side of the divide we might then be on.

Of course, we were aware that unless we should be fortunately brought to the Republican river at some place where we had been before, we should not know which river we had come to; but, there *was* a chance of striking it at such a place, and a certainty of shelter and getting fuel to cook with on either river. But at best a long march was before us; and so our meat—excepting a few pounds—was thrown away, and we jogged on, wet, cold, hungry, and forlorn. Well we knew how the surface water would meander back and forth, and wind around, ere it grew to little creeks, how the little creeks would twist and twine for many a weary mile ere they would lose themselves in the river they would help to swell.

We journeyed on for miles—for hours. It began to get dark. But unquestionably we had got on the course of a defined prairie stream, for occasional clumps of willows and beds of reeds showed where, even in the dry season, there was always water. As we went on, the intervals between the clumps became gradually shorter and shorter, the willows larger and larger, and at last the reeds became a continuous bed, with a miniature river flowing through them. It got darker and more dark, also muddy and more muddy, and the wearied horses commenced to slip and stumble. All at once one of us came a cropper, horse and man rolled over together. The man and rifle fortunately unhurt, but the former badly shaken; and though a careful inspection of the horse revealed no serious strain, it had clearly become a case of walk and lead, or of probably breaking our necks. To have to walk was indeed to have bad made worse, for we were shod with moccasins, which, though most comfortable for riding in, and in dry weather by all odds the best arrangement for the feet for walking, are, when the ground is wet, utter abominations for such purpose. Then they stretch until your feet seem cased in pudding bags, they slip all ways, they pick up mud until your feet are like those of elephants, they are simply killing; and besides, our tired beasts, who had been difficult enough to urge along while under us, when being led, hung back on their bridles instead of following, and brought us to a stop. We tied them together, one of us took the end of the "lariat" over his shoulder, threw his weight on it and trudged on; the other, furnishing himself with a long willow *persuader*, floundered along behind, *arguing* with the horses. I have heard people say that going out on a buffalo hunt is "no end of fun, you know;" well, so it is, but it has its averages. By-and-by the rain decreased to a drizzle, and though it had been for some hours night, the light increased, and the range of our vision extending, allowed us to perceive we had got into a little valley. We were descending more rapidly, the prairie rolls on either hand began to present to us abrupt continuous slopes, and to be getting higher. Soon they commenced to recede, and assumed the appearance of miniature cliffs, and the creek to be bordered with thickets of willows, wild-plum, underbrush of all kinds, brambles, and vines. A little farther on we got into a gorge where the creek was sixty feet wide and belly-deep to a horse, probably its gateway through the bluffs of the river it was about to join; there we found ourselves obliged to ford and re-ford it many times as it crossed from point to point of its lofty and precipitous banks. Occasionally too, we had to cut our way through the matted jungles which bordered it, to the sore trial of our tempers, and the injury of our clothes and morals. The light continued to increase, the rain nearly ceased, and a star or two was to be seen above us. Suddenly the banks of the gorge broke away right and left, and we were in the main valley of a river. There was the long dark sweep of the timber, and away beyond it the opposite bluffs. We halted and took a good long look round. Which river was it? If it should prove the Republican, which way should we go when we reached the timber? How know whether we were above or below our camp? The heavy rain had washed out all tracks: we had better halt for the night in the first timber we got to.

As we stood undecided, a far off twinkling glimmer showed itself on the timber's edge—away, miles from us! it went out, it brightened up, it gleamed steadily awhile, was seen no more, then glimmered again. It must be a camp fire! Our usual one could not be seen, but the boys in camp might have built a signal beacon in the open for our benefit. We started towards the light. In a fitful way it brightened as we neared it. By-and-by a scarcely audible noise, like the distant report of a rifle, came faintly to our ears. Instantly a watch was out, a prairie match struck, and by its light, the seconds hand attentively regarded. Thirty seconds—another report! Fifteen— another! Then no more. There could be no mistake. It was "the recall" of our long since preconcerted signal code. Careless of danger to themselves, and in spite of the rain, the boys had made an immense beacon, and, as we afterwards learned, had fired since nightfall at intervals of an hour, the recall.

Climbing into our saddles—there was "nary a jump" left in us—we remounted, and at the best pace that humanity to our animals permitted, rode into camp at half-past two in the morning, to the great relief of all there. We declared ourselves to be too tired to eat, and so, stripping off our soaked clothes, rolled ourselves up in our blankets to sleep. But our irrepressible *chef* soon roused us to drink some coffee, steaming hot and strong, with something in it besides, which, together with the warmth of our beds, put new life into us. Our hunger returned, and we polished off a hearty meal. The horses were taken equally good care of, and ten o'clock next morning saw us well recruited, eating our breakfast, and telling, with many a laugh and jest, the misfortunes of the previous day.

Of course that morning we did not take our horses out, so we remained in camp and gave our men a chance to amuse themselves by going stalking, and employed our time in repairing damages to wardrobes and accoutrements, in cooking, and attending to the jerking of the buffalo meat.

There are several ways of jerking meat. We had been instructed in the best method by old Connor, and it is as follows:

An oblong frame of light poles, of proper dimensions, is supported, four feet from the ground, on forked posts firmly planted in the soil, and crossed with light sticks, thus making a big wooden gridiron on legs—thirty feet long by ten wide is about the usual size; under the middle of the frame and of the same length, a shallow trench is made for the " smoke-fire," and filled with cedar-chips, or, if the neighbourhood does not afford such, with the next best " smudge-wood "—anything will do that will make a smoke if you are not particular as to the flavour of the meat—and your " jerking-table " is ready.

The meat is either cut off the carcass by "fleecing," or off the joints and pieces brought into camp. It is cut in ribbons two inches wide and three-quarters of an inch thick, and as long as practicable. An expert fleecer can cut off a carcass, strips averaging ten feet; but the choice pieces of meat furnish only shorter lengths, and the chief art in fleecing is to cut all the strips of an equal thickness, so that the meat may cure evenly.

A camp kettle, full of brine, is boiling on the fire, and into it, for a few seconds (two or three), the ribbons of meat are dipped, and then laid on the jerking-table.

When the table is covered with meat the wood in the trench beneath is kindled, and thereafter kept burning gently until the " jerky " is done.

The object of the fire is only to make a smoke or smudge that will keep flies and other insects away during the day, and lessen the cold and damp of night, and it must never be allowed to burn sufficiently fiercely to heat the meat, as it is the dryness of the prairie air, and the heat of the sun, that really cures it. I have often jerked small quantities of meat, well enough for all practical purposes, by simply cutting it off the animal, hanging it on a bough in the hot sun, turning it a few times, and in a couple of days called it done. But when a quantity is to be jerked, it is well worth while, if practicable, to do it in the best way possible, which, as far as I know, is as above. If ants make their appearance some grease round the uprights is sufficient to fend them off; the smell of the meat, however draws larger pillagers around the camp; coyotés, wolves, wild cats, and perhaps a panther or two, will make night cheerful for the lonely sentinel.

CHAPTER VI.

Skinning a Buffalo—A Panorama of Life and Motion—Another Rogue Bull—an Escape—A good Shot—Trying to turn him over—The Virtues of a Pipe—" Catch him by the Hind-leg and throw him over"—How to get at the Tongue.

BEFORE describing how the flesh of the buffalo is jerked I ought perhaps to have told how the animal is skinned. For though such preliminary operation is easy of performance to the expert, to the uninitiated it presents a difficulty; unless he has a horse with him, which on my first essay I was without, for my hunter was having a rest, and I had gone out on a quiet stalk a-foot—not to get meat, for our jerking table was full, and it was no use wasting it, but because I wanted a good buffalo robe of my own dressing from a bull of my own killing. This was rather a difficult achievement, for at that season of the year only a few old bulls were well furred—those who were very fat and had been calved in the autumn.

The boys had hitherto always gone with the waggon and a pair of mules to fetch in the meat after each run, and it never occurred to me I should find any difficulty in skinning an old bull without assistance.

After a couple of hours quick walking I sat down on the highest knoll I could find, to rest and reconnoitre.

I was surrounded by the scattered bands of bulls that always fringe the main herds, and it was most interesting to sit and watch them.

Some of the buffaloes were feeding; some lying down chewing the cud; some dusting themselves by rolling over and over in the little hollows known to "plainsmen" as "buffalo wallows;" others were pawing the dry dusty ground up with their fore-feet and throwing it in little puffs over their shoulders; others quarrelling and fighting.

There were sometimes as many as twenty single combats going on at a time in as many different directions. More than once, while I remained a watcher, a general *mêlée* was, to my great entertainment, performed. Occasionally gray wolves would be seen trotting leisurely along some hollow, and a distant flock of antelopes wheeling and playing around in graceful evolutions.

Above, numerous vultures and turkey-buzzards circled in endless gyrations; some near me, some almost invisible specks against the clear blue sky.

The little prairie-dogs sat up and barked at the strange intruder on their settlement; while their queer fellow-lodgers, the burrowing-owls, regarded me with looks of comic wisdom; the grasshoppers chirruped, and the bulls roared.

The proverbial solitude of the wild prairie was changed into a panorama of life and motion. I looked around me and felt happy. The bright warm sunshine, the clear bracing air, the sense of freedom, were so many elixirs and tonics.

Before long a rogue bull, who looked almost black—sure sign of fatness—caught my eye. I watched him a long time as he wandered about grazing. As well as could be judged from a distance, his hide was just what I wanted. A short careful stalk brought me nearer to him. Yes, I was right. I slipped along a hollow, and got still nearer. When I took another observation the bull had left off feeding, and was walking straight along with an air of quiet deliberate intention, just as if he was going somewhere. Undoubtedly he was on his way to a watering place to drink. A judicious ambush and ordinary luck would ensure me a close shot. I took his direction, made a long detour at the double to his front, and laid myself down to await events.

I had chosen a hollow, so as to get as long grass to lie in as possible, but on the upland prairie it was everywhere very short; even where I was it compelled me to lie as flat as possible, and trust entirely to my ears, for a head slightly raised even would have been instantly seen by an advancing animal.

By-and-by I got tired. I had heard nothing but the distant noises of the herd and trifling local sounds. Perhaps the bull had altered his course; perhaps—but under such circumstances it was no use perhapsing. I gently raised my head.

There he was. *Not* a hundred yards off, but *there*, right in front of me, close to me.

So quietly, so gently had he strolled along on the close carpet of grass that the sound of his footfall had been undistinguishable from the general noises.

The bull stood before me as though he had been an apparition.

The huge head was lowered, his beard reaching to the ground. His monstrous mane hung round his neck bigger than that of any lion's. His keen, wicked eyes glared at me. His strong, short, sharp black horns stuck viciously out in my direction. He at once commenced to paw the ground and bellow.

I found out afterwards he was not as large as the universe, that he was only an ordinarily fine bull, but at that time he suddenly grew and spread, until space became one mass of black curling hair, bristling with horns, and glowing with eyes.

Slowly and gently I lowered my head, flattened myself out like a burrowing beetle, and held my breath. The least aggressive movement and the bull would have charged; and he was so near there would have been neither time nor room to handle a rifle.

For a quarter of an hour I lay perfectly still—perhaps it was only two minutes and a half, but it seemed a quarter of an hour—then I tried another look. He was *not* in front of me. I sat back on my heels and gave a sigh of relief. My life had not been worth a pin's point. I looked around and saw him. He had got quite small again, and was making off, walking slowly up the rising ground to my right.

Now was the time to get even with him for nearly scaring

me to death. I gave a shrill whistle through my fingers. The buffallo stopped, turned his body a quarter round and his head half round to look at me. Standing there, relieved against the clear, bright sky, he looked as if done in bronze, and offered a splendid target.

I drew a coarse sight upon his off fore-leg, raised my rifle steadily until the ivory "bead" showed like a ball of snow on his dark body two-thirds up, moved it a trifle to the left, touched the hair trigger, and the sharp crack of my rifle was answered by its welcome echo—the thud of a striking bullet.

The bull staggered, swayed to and fro, dropped on his knees, fell on his side, and rolled on his back; then his legs straightened in the air with a jerk, and he fell back on to his side again—dead. Killed with a single shot at a distance of two hundred and seventy odd yards.

Considering the circumstances, I think that was as creditable a shot as was ever fired by me. Lying flat on your face, waiting for the commencement of a trampling and goring process, that is to break every bone in your body and make a mangled corpse of you, is *not* conducive to steadying the eye and finger for shooting with a fine-sighted hair-triggered rifle.

And now for the skinning. I had "stripped" plenty of smaller animals before, and knew quite well how to make the cuts for an open skin. Bag skins are cut differently. First a circular sweep round the neck, and then four round the legs, above the knees and hocks. A longitudinal cut for the whole length of neck, breast, and belly, two transverse ones at right angles to it, from knee to knee and hock to hock, and you have eight right angles on your centre cut. Catch hold of the skin at any angle you like with your left hand, and using your knife in your right to loosen the skin from the flesh, skin away. Quite easy, you see.

I went to work with confidence, but soon found that if I had not an elephant on my hands I had the next thing to one. I could not lay a buffalo-bull on the flat of his back as I could a specimen dormouse; and if I could, his hump would not let him stop in such a position. That was why he had fallen back on his side after dying with his legs in the air. But what could be easier than to skin the side of the buffalo lying uppermost down to the ground, turn him over and finish the other side?

With many sharpenings and re-sharpenings of my hunting-knife—for the old bull had a tough overcoat of his own—that much was accomplished, and I rolled the half skin neatly up past the backbone, so that it would be free from the buffalo's weight when he should be turned over, and then sat down on the carcass to take a comfortable rest, for my back had begun to ache with stooping.

I now looked round me with feelings of satisfaction. I was getting on famously. I got up and attempted to turn the bull over. Turn *him* over! Why, I might as well have tried to lift myself off the ground by pulling at my moccasin strings. I pushed, I pulled; tried one leg, tried another. I perspired and I strained. I sat down and felt very small indeed. If I only had a horse, it would be quite simple. The loop of a "lariat" thrown over the bull's legs, a few turns of its slack round the horn of my

Mexican saddle, a touch of the spur, and over it would have gone. But I had no horse, had no rope, and not a "stick," to make a handspike from, was within miles.

Then it struck me—why, the brute is lying the wrong way of the slope! I will haul him round.

I could *not* haul him round; he would not haul "worth a red cent." Desperately I tugged at him again. Taking hold of the front leg next the ground by its hoof, I stood on the carcass just behind the elbow of the other leg, gave a few preliminary sways, and then threw my whole weight backwards; but the leverage of his big hump and his horns stopped the turn just as it appeared about to be made, and "soss" back he went!

Of course I could cut the animal up, skin him from his hide, instead of his hide from him. But that was no way to skin a buffalo; besides, I had started in to do it, and was bound to turn him over.

There is wisdom in counsel. My counsellor hung from my neck like a lady's locket. It did not hang from my neck by a gold chain, but by a greasy old buckskin "whang," and it was not an affair of gold, glass, hair, and photograph. My faithful counsellor was a well-seasoned, chocolate-coloured, large-bowled, short-stemmed, old briar-root pipe. And why did I hang my pipe from my neck, like the ornament of a fashionable siren or the fetish of a Hottentot Venus, instead of having a case for it, and carrying it in a pocket, like every other respectable member of society? For more reasons than one. A pipe is a valuable and irreplaceable treasure on the Plains, whose loss must not be risked by taking the chance of laying it down and forgetting it, or by carrying it in pockets liable to have holes made in them by the rough usage of frontier service, and not likely to be carefully mended; and because—now this is personal and confidential—I suffer under a physical disability, or infirmity, or malformation, or whatever its name is, and can *not* hold a pipe in the left side of my mouth and smoke comfortably. I have a right-handed mouth for smoking. I have seen plenty of smokers with left-handed mouths, some few with double-handed mouths. I am not one of those kind of men, and consequently, as a smoker and sportsman, lie under a disability, the magnitude of which may be easily ascertained by experiment. Fill a pipe, light it, put it between your teeth on the *right* side, begin to take a serene smoke, and then pick up as quickly as you can a heavy rifle, throw it promptly to your shoulder, and simultaneously bring your head down to catch the sights; and if the experiment is successfully performed the pipe's stem will be smashed, its bowl fly into the air, the fire from it into your eyes, and a tooth or two be broken. Possibly it may require practice on your part to enable you to do so many things simultaneously and neatly, but you will infallibly do most of them every time. And what sort of a sight do you suppose you could take at a running deer or hostile foe under such difficulties? Now it might easily happen, in an Indian country, that a shot required to be fired so suddenly there would be no time to get an obstructive pipe out of the way, excepting by letting it fall out of the mouth and losing it. Was I therefore to refrain from smoking on the line of march? Certainly not, while a string of any kind was to be got or made.

My counsellor having received his *charge*, I sat down to

deliberate. The thing could be done—was indeed done every day by ignorant savages. What a duffer I am, I thought, while smoking, to have tugged and pulled senselessly and stupidly, instead of sitting down first and applying to the great Genius of tobacco to stimulate invention, to show me how to tackle the horns of my dilemma! Hurrah for tobacco, the great revealer! Take the bull by the horns —plenty of leverage to them—twist his head round the way I want him to turn, as far as possible, stick a horn well in the ground, to hold his head from going back, and a strain in the desired direction will be established along the whole length of his spine, like a spring cable; catch him by the hind-leg and throw him over! It is "as easy as falling off a floating log."

Now for getting at his tongue! Perhaps some reader innocently thinks there could not be any trick about getting at that. "You have only to open his mouth, you know." Well, try it! I did. Took his upper lip in one hand and his beard in the other and pulled with all my might, but open his mouth I could not. Grim death had shut it too hard and fast for my strength to avail. I broke the point of my good bowie between his jaws, trying to pry his mouth open with it, then a corner off the blade of my tomahawk. Then I *very faintly praised* "everything an inch high and an hour old." At last I cut the bull's throat, put my hand into the opening, pulled his tongue through, cut it off, and gathering up my spoils and tricks, went to camp rejoicing in success.

CHAPTER VII.

A solitary Elk — A careless Sentinel — Preparations for Departure — A phantom Horseman—A striking Picture—A narrow Escape—a Consultation—Our Chances—A new Sensation—Precautions—The Videttes —Safe at Fort Riley.

ALTHOUGH, while we remained in Camp Gibraltar, we were on the direct line of the semi-annual migration of the elk—indeed, not very far from where, on a subsequent occasion, when hunting with a party of Delawares, I saw a drove of over three hundred of them—only one was seen during our stay, and that by the sentinel alone.

About eleven o'clock one fine moonlight night the sentinel, while lying in his *form*, heard a splashing in the water to the rear of the camp; and though he ought certainly not to have left the unprotected side of our position for a moment unwatched, in order to go to the safe one, he did do so. The feeling that continual vigilance is an unnecessary bore made him for the moment careless. Peeping through a bush, he looked towards the river, and saw near its opposite side, standing up to his knees in it, and in the full moonlight, a large buck elk pawing the water. Excitement banished all reflection from the guard's mind, and he immediately cracked away at him. The shot started everyone to his feet. Arms were snatched up, and we rushed to cover, thinking, of course, we were being attacked. It was very stupid of the guard, and we told him so, singly and in chorus, and often, and that it was more especially stupid because he had made a miss of it.

A reflection that has often occurred to me recurs now. How is it that men, camped out in the wilderness, in places where, without warning, they may at any time find their lives in imminent peril, sleep most soundly, and yet quite lightly? How is it that, while lying in the deep, dreamless sleep that is induced by a day of hard exercise, a warm bed, and the free air of heaven, a slight *unusual* noise awakens them at once? and not only so, but they seem to have heard it mentally as well as physically. I mean by this that not only has the noise awakened them, but they know what the noise is. Now, as the sleep was sound, and the awakening subsequent to the noise——But I give it up, and must remain satisfied by knowing that the fact is so.

That elk was the last head of game shot at while we remained on the Republican—indeed, we then had already commenced making preparations for our start for home. The barrels of tongues had been headed, filled with brine, and placed in the waggon; the jerky sacked and packed away; the buffalo tallow rendered out, allowed to get cold and hard, wrapped up, and loaded also into the waggon. But though the buffalo had been gradually moving farther and farther off, and it had become a long day's work to get to them—make a "run" and return; and though our horses were showing signs of being done up, their corn all eaten, and acorns its poor substitute, we still had lingered.

It was such a free, jolly life to lead; we looked with regret to a return to the cares and worries of civilisation. Uneasiness on the score of Indian danger was felt no longer. Freedom from alarms had given us a sense of security, had lulled our anxieties to rest. We were as yet young hands at that sort of thing. We had not learned that hard lesson to remember, that maxim of Indian warfare: "There is most danger from Indians when none are to be seen." Nevertheless, we kept up camp discipline, and the regular guard went on each night; and as there were only five of us, while two hours is *quite* long enough a time to have to watch with the vigilance necessary against Indian subtlety, each had to take a turn, so running the night through; for the first man came on at seven o'clock in the evening, and the last went off at five the following morning. The first watch was only a nominal affair, as far as hardship went, for nine o'clock is not a late hour for a man to go to bed at, even after a hard day's hunt, and for him there was unbroken rest until breakfast time; but the other watches were not liked, and so to make it even all round, that there should be no feeling of dissatisfaction in camp, that everything should be lovely, we ran a roster: no man took his watch two nights alike, and in the course of five nights each had run through all the watches. Want of incident had rendered these watches tiresome and monotonous; but at last one came that was interesting enough, and decided our immediate start.

The one o'clock relief was made as usual, and also the report, equally as usual: "All quiet: nothing happened." We were getting tired of this regular song of "All quiet," &c.; it had become a byword. The night was clear, but raw. A mist had crept up from the river, rolled across the valley, and settled in and over its depressions and hollows, making the higher portions of the ground look like low islands in a ghostly sea. The moon was still up, considerably to the west of south, and she threw a flood of light down the valley. It was a cloudless night, and the silvery mist, the bright moonlight, the dim shadowy distance, gave a vague poetic look to the whole scene.

The regular nightly serenade was too familiar to receive attention, and an hour had passed uneventfully away, when a dim and distant object emerged from a veil of mist far up the valley. As this object approached it began to resolve itself into a resemblance of some large moving animal; then it was lost to view; anon it appeared again; larger, a little less like a fancy of the brain; and again it was lost. When it emerged once more it looked like a phantom horseman coming at a swinging canter. As it neared it became more and still more distinct. Suddenly it stopped, went on again at a walk, broke into a canter, slackened into a trot, and dropped into a walk again. Its motions looked very much like those of a man on horseback tracking an easily-followed trail. As it got still nearer, all doubts vanished, and on its arrival abreast of camp—where the different trails we had made going and coming came together—it stopped, and the bright light fell on a striking picture.

A black powerful Indian pony, gay with trappings and plumes, and mounted on it a stalwart Indian. His bow and arrows, and his long slim lance, hung crosswise at his back; his rifle lay athwart his saddle bow; the fringes of his hunting-shirt, and the stained feathers of his head-dress, gently stirred and fluttered in the night air. He turned in his saddle at right angles to his horse, and became motionless, gazing fixedly in the direction of our camp.

Now was the opportunity. While the Indian had been approaching, the sentinel, in anticipation of possible eventualities, had taken off his hat, rolled it tightly up, and laid it as a rest for his rifle upon the stone before him—to prevent the jar that, should he have occasion to fire, would otherwise affect the direction of his ball—and on it the rifle had been laid. The rifle's lock was at full cock, its hair-trigger set; its long, thin, ivory front sight showed in the strong moonlight clearly and distinctly, and was drawn well down into the fine semi-circular notch of the buckhorn hind sight—a notch no bigger than half the eye of an ordinary sewing-needle. It looked like a small shining china bead of the Indian's hunting-shirt. The stock of the rifle was slowly depressed, bringing the line of sight carefully, steadily upward. The small white bead was in relief against the darkness of the Indian's face, and the index finger of the sentinel's right hand was laid to the side of the hair-trigger. The movement of a muscle would send an ounce-and-a-third of lead crashing through the

A NARROW ESCAPE. 61

brain of that prying bloodhound who had so surely tracked us to our lair.

Was it best to kill him or let him go? Hard question to decide, and little time to do it in. Under such circumstances a man thinks quickly, very quickly. Why had that Indian ridden more than half a night to ascertain our whereabouts? not for curiosity—curiosity is not an Indian characteristic. Was not the probability of his being one of a band of raiders, anxious to gain the knowledge that would enable him to bring his murderous companions to our massacre and plunder, and now possessing it, reason sufficient to shoot him? Nay, was it not the *duty* of the sentinel to shoot him? It was not simply a question of his own life. Were not the lives of his sleeping comrades entrusted not only to his vigilance but to his judgment? Was he not bound, as a necessity of the situation, to assume the responsibility of homicide? But the Indian might not be there with hostile thoughts; it was just barely possible. And then it looked so like deliberate murder—that settled it.

The finger was removed from the trigger.

Little did that dusky spy wot of the danger he had been in. He never was nearer death before, never will be again, until he is "called."

After a few moments of motionless regard the Indian recovered his riding-seat, cantered diagonally to the river's bank, below our encampment, turned his back to the river, and slowly described a large semicircle around us until he reached the river's bank above it. He was cutting all our tracks to see if there was any indication that we had left.

It looked very bad indeed. Then he wheeled round and galloped off.

Camp was immediately aroused, and a council held.

The theory that we were in immediate danger was the most prudent one to make the basis of our deliberations.

Where? when? how? had our night visitor struck the track he had so successfully run to its termination?

These seemed the most probable conjectures: the Indian came across the trail he had followed while hunting —consequently by daylight. Fifteen miles or thereabouts in a direct line was as far off as any of us had lately been in the direction whence he had come; when seen he was tracking at the rate of six miles an hour, including checks. He was seen at about two o'clock; therefore it had been half-past eleven that night or thereabouts when he started on the trail. If he had known of the trail before sunset why had he lost five hours? Because when he had first seen the sign his horse had been loaded with buffalo-meat, or tired, perhaps both; and as the Indian could not tell how far he would have to go on the trail, or whether he might not have to make a run for life before he got back, he had returned to his camp for a fresh horse; indeed, it was almost certain he would have done so. Making the calculations against ourselves, the Indian first saw our sign at sundown, and it had taken him five hours to get to his camp and back to it; half that time with a tired horse, half with a fresh one that he would be saving for a possibly long ride, perhaps a race. Eight miles an hour would be about the speed he would have averaged; therefore, his camp must be twenty miles beyond the allowed fifteen—say thirty-five miles off. The Indian would hardly go straight back; the necessity was not pressing enough to induce him to make his ride a seventy miles one after a day spent in hunting; he was probably fast asleep in some thicket, his hobbled horse feeding or reposing near him. If so, he would certainly sleep six hours, then arise, eat a few yards of jerky, take a drink from the river, and start out to rejoin his party, reaching them about two o'clock in the afternoon. If we moved immediately, we should have a start of thirty-five miles and nearly ten hours. Our mules had done nothing but fetch meat into camp from time to time since we had lain there. They were as fresh as paint. Our horses were in hard condition, and we knew our way back. Though loaded, we could easily do forty miles in the ten hours. Thus we should have a start of seventy-five miles.

"A stern chase" is proverbially "a long one," and such a start was a big bite out of the distance to Fort Riley. The odds were we could beat a pursuing party there easily if we had no breakdown and did not spare the animals, and *if* our conjectures and calculations were only correct.

We might be frightening ourselves for nothing. We might be attacked before daylight; but we decided on immediate flight. We had come out for a hunt. We had hunted. We were about to try the experiment of feeling that we were being hunted. Novelty is the spice of life. Galloping after buffaloes had become monotonous. There was a fine chance for a new sensation.

Everything was quickly packed and loaded into the waggon, the mules harnessed and hitched up, horses saddled and tied behind, and we started on the back track. I believe the mules considered we had gone crazy; a start in the middle of the night was a novel experience to them, and they showed their disapproval of such a proceeding most unmistakably.

At daybreak we halted well in the open for a short rest to water the animals at a little prairie creek we had just crossed, and to eat a hasty meal ourselves. Breakfast consisted of some fresh meat that had been hung to the waggon bows, boiled in a fryingpan, and the strongest of hot coffee; bread we did not bother with, there was none made and no time to make any.

As it would not do to trust entirely to our conjectures, and as there might be unknown Indian dangers in our front, it was decided to commence taking proper precautions.

The horsemen should mount, ride forward a mile or two, one of them take up a commanding position on some eminence as a vidette or look-out; the other ride still farther forward and do likewise; when the waggon should get abreast of the farther one the vidette who would then be the rearguard should push ahead and become the advance one; and so, if danger was descried, there would be time for deliberation and preparation. If the vidette in the rear should see a party of Indians in pursuit, whose strength rendered the chances of defence desperate, he was to discharge his revolver thrice with the utmost rapidity; at that signal the traces were to be cut, the three best mules mounted, and it was to be considered a case of *sauve qui peut* —a run for our lives: "Every man for himself, and the devil take the hindmost."

Wonderful is the feeling of conscious energy, of self-confidence, of personal courage, that results from a combination of youth, perfect health, freedom from the petty cares, annoyances, and toils of ordinary civilised existence, and the exhilarating effect of life in the open air! I am certain that not a single individual of our little party but regarded with feelings nearer akin to pleasing anticipation of excitement than apprehension the chances for either a desperate conflict or a headlong flight; but the occasion for neither arose, and our precipitate retreat soon ended in safety within the stockades of Riley.

CHAPTER VIII.

We make a Sensation—Indian Hostilities—A kind Offer—Our new Camp Ground—Our Visitors—Frontiersmen and Frontiersmen—An Attempt to give Advice—My Rebuff—A good Laugh—What would be said.

OUR arrival at Fort Riley made quite a sensation. The mules were hardly pulled up before our waggon was surrounded by an inquiring crowd.

Leaving the boys and crowd to talk, we repaired to head-quarters to pay our respects. The officer in command seemed to be really glad to see us once more, and as he shook our hands cordially, assured us he had not expected to have that pleasure again. He had supposed we had been "wiped out."

That "military necessity," a demijohn, was produced, and the frontier toast, "The hair on the top of your head, long may it wave there," was drunk in a bumper and with a "repeater." We gave a concise relation of our adventures, and heard the news.

All doubt as to Indian hostilities having commenced was at an end. Official information had been received that a mail-station on the Overland Route had been attacked, the stock captured and driven off; that several express-riders had been shot, and that emigration was stopped *par ordre*. The Kiowas and the Cheyennes were certainly on the warpath, the Sioux probably "out." There was a rumour also, believed to be true, that the Indians had been fighting amongst themselves. He, the commanding officer, was then expecting reinforcements from Fort Leavenworth, to enable him to put a scouting party in the field.

Our gallant friend further told us he thought we had "crowded our luck," and would be wise to take no more chances; that he was going to send a small escort off in a couple of days with despatches to his district head-quarters, and we had best wait for them and avail ourselves of their protection as far as the Pottowattomie's country; and that if we chose to do so, he would give them orders not to travel faster than we could conveniently go, as they could make up any lost time after parting from us. Such an offer was too good to be refused, and was gladly accepted.

The interview closed by an invitation to spend our spare time with him and his officers—especially the evenings —our friend adding that though their resources for amusement were quite limited, he could ensure us hearty welcome, good cheer, and pleasant company, and he would immediately see what could be done for us in the matter of quarters and stabling. We begged, however, he would give himself no trouble about our accommodation, since we much preferred camping out in our usual way until we should arrive at home again. He then told us there had been a hay-camp just below the Fort in the river bottom, and as several large ricks were still there, he had, fearing they might be burned, placed them under guard since the

"Indian difficulty," so had no doubt we should find it a safe place to camp at, and that grass, wood, and water were there in plenty.

Such a camp ground was all that could be desired, and as we much preferred it to being close to the wretched little settlement farther down, we established ourselves there without loss of time.

Though we did not trouble the "city" with our presence, some of the citizens seemed to consider themselves quite free of our camp. They were there all day; they were there nearly all night. They seemed to think we existed only for their special benefit, that our *raison d'être* was to be listeners to their interminable yarns, to believe their outrageous braggadocios, to shoot against them for whisky, and to keep a roaring camp-fire burning all night for them to drone and doze over. They wanted to trade with us for every thing we had. But for the novelty of the thing, the certainty of its being soon brought to a close, and that after all they were entertaining rascals, for a time, we should soon have brought things to a crisis, and "discommoded" some of them.

Our visitors belonged to that class—border ruffians and loafers—who have made the name of frontiersman obnoxious to the ordinary run of English sportsmen who have made hunting excursions in the Far West; because from such as they, and the very worst of them too, have been almost invariably procured their camp-followers, their guides, their "professional hunters." Save and defend us! These are they of whom we hear stories of low profanities, drunken quarrels, insolence, and dishonesty. All such call themselves frontiersmen, and how is the foreign stranger to know that there are frontiersmen and frontiersmen, or wherein is the difference?

The non-producers amongst the border settlers, the floating population of non-labouring unprofessional males, may be roughly divided into two portions—those who are there from an unrecognised but no less imperative compulsion, and those who are there because they choose to be.

To the former division belong all whom the genius of industry and competition has crowded to the borderland— men who from their innate worthlessness are incompetent to hold a place within the pale of the ever active energetic civilisation of the great American people; the low, cheating gambler, who has been found out too often; the cattle-lifter and the horse-thief; the man who has "served his time;" the bar-room loafer and the escaped jail-bird.

The *true* frontiersman is to be found amongst the latter division. A love of nature, a sturdy inborn independence of mind, a thirst after adventure, the love of sport, an impatience of the petty restraints, annoyances, and small meannesses inseparable from a high state of civilisation, send *him* there. These are *his* impelling motives. Such feelings, such motives, have sent the pioneers of civilisation to every clime—Columbus to the discovery of a continent, Cortez to the conquest of an empire.

The English tourist-sportsman necessarily carries with him his habitual British manner; unconsciously he treats at their first interview his supposed social inferior—that is to say the man who is worse dressed than himself—with abruptness, hauteur, or condescension, according to his individual disposition or the temper he may be in; but whatever way he may treat him, he permits it to be plainly seen he considers himself very much the superior being. Such a manner is the natural result of the construction of English society, and in England is not offensive. But the true frontiersman will allow no such pretension, for such he considers it. Self-respect and independence of character are his leading characteristics. Acknowledge the honour which he considers due to the dignity of his manhood by treating him frankly as an assumed equal; let him see by your manner, you consider, as he does, that wealth, titles, and social position are accidents, that truth, fortitude, and courage are the essentials in questions of relative worth between man and man, and he will do much to serve you. "Put on airs," as he calls it—though, unrecognisable fact to him, you are really acting quite naturally, having no intention to offend or assume superiority—and he will feel insulted, and when recounting the interview, say: "I am as good a *man* as he is." From his standpoint he possibly *thinks* himself a better; and he will probably add, but expressing himself with a difference, putting the idea into the shortest, plainest, most forcible, most Saxon form: "The individual be condemned. The individual can depart unto Hades." On the other hand, the moneyed foreigner in pursuit of sport is just the man for unprincipled border idlers and roughs —men who live anyhow and anywhere and on everybody; men with but one leading principle, and that not to earn an honest living by work, though they often work hard enough at villainy. By the nature of his vocation a bird of prey, as a necessity of his life a parasite; from acquired dexterity, as a solicitor of favours, a sycophant; a man of this class is a plausible, cunning, and when requisite to gain a point, deferential rascal. He has no self-respect to be wounded by mannerisms. Most of these men have during their roving careers been many times across the Plains. To loaf round camp-fires is their delight. It is to them as the blacksmith's shop is to the idlers of many an English country village. From the mouths of the actors in them they have often heard tales of hunting, of trapping, of Indian warfare. The unwritten romances of the wilderness, the half-legendary folk-lore of the border, are oft-told tales to them. They are thoroughly qualified to cajole, humbug, and impose on an open-hearted, ardent English sportsman, who, knowing nothing of what he is about to undertake, thinks he knows it all.

I had once a little experience with a party of my countrymen who had chosen Leavenworth city, then a straggling frontier town with a very uncertain future, as their point of departure on a sporting trip to the neighbouring prairie. I daresay they were first-rate fellows, and that I should have found them to be so had we become *properly* acquainted. They were gentlemen by birth, rank, and position. I do not know that the affair is worth telling, but, like the story of Little Red Riding-hood, "it has a moral, and may teach a lesson."

Having occasion to go to Leavenworth to see to the due fulfilling of an army contract, I took up my quarters at my usual resting-place, "The Planters' Hotel," then owned and "run" by one of my warmest partisans. I was an old *habitué* of the hotel, and there was not a woolly-headed "boy" or "yellar gall" about the place who did not bestow upon me the grin of recognition. On the occasion I am writing about, the hotel hall presented, as I entered, a most unusual appearance. One corner was filled with a pile of gun and rifle cases, saddles sewn up in canvas covers, boxes and packages of every shape and size, all unmistakably English, and suggesting strongly a "hunting" party. I stepped up to the desk, bid good-day to the hotel clerk, and asked him what was up. "Tell you what's up? there is a parcel of English a-*ri*stocrats arrived, who are going to kill all the game in the country. They have brought their dogs, their weapons, and their mountebanks with them, and they have got a kit of everything in the universal world that is of no earthly use in this country. They are in No. 8, and there is nothing good enough for them in this 'blársted' hotel!"

I turned to the hotel register, and read their names and titles; while doing so the "mountebanks" came in—four English men-servants *in livery*—two grooms, a gamekeeper, and a body-servant; clean, smart-looking, well-appointed, good-style retainers.

My heart warmed towards the occupants of No. 8; they were my fellow-countrymen, and they were sportsmen. They had come thousands of miles in pursuit of the pleasure I loved best. Had I not been tied for time I should have proposed to join them; as it was, I would manage to spare them a few days to get them properly started. Acting on the impulse of the moment, I gave my card to the hotel clerk, and asked him to send it in to the gentlemen in No. 8, with my compliments, and that I should be glad to learn when it would be convenient for them to receive a call from me. While I was exchanging a few words with the gamekeeper, the coloured boy returned. "Marssa, de genelmen ul see you instander," he informed me, as he made a leg and pulled his woolly forelock with his right hand ; so, preceded by him, and duly announced, I entered.

A small party of men of unquestionably British cut were standing together before the spot where, in an English room, the fireplace would have been. The centre one stood with his feet wide apart, his left hand in his trousers' pocket, and his right one extended with my pasteboard between its thumb and first finger. He bowed stiffly, waved the hand holding my card towards a chair, and said : "Mr. Er—r—r ;" then he glanced at the card and addressed me properly : "take a chair, and state your business with us."

I took a chair. I expected they would all take chairs; but no, there they stood, with their backs to the wall, their hands in their pockets, balancing themselves forward on their toes, and then back again, and staring at me. I told them in effect I had heard they were a party from England on a sporting trip, and that I would never forgive myself should they suffer disappointment or failure from want of the information that could only be given by a person who not only was a sportsman but acquainted with the country, its people, the necessities of the case, and local resources to meet them ; that I had not much time to spare, but could give them a few days to put them in right hands ;

to assist them to buy horses and mules, waggons, camp equipage, and commissary stores; and to look up the *personnel* required for their contemplated expedition—in any case, my best advice was theirs to command.

Now what answer will the reader suppose I got?

"Thanks very much, ah! very much obliged indeed—most *disinterested* of you—but, ah! we never take advice from an *entire stranger*. We have letters to the first banker here. We shall rely entirely upon him in the matter. He will have our full confidence. Ah! Good-morning. Ah!"

I bowed myself out of the room in silence. I did not dare to open my mouth, for I did *not* want to laugh in their faces. Then I entered the empty billiard-saloon, threw myself into a settee, and roared aloud. I know it is a very bad habit to laugh at one's own thoughts, but, bad as it is, I have done it all my life. I have just as much right to my bad habits as anyone else has to his, and I am continually saying and doing things that are not apparently *à propos* to the time and place. I believe that if I were lying on my death-bed, awaiting dissolution, and the undertaker came and began to measure me for my coffin, I should say something that *he* would consider quite inappropriate to the solemnity of the occasion.

"An entire stranger." I tried to contemplate myself in the character of an entire stranger in Leavenworth, where every man, woman, child and dog, knew me. Why, *they* were the entire strangers. I had read their names and titles, had seen their servants, had seen them. I was well enough satisfied that they were what they professed to be, but to everyone else in that community they were in the fullest sense of the word strangers. To them their looks were strange, their accent ridiculous, many of their expressions hardly intelligible, their technical and slang phrases enigmas, their nobby servants "mountebanks." The whole lot would be looked upon as possible anybodies or anythings. I was a judge of that class of men, but who else in that city was? Verily to all others they were indeed black swans.

And the deliciousness of the slight emphasis on "disinterested." The delicate way in which it inferred so much. That I was either a "Galvanised Englishman," or a "Whitewashed Yankee," and calculated to *do* them, to make a commission out of them on their purchases. And how plainly it expressed that *they* were not to be gammoned; that *they* were too fly for Yankee tricks to be played on *them*. Oh, it was killing! And the lofty allusion to "the first banker here," who had their "full confidence," to whom they had "letters." Why, for all practical purposes—as far as sporting matters were concerned—such were, in effect, letters to me. I knew what "the first banker here" would say. It would be this: "Gentlemen, I *will* be pleased to do all I can for you in any way, but in all things pertaining to sport, I am quite ignorant; never fired a gun in my life, or got upon a horse; but I will give you an introduction to my friend" (that's me). "I have the fullest confidence in him" (I should think he had, if allowing an account to be heavily overdrawn more than once was any sign of it); "he knows this country, its people, ways, and all about it, and has hunted every kind of game in it, from snipe to Indians. He is 'posted' in sporting."

I had been much amused by my interview, but was sincerely sorry for its result. Here were a number of representative men, members of a class of whom specimens had then been rarely seen on the American frontier. In as small a place as Leavenworth then was, they would be observed by everyone. Numbers would ask me what *really* was their standing in the "Old Country?" I should have to say they belonged to the upper class. Of the upper class they would be considered types. It would have been so pleasant to have been able to say to my questioner: "Don't talk to me about effete, played out, old countries, and the enervating effects of their institutions. Look at those men. They were not born to toil. There is no necessity laid on them to compel to energy and enterprise. They have plenty of money, and can indulge in idle luxury, in dissipation, in lordly ease. And here they are, strong, hearty fellows, courting hardship, toil, and danger, for the love of it, and calling it sport." And instead of having this pleasure, I felt morally certain I should see them made the laughing-stocks of the whole country; hear them described as "Cockney sportsmen," as "Battue lordlings." Why, even the hotel clerk had already begun to ridicule them. I should have them and their doings flung in my face until I made a "serious difficulty" with some fellow about it, *pour décourager les autres.*

CHAPTER IX.

The Pottowattomie Country—An Indian Camp—Old Acquaintances—Captain Connor's Adventures—His Speech—The surprise Party—The Design—Night Attacks—Captain Connor's Success—The Festivities—" Let it alone."

BETWEEN Fort Riley and the Pottowattomie's country nothing of special interest occurred, and immediately upon entering it the escort left us, for they had lost time to make up, while we were wishful to jog easily along and travel by short stages, having taken it out of our animals considerably in our rush from Camp Gibraltar.

Our road ran through the main Pottowattomie settlement, the site of their council lodge and other tribal erections, which towards evening we found ourselves in sight of. That something extraordinary had happened— that events of unusual importance were in progress or being prepared for—became at once apparent. The whole nation seemed to be assembled. Buffalo-skin "tepees" (Indian tents) were thickly clustered round the council lodge, and dotted up and down near the stream's banks, and the prairie on each side of it was covered with bands of Indian ponies (about two thousand head), then being gathered together by their respective herders—picturesque-looking, half-naked young Pottowattomie bucks.

Our course led us between the council lodge and two tepees, which were, judging from their size, emblazonments and the lance hung with "totems" and trophies that stood upright before each of them, the head-quarter tepees of chiefs of eminence. As we drove slowly along we continually encountered or passed groups of braves, squaws, and paposes, who gazed stolidly at us. Among the braves was a considerable sprinkling of Delaware warriors, some of whom we thought we recognised, and a crowd of Indians stood talking together between the council lodge and the chiefs' tepees, quite blocking-up the roadway. Arrived at the crowd it parted right and left, and we beheld approaching, with a smile of pleasure on his countenance, and his right hand extended in welcome to us, an instantly recognised face and figure, but in strange guise and metamorphosis. It was Captain John Connor, arrayed in the state full dress of an Indian head chief! Nothing was lacking but the paint and scalp-lock, he was too civilised for these. The dainty French kid boots in which we had been accustomed to see his feet encased were replaced by buckskin moccasins, stiff and brilliant with coloured beads; his lower limbs were covered with Indian-tanned buffalo-hide leggings, heavily fringed with buckskin strings and human hair. The neat frock-coat was exchanged for a buckskin hunting-shirt, every seam fringed like the leggings, and further ornamented by bead embroidery and stained porcupine quills. His *chapeau de Paris* was a plume of war-eagle feathers;

his gold watch and chain changed into the badge and totem of his tribe and office. Truly the contrast was most striking between the gorgeous savage before us and our recollection of the middle-aged swell, dressed with quiet fastidiousness, we had but lately parted with. It was like the transfiguration of a pantomime. We jumped down at once, shook our friend cordially by the hand, and received a most pressing invitation to become his guests for a few days. He said he had a long story to tell, and there would be much of interest for us to see. He was only waiting the arrival of a delegation of his own tribe to properly celebrate in ancient form a great victory recently achieved over his enemies. As he said this he straightened himself, and waved his hand towards the standard spears, which we then observed had many fresh scalps swinging from them. He further said he much wanted an account of our adventures; he had heard of our having gone buffalo hunting, and had had great misgivings that he should never see our faces again, but, beholding them, was made happy once more.

An invitation of such a nature was absolutely irresistible, and having immediately accepted it, a place of honour near the council lodge, whereon to pitch our tent, was assigned to us, and we encamped forthwith, turning our stock over to the charge of a young Delaware, who had received his chief's orders to take good care of them.

At sunset my comrade and I joined Captain Connor's mess, of which we were expected to remain members until our departure. We found it undeniably excellent, as indeed was to be expected, considering our host's antecedents and resources. Over his camp-fire, behind his glass of grog and glowing meerschaum, he told us the story of his late adventures.

He had started out, three weeks before we had, with a small band of picked hunters—twenty—and as many boys to wait upon them, herd the hacks, buffalo-runners, and pack-horses, and perform camp duty.

The Delawares being at peace with the tribes of the Plains, no hostile acts were to be looked for from them; indeed the Delawares did not expect to be molested in any way, as it was their intention to confine their hunting to a district which through long prescription and usage had in a certain sense become their special hunting-ground. They had met with the success a party of such able and experienced hunters were entitled to calculate upon, and were nearly ready to return, when, one night at twilight, while eating their supper, they were swooped down upon by a large well-armed band of Cheyennes and Kiowas. A cloud of arrows and some rifle shots were discharged at them at long range by their assailants as they swept round the Delawares' camp; the stock surrounded, two herders killed, one taken prisoner, and every hoof "lifted" before their eyes. The whole thing done, too, so suddenly and quickly as not to afford a chance of resistance. And Connor and his men found themselves set a-foot in the wide prairies, over a hundred and fifty miles from the nearest point of safety—the Pottowattomie encampments—encumbered with two wounded men, and with a loss of as many boys killed and one taken prisoner.

The position was not only humiliating but dangerous.

The capture from them of their means of transport might be followed up by a crushing attack by overwhelming odds from the Indians who had broken the peace; or the Delaware party might be daily and nightly harassed, worn out, or cut off in detail, during the long and tedious march before them.

However, Connor's party was not further molested. They travelled and camped with every precaution, taking all the advantages that experienced braves, led by such an able old leader, might be expected to do—and certainly eighteen picked Delaware warriors so led, each armed with a good Hawkins' rifle, Colt's revolver, bowie and tomahawk, and seventeen youths, expert bowmen, proud of their position as squires to such knights, and keen for a chance to distinguish themselves under the eye of their respected chief—anxious, in fact, to earn their rank as braves, and be boys no longer—were not a party to be unadvisedly brought to bay. Probably their plunderers considered it would be sheer folly, after securing the spoils of a victory without the loss of a man, to risk their lives by an attack on well armed and desperate warriors, from whom, except their weapons, no further plunder was to be obtained.

I learned afterwards that when John Connor arrived at home with his little band, he called his council together, and made the most stirring and bitter speech any of them had ever heard him deliver. It was reported to me that he had said : " I went out well-armed, mounted, and equipped ; my return, loaded with the trophies of the chase, was looked forward to with pleasure. I had promised to come back with meat for feasting and with robes for wear—I have brought back lamentation for meat, wounded brothers instead of robes. I went out a mounted warrior, and have returned a fugitive on foot. The spilt blood of my children cries aloud for vengeance. How can I look their mothers in the face when they say to me 'Where are my sons? Show us our sons or the scalps of their slayers!' What must I say to them? That I, their chief, I, the father of my tribe, have seen them killed before my face, without striking a blow for their defence and for the honour of my nation. But they shall be avenged. Is the spirit of the great Leni-Lenape nation dead—the spirit of the father-nation of all peoples? No! Those cowardly dogs of Cheyennes, those sneaking Coyotés, the Kiowas, shall find the Leni-Lenapes' arm reaches far, his knife is keen, his vengeance certain. My allies and brothers the Pottowattomies shall go with me. Disgrace shall be wiped out in blood. The face of the old men in the Cheyenne and Kiowa camps shall wear the black paint of mourning; their young women be widows, their old ones childless."

In such strain the old chief had continued to speak for an hour, delivering himself with the fluency and vehement gestures of an accomplished Indian orator, and concluding by a furious peroration, lashing himself and audience into a perfect frenzy of passion. Of course his address ended with a yell for immediate war, and runners were forthwith despatched through the nation, calling the braves to arms; and a deputation of "Sagamores" sent to the Pottowattomie chiefs asking for a contingent—such compliment being due to that tribe as treaty allies of the Delawares.

In three days Captain Connor took the field with something over two hundred men, the pick and flower of Delaware and Pottowattomie chivalry. This number did not represent the effective aggressive strength of those two nations. They are estimated to be capable of putting, if considered necessary, a united force of from one thousand to twelve hundred thoroughly armed and efficient horsemen in the field; but the old chief was confident that, considering the material at his command, and the plan of campaign he had determined upon, two hundred men were enough; and his greatest difficulty was in keeping his party from being larger than he wished, so eager were the braves of the tribes to be led to what they considered certain victory.

Connor's intentions were, as soon as he should arrive where there was danger of any hostile Indians perceiving the expeditionary party, to travel entirely by night, lying in the daytime in the closest cover he could find, keep a few of his most experienced men scattered as scouts well in advance, but in continual communication with him, and use every Indian dodge and wile to prevent the enemy from discovering he was "out." In short, the expedition was to be a surprise party. This was Captain Connor's chief reason for limiting his force; and indeed it would have severely taxed a less able Indian leader to take so large a hostile party as he started with into the heart of the prairies, unsuspected by the Indians wandering over them. But he knew the twists and winds of every stream, hollow, and valley of the ground he was going to operate on;

every unfrequented water-hole, every clump of timber. The Delaware chief's first aim was to strike the *cold* trail of the main hunting-party of his enemies well behind them; to follow it rapidly up, ascertain through his scouts where their camp was, its disposition and strength, where their band of horses was being herded, and then make a night attack.

Night attacks are not at all in the ordinary course of warfare between Indians of the Plains. Indeed, all the *wild* Indians seem to have a great aversion to making one, while it is quite out of my experience for *any* attack to be made by North American savages, except when they have the advantage of overwhelming numbers. When they do attack a camp their usual course is either to surround it towards morning, leave their horses under guard, crawl up in the grass as closely as possible, lie still until there is light enough to aim by, and commence the action by a sudden volley; or to ride up in range of the place to be attacked, and circle round and round it on horseback, keeping up a continual discharge of arrows and rifles.

It is probably as much from the complete want of discipline among the wild tribes, and their individual "ownhook" style of fighting, inducing a consequent want of confidence in their supports, as to their superstitious fears, that make night attacks almost unknown amongst them. But their very infrequency causes one, when properly delivered and sustained, to be all the more demoralising and effective; and it was the only way in which a party of two hundred could, with hope of victory, attack a camp of perhaps as many tepees. Connor had not gone through the Seminole campaign and Texan war of independence for nothing; nor had he instructed and led his braves for forty years without teaching them discipline, reliance on one another, and confidence in him.

The Indian tribes of the Plains make their great annual buffalo hunt in large bodies. The whole nation goes to it. It is the opportunity for every man to lay in the winter's meat and clothing for himself and family. The women and children who are able to assist do the skinning and cutting up, carrying and jerking, curing and dressing; and busy enough they all are when the edge of the great buffalo herd is reached and the slaughter has commenced. Besides, it is their golden opportunity to get all they can eat every day, to fatten themselves up after past privations. The encampment of a prairie tribe on its annual hunt is a city of tents, and their buffalo-runners, their riding-hacks, their pack-horses, cover the ground round about it. As they move along from time to time, following the slowly migrating herd, they make a trail as plain and easy to see as the Queen's highway—one that an Indian can follow at a hand gallop on the darkest night.

Captain Connor was on his mettle, and he made a great success of the expedition. An evening arrived when he called his little band around him, and informed his braves only half-a-night's easy riding lay between them and a large encampment of their foes, and that they would shortly have another opportunity to make the name of Delaware a sound of praise.

When close to the doomed camp, he halted his men and explained the plan of attack. The entire force would approach to charging distance. Twenty men, told off for the purpose, would detach themselves from the rest; their duty would be to find and stampede the enemy's troop of horses, drive all they could into a ruck, and start them at full-speed straight for home. The remainder would form in double line, open order, with intervals of ten yards between the men. Every man in the first line would hold himself in readiness, provided with a bundle of dry sticks of the resin-weed, enclosing a greased rag rubbed with gunpowder, wound round a bunch of prairie matches, head down, with a well-lighted piece of touch-wood stuck in their butts. Every man in the second line would have his revolver in his right hand.

The stampeding party would show a light when they started the horses. Immediately the first line was to charge, yelling, through the camp, whirl their fire-bundles in the air, and, as the draft caused them to burst into flame, hurl them against and into the tents, so as to set them or their contents blazing. At the report of his (Connor's) pistol, the second line was to follow the first, and as they charged through the camp, to fire their revolvers into the tents, shooting down every enemy indiscriminately. No quarter; no prisoners; no unnecessary time to be lost in scalping. The front line, when clear of the encampment at its farther end, to wheel round, draw their pistols, charge back, scatter through it in fours, and keep killing until they should hear the recall. The second line, when clear of camp, to form column, re-load, and await orders.

These commands given, the chief called up his head

men and privately imparted further directions, thus providing for the possible contingency of his being killed in the action.

The plan of attack was as ably executed as conceived, and a scene of the wildest description ensued. The surprised enemy, taken at every disadvantage, aroused out of sleep by savage yells, their tents blazing over their heads, shot down in numbers, and bewildered by the firing, were struck with panic and dismay, and made at first but the feeblest attempts at defence. But soon their best warriors armed themselves with such weapons as in the confusion they could lay hands on, and bravely rallied in a body several hundred strong round their chief in the centre of the camp. It was the moment waited for by Captain Connor. At the head of the reserve, charging in column, he tore through them like an avalanche, opened out right and left, and scattered his foes as a tornado would a forest's autumn leaves, and the blazing camp threw a glare of light upon a scene of massacre and carnage.

The party with the stampeded horses were already well on their way; the recall was sounded, and the victorious allies drew off and followed at a canter.

After a run of ten miles, the terrified band of steeds stopped, having then recovered their courage or lost their wind, and their drivers gladly halted and awaited the arrival of the main body. When this came up, lassoes were brought into requisition, some horses captured out of the band, saddles changed, and every man having got a remount, flight was recommenced, and with only the shortest possible halts for rest and refreshment, and with many a change of horses, continued until all were safe in the Pottowattomie nation, where the victorious old chief arrived with a loss of only three killed and seven wounded, and with over eight hundred captured horses, numerous scalps, and a tale of victory and triumph. We had arrived just as the preparations were finished for the celebration of "the late glorious victory."

This brilliant and dashing night attack was made when we were at Camp Gibraltar, and occurred not twenty miles from there. Probably it was the real reason we had been allowed to hunt in peace. While we were taking our sport and pleasure, the Indians, who would have been following the buffalo herd that afforded us our pastime, were howling over the slain, and dancing the solemn death-dance for their departed.

An attempt to describe, *interestingly*, the ceremonious dances and festivities of the North American Indians east of the Rocky Mountains has been often made; but description can hardly give an adequate conception of them, and not be tedious. Such things are, from their nature, very different to see and to read accounts of. To illustrate, I have no doubt but that a sight of *our* dances and festivities, of a well-appointed and executed European ballet or a Lord Mayor's feast, would be highly entertaining and interesting to a travelling gentleman from the Flowery Land; but his written description of the performances to his friends in China, would, I am certain, convey to them a very vague and uncertain idea of such spectacles. And the account could only be rescued from dreariness by seizing on its points of ridicule, poking fun at the performances, their executants, and their audience, or making it a text for philosophical disquisition. But Indian ceremonies are not funny, they are not ridiculous; they are wild, fierce, and earnest, ofttimes cruel and bloodthirsty. They are semi-religious rites, not celebrated in a perfunctory way, by a salaried pagan priesthood; but are the solemn, earnest exercises of grim, determined savages.

Clearly then, a light, jesting, joking account of them is out of the question. Philosophising is not exactly in my line; an attempt at it might be dangerous to my peace of mind. I might, like some others, bring up in a fog of limitless nonsense; I might end by confusing or multiplying my individuality, become a man beside myself. A friend of mine once succeeded in achieving that spiritualistic feat, through trying to seriously explain why tables turned at mystic séances. No, I cannot go into a disquisition on Indian war-dances, from a philosophical standpoint. I must let them alone. First-rate idea that. There is more money than the thoughtless imagine in "Let it alone." "Never do to-day what can be conveniently deferred until to-morrow," is another very valuable and much underrated maxim. Just think for a moment of the multitudes of suicides it would have saved, had this idea been properly impressed on our ancestors' youthful minds, say by its being made a standard copy-book heading, or a motto for book-markers! It is a short step in the direction of that higher conception, "masterly inactivity," the Hindoo idea of ultimate perfection.

In a few days we bade adieu to our wild friends, and

without the occurrence of any incident worthy of record, arrived at home. Our trip had been a complete success. It is rarely that a prolonged pleasure excursion does not either break down totally, or terminate with a feeling of disappointment and regret; that some unlooked-for misfortune does not occur, or that an anticipated pleasure does not prove, on experience, a hardship, a worry, or a delusion. Our first buffalo hunt had been a bright exception to the usual course of human events. We had made for ourselves a rash and hazardous programme; one beset with innumerable contingencies, with a certainty of danger, open to grave doubts as to the possibility of its achievement, and its successful fulfilment to the very letter had become an accomplished fact—a thing of the past. It had not only been fulfilled in outline and detail, but such fulfilment had been accompanied with, to us, many unlooked-for surprises, startling effects, and unrivalled scenery; and had, moreover, been performed with great (self) applause. Taken in its entirety as a pleasure trip, of the kind it was unparalleled, and we were fully satisfied.

CHAPTER X.

Quarter-racing—Old Double S.—The Wager—The Colt—The Race—Denver City—The Murder.

LIFE on the frontier brings a man in contact with strange characters, as well as into stirring scenes, of which fact the following sketch of a neighbour will serve as an instance; and an account of a race run by a colt of his soon after my return from the buffalo hunt narrated, besides being interesting in itself, will afford an opportunity to describe "quarter-racing," a style of "running" horses but little, if at all, practised out of North America.

Old Simon S—— was a "leading card" in the young Western city near which he resided—he was, in fact, one of the "institutions" of the place. He was well off, followed the profession of "gentleman at large," and his chief pleasure was horse-racing. He was an old bachelor, with a pretty niece who kept house for him, and he had the best stud of horses in the country. Old Double S., as he was familiarly called, was addicted to the "flowing bowl." His flowing bowl was four fingers of whisky straight, taken irrespective of the time of day or when last indulged in.

Habit is said to be second nature. This trite observation was finely illustrated by the gait, manner, and speech of Double S. Except by his most intimate associates Simon sober had ceased to be distinguishable from Simon tight, and its not being the eleventh hour of the day was, in his case, no safe rule to go by. But he was *most* notorious for his swearing—not common, ordinary, vulgar oaths, but elaborate, complicated, original, three-volume-novels of profanity.

Old Simon S. attended, as he had often done before, a "quarter-race," a name applied to races of a quarter of a mile straight run.

To a person only familiar with long courses a quarter of a mile dash seems absurd, but an afternoon spent witnessing several such is entertainingly passed; and in places where quarter-racing is in vogue it takes a tip-top horse, of the kind, to be a frequent winner. He must be compact, well-muscled, and active; long in his "jump," and quick in his "gather;" and, above all, his temper must be good, for, in so short a distance, much depends upon the start, of which there are generally many false ones, often made intentionally to worry and fret the horse of an opponent.

To dispense with every pound of weight possible the horses are always ridden barebacked, there being but a surcingle round them, and by the lightest of boys, the only use of riders being to steady the horses' heads, keep them in the course, and pull them up when the race is run.

The riding costume of the "race-boys" is white cotton stockings and ribbon garters, no shoes, a close-fitting pair of web drawers, a tight web shirt, and very small jockey cap—nothing to catch a particle of wind, no spurs, and a light keen cowhide whip.

The start is from a "scratch," behind which each horse is held by a "starter." The race-boys being mounted, the "judge" at the scratch asks: "Are you ready?" If the starters all say "Yes," he glances along the scratch to see none of the horses have a leg over it; if not, he says "Go!" The starters leave hold of the horses, hit them a good cut of a whip if they think it advisable, and, getting off at their quickest pace, the nags rush through "on the jump," and the *two* judges at the "outcome" give their decision.

A considerable amount of money often changes hands immediately after each race, the invariable custom being for all settlements to be made directly, and for all stakes and bets for the next race on the day's programme to be placed in stakeholders' hands before it is started for.

There is the inevitable "bar" on the ground, and "Let's take a drink" is heard on all sides between each event. Quarter-races are scenes of much sharp practice, if not of downright trickery, and at them all kinds of characters are to be met, the only exception being they are never attended by ladies—that term being used in its strict and exclusive sense.

On the occasion referred to, besides several minor matches, there was one of unusual interest to come off. A "crack" quarter-horse from a neighbouring State was to run against Chieftain, a local favourite. Double S. backed the local favourite liberally. The crack won easily, and the old squire mollified his feelings with several "four fingers of it," and by improvising and delivering a full, elaborate, and original commination service against the local horse, his owner, his rider, his starter, the judges, and everybody and everything, ending by saying that the local horse was a "bilk," and that he, Simon S., had a sucking-colt not yet six months old, who could that day week, over that very course, beat him for double the money. As he said this he produced a fat pocket-book, pulled out notes to the amount, and flourished them in the air. He was told to "shut up," and not talk stuff and nonsense. Everybody knew a colt of that age could not carry a rider. This only seemed to aggravate the squire. He rejoined, with a fresh string of new oaths, that his colt had more sense than Chieftain and his owner taken together; that he could run against and beat him without a rider or being led; and if anybody thought he (the colt) could not, and that he (Simon S.) was a —— fool, why, let them just "cover his money." Old Simon was evidently *very* drunk.

The owner of the losing horse, nettled by these remarks, smarting under his late defeat and loss of money, and considering that it was old Simon's look-out that he was under the influence of liquor, not his, produced the necessary coin, and took the bet. Of course a crowd had gathered round, and the squire's friends interfered, insisting he was not in a responsible state, and the bet must be considered off. Upon this old Simon got in a rage, and stated, in his usual impressive style, he would make it "a personal matter" with anyone who interfered.

In that country in those days such a threat meant mischief, and out of the squire's mouth was no joke; he had the reputation of being a "fighting man," and, considering how his hand habitually shook, was an extraordinary good shot. The stakes were consequently taken charge of by a stakeholder, with a private arrangement that, should old Double S. on the following day declare on honour he had been too drunk to know what he had been doing, they were to be returned; if not, it was a match P. or P.

But as there was general doubt as to this race coming off at all, and as nobody wanted to lose their time by attending a blank day, some other engagements were made for the same date, to secure a certainty of sport on the occasion.

The following day, when spoken to on the subject, the squire declared he was not drunk when he made the match between his colt and Chieftain, that he never did get drunk, that to do so was not a habit of his, that moderation in all things was the rule of his life, and further, that had he been drunk it made no difference; Simon S. sober would never turn his back upon Simon S. tight. No! he had always, and under all circumstances, stuck to his word, and always should; and then he made illustrative remarks not necessary to repeat here.

The universal opinion was that the old fellow would sooner lose his money than give a chance for it to be said he had "backwatered." Nevertheless there was some curiosity evinced about the "sucking colt." It was a very promising young thing—the first foal by a horse of celebrity out of a famous mare who had been recently retired, because her superiority as a quarter-runner caused her to be barred at all neighbouring races.

The day of the match arrived, and the attendance of "sports" and general public was quite large. One of the events had come off. Nothing had been seen of old S. S. or the sucking colt, and the odds were "The National Debt to a postage-stamp" against him—no takers.

The appointed hour had passed, and the thirty minutes grace was drawing to a close, when the squire appeared, riding his well-known cob, and leading the colt by a draw-strap, accompanied by the mare, its mother, ridden by a boy. On arrival he was greeted with a cheer, and without loss of time dismounted and led the colt up to the scratch.

The colt was a splendid little fellow, promising to be a dark bay with tan muzzle and black legs and feet; in tip-top condition, and was lunging and pulling to get away to his dam, who had stopped a little way off. I and some others lounged up to the mare to take a look at her. For a mare in milk she appeared very much like having been put in racing condition. I looked at her rider. He had a long great-coat on; he was one of the squire's race-boys. I glanced down at the mare's feet—*she had racing-plates on*.

As I walked back to the scratch I began to smell a very large rat. Somebody offered long odds against the colt. I took him, and offered to double.

Chieftain and the sucking colt were already at |the scratch. "Are you ready?" calls the judge. "Yes," answered Chieftain's starter and old Double S. Before the squire said Yes, I noticed him give a quick look down the course; I did so too. The mare was standing almost in it broadside on, a hundred yards in advance. The boy's coat and boots were off. He was in full racing rig. As the judge called Go! and Chieftain started, the mare's head was turned down the course, and away she went. The colt, liberated by the squire, rushed after his mother, and galloped past the judges at the outcome—a winner, with a gap of daylight between him and the Chieftain; and Simon S. claimed and received the stakes.

It is known to those who have hunted wild horses, but may not be to all readers of this book, that so soon as a foal gets the full use of its limbs it can always gallop as fast as its dam for short distances; as I knew that fact, seeing running-plates on the mare gave me "the straight tip."

When I next saw "the Colt" he was owned by a racing man at Denver City, and was the best horse there.

Denver City is associated in my mind with many a striking episode, and was, when I first knew it, the greatest possible contrast to the well-ordered, prospering railway centre it now is. Then, to use a localism, "we *was* not two boards nailed together of a town." It was a lawless, straggling encampment of pioneer adventurers, and a heterogeneous mob of the scoundrels that live upon the credulity and industry of "the honest miner." As they themselves said, but in far stronger language, it was a camp wherein the shadow of every bank was a drinking saloon, each tree a gambling-house, and all the bushes man-traps. And the *ladies* of the community having nearly all come there under the protection of low gamblers, Mexican horse-thieves, Texan outlaws, Yankee absconders, *et al.*, the morals of the place were decidedly "mixed."

There were some queer incidents always happening. For instance, there had been a row over a game of cards—no unusual thing—and of course there was no getting at the particulars. Everybody told a different tale; but one thing was certain, it had led to a "free-fight," and a man had been killed. Well, it turned out deceased had no friends and no money. When the man who had knived him heard that, he expressed his sorrow, adding—to prove he bore no animosity to the departed—he did not mind "standing" a first-class funeral for him, which he really did, and attended himself in the character of chief mourner.

CHAPTER XI.

More Denver—The Indian Scare—Preparations—My Camp—The Effects of Fear—Panama—The Railroad Journey to Colon—A Fright—The Sensitive Plant—A Pointer.

DENVER has seen many vicissitudes and strange occurrences. I was there during what was known and long talked of as "The Indian Scare," being then encamped only two miles below town, upon the south bank of the Platte river.

For some time all kinds of alarming rumours concerning the Indians had been circulating. The newspapers had been full of accounts of the "Minnesota massacre," and the mind of the public was altogether in a morbid state about Indian dangers. Denver was past its first stage of existence. It was full of storekeepers, eastern emigrants, Jew dealers, and freshly-arrived Europeans—people knowing nothing about the savages or what they were or were not capable of undertaking, and as frightened of them as small children are of bogies.

A Kansas City "bull-train," lately come in, had passed an encampment of over six hundred tents. Four or five of the tribes of the Plains were having a big talk together. Indians belonging to the tribe who had committed the massacre in Minnesota had been recognised among them; doubtless, therefore, a conspiracy was hatching for an organised assault in force on the whites. The most timid among the shopkeepers and dealers of Denver were sure their town would be attacked, captured, and sacked, and the more they talked the more they frightened themselves and each other. By-and-by the climax came.

A day's journey from Denver, on the road known as The Cut Off, was a road station, kept by two Germans, family men, each with *vrou* and *kinder*, but still not considered good settlers, for they were strongly suspected of being habitually guilty of that least tolerated of frontier crimes, trading whisky to Indians, a disreputable lot of whom were always hanging about their place; and while the Denverites were alarming themselves about the probability of Indian hostilities, the drivers of a passing mule-train discovered the scalped and mutilated bodies of these German families lying in their plundered cabin, and bringing the corpses with them into Denver, turned alarm into panic.

I happened to ride into Denver the evening of that day, and found everybody apparently crazy. The mayor had "gone off his head," and issued a proclamation calling upon all able-bodied men to assemble at the Town Hall with such arms as they might have. The gunsmiths' shops had been taken possession of by the authorities, all their arms and ammunition requisitioned, receipted for, and were to be distributed amongst those citizens who were unarmed.

The windows of a block of brick buildings were being boarded up for the women and children to take refuge in when the attack should commence. Everybody was in the streets, most of the women crying and the children howling. There was no possibility of doing my business that evening, so I returned to camp. The infection, however, had spread to it, and I found my men anxiously waiting for news. They begged me to let them hitch the mules to the waggons and drive for safety to the city. I peremptorily refused, and told them the idea of Indians attacking or even coming near with hostile intent such a big place as Denver City was utter nonsense. Though were they to try to take it they could do so easily enough, since in their present state of mind one half of the citizens would die of fright, while the surviving one would run away. That as to the murdered family, I believed selling whisky to Indians had been at the bottom of that affair. But if they liked they might park the waggons in good defensive shape, discharge and then reload their arms, and thus generally prepare for defence.

This I did for no other reason than that I thought doing *something* and firing off their weapons would inspirit them, and make them feel better contented and more satisfied. Two or three old hands were cool enough, but some of the rest were in a tremble of excitement. What does the reader suppose one of them did? He was a fine young fellow, considered to be of good courage, and from boyhood had been accustomed to use both rifle and shot-gun. He discharged his weapon in the air, took a box of Ely's caps out of his waistcoat-pocket—a full box—deliberately poured all the caps into his rifle-barrel, placed a greased patch on the muzzle, the ball upon it, rammed it down, withdrew the ramrod, and was pouring the powder out of his flask into the gun in a continuous stream, when I took it from him, and ordered him to sit down and keep quiet until he had my permission to stir. The young man sat down without a word, and I gave him a big dram of brandy, and told him to "get outside of that." This dose had the desired effect, and he recovered his senses. Fortunately for him, none of the men had perceived what he had done, and I took care not to mention it, for had the performance become known his life would have been rendered unbearable by their jeers and ridicule.

The effects of fear seem to be strangely various. I have had my experiences of that emotion, but never for long enough at a time to influence my conduct beyond some sudden gesture, while the reaction therefrom has in my case usually increased clearness of perception, intensified determination, and stimulated to action—most fortunate results of temperament to which I owe my life on more than one occasion.

Once, when travelling from Panama to Colon, I was as badly frightened—in my way of taking that affection—as were the Denverites by the "Indian scare," and with about equal reason. As the trip across the isthmus is, from its scenery and little incidents, always an interesting one, some account of mine on that occasion may prove entertaining.

Of my place of arrival, Colon, I shall say nothing; bad language is not my style, and its use is certainly unavoidable when describing that miserable hole. My point of departure, the port and town of Panama, is one of the oldest, quaintest, most picturesque of all Spanish-American cities; a place full of medieval-looking convents and monasteries, having a most unique and handsome cathedral, a fine old college, a hospital, and many curiously constructed and decorated churches. Surrounded with a city wall, built as a defence against the piratical sea-rovers of those old days when it was the emporium for the precious merchandise of Peru and Chili, and Spanish galleons carried the treasures of the world, it has also an ancient fort, whose crumbling walls are laved by the bright waters of a bay yielding the pearl of price.

The run from Panama to Colon is only forty-seven miles, and the highest point surmounted by the railroad two hundred and forty feet above the sea-level; but the gradients are occasionally rather steep, and the trains run quite slowly.

Soon after leaving Panama, the railway follows for some miles the course of the river Chagres, a slow muddy stream (about twice the size of the Usk at Brecon), abounding with alligators, through dense forests, with only occasional clearances near the villages or collections of huts at the various stations. During the last eight miles, before reaching Colon, the railway passes through a swamp covered with a rank growth of coarse grass, brushwood, and sedge, and which at most seasons is under water. At both ends of the line there are expansive sidings, and large warehouses for sheltering goods awaiting for transit. The railway works, taken throughout, are very heavy in cuttings, banks, and works of art on streams and dingles. All the bridges are of stone or iron, or a combination of both. The line is laid throughout with longitudinal sleepers of hard wood; but the destruction by white ants is a very serious item in the renewal. A plan has been adopted (and I believe successfully) for concreting the telegraph poles—that is, covering the poles entirely with a coating of cement concrete, so as to prevent the ants getting at the timber. At all the stations there are commodious houses built for the employés of the company, which are in grounds in most instances very tastefully laid out and neatly kept. The first train each morning carries the supply of meat for the employés along the line, and it is left at the various stations as they pass. The summit of the line is at thirty-two miles from Colon—so that the gradients between Panama and the summit are steeper than on the other side — though there is probably no gradient steeper than about 1 in 100. The western slope is far more beautiful and varied than the eastern, and the line winds about in a remarkable manner, to secure an even descent to the plains about Panama. We started early on a lovely morning, towards the termination of the rainy season, and vegetation was in its fullest luxuriance. We passed through fern and bamboo swamps, amongst low accidented hills, along a river's winding banks; a recent shower had cooled the air—that is to say, made it cool for that place; and rain globules, glistening in the sun, gemmed the surrounding foliage. Over hill and dale, in swamp and fen, crowning the distant eminences, opening in glades and savannas, to our right and left, their branches draped with the waving tresses of the Spanish moss, their stems covered with parasitic ferns and myriad orchideæ, whose blossoms loaded the air with a thousand sweet perfumes, grew Flora's loveliest forms. Majestic mangoes, mimosas, and huge wild fig-trees threw their welcome shadows on the ground. Creepers of every hue and form dappled the verdure with flecks and flashes of brilliant colour. The elegant green tracery of the tree-ferns' feathery plumes showed sharply against the clear blue sky. Symmetrical columns of dates, cabbage-trees, and cocoas, garlanded with convolvuli, stood in long vistas of fairy architecture; and towering palms of many kinds added their stately beauty to the scene. Pretty villas—white, cool-looking buildings with wide green verandahs round them, embowered amongst the choicest ornamental plants of the tropics, with little plots of bananas, with orchards of oranges and limes, pomegranates and spices, fields of sugar-cane and groves of coffee-trees: the residences of planters, railway officials, and the country quarters of rich Panama merchants—were to be seen from the road; and many a group of huts built of bamboo reeds, and thatched with palm leaves, villages of the natives. As the train passes these, women and children hasten from them to the side of the road, the "cars" are stopped, and delicious fruits, cocoa-nut-milk, palm fans, curiously-carved cocoa-nut bowls, and various other articles of native manufacture are offered to the passengers for sale. The costumes of these villagers afford no material for description. As we followed the course of the Chagres river we surprised several bathing parties with nothing on them. They were about as much dressed as the majority of the vendors of fruits and " notions."

Altogether, it was an interesting and delightful trip. There was but one drawback—Panama fever was reported very prevalent, and unusually malignant. There had been several recent deaths from that epidemic, and everyone in the train *would* talk about it. When passing some splendid crimson flowers, a lady, to whom I was temporary escort, expressed a longing to possess them, so I went forward and asked the conductor if he would stop the train while I got out and picked some. He knew who I was well enough, and most obligingly pulled the check-string; the engine was stopped, and the conductor offered to send one of the brakesmen for the flowers; but I preferred gathering them myself. It was the middle of the day, and the heat had become intense. The sun was quite vertical. A man's feet covered his shadow. After plucking a sufficiency of the crimson beauties, it occurred to me a border of green round them would be an improving addition, and noticing a large bed of plants, about knee high, of delicate form, and of a beautiful green shade, I walked to where they grew, stooped down, plucked a fine spray, and placed it alongside the flowers. To my amazement, I saw that I had gathered a withered, shrivelled, brownish weed. I chucked it away, carefully selected by my eye a large bright green plant, and plucked it. Again I had in my hand a bunch of withered leaves. It flashed through my mind that a sudden attack of Panama fever had struck me delirious, like the mayor of Denver. I went "off my head" from fright. I have no recollection of throwing the flowers down, but I did, for on coming to myself I saw they were lying at my feet. I looked around, nothing seemed changed or strange. I put my hand on my forehead, it was perspiring profusely. The air was hot enough to have made a lizard perspire. I felt my pulse, it was beating fuller and faster than usual, but as steadily as a chronometer. Clearly I was all right. I looked down at the flowers, and as I did so noticed that the plants I stood on were shrunken and wilted. An explanation occurred to me. Carefully I approached the tip of my finger to a luxuriant plant growing in front of me. As my finger neared it its leaves drew back, commenced to crumple up, to change colour. I had been frightened by sensitive plants. Of course I kept my counsel, but felt utterly disgusted with myself.

For years I had been used to danger, and so often, on finding myself in great and sudden peril, had I been stimulated, not alarmed, that I had deluded myself into a belief, no matter what happened, I should never more feel frightened. I shall not have such confidence in myself again. Like the Denverites, during the "Indian scare," I had been terrified by an imaginary danger, for—oh, most lame and impotent conclusion!—Denver was unmolested, and soon its citizens were heartily ashamed of themselves. To say "Indian," was to say a "fighting word," and the mayor went about telling everybody—in confidence—that he never had any apprehension of an attack; had only issued the proclamation to inspire confidence and allay fear. It was on the Platte route, from Denver City to the Missouri, that I got possession of the best pointer, by all odds, I ever fired over. A dog whose memory well deserves the slight tribute of his being made the hero of a chapter in this book.

CHAPTER XII.

The Bar-room—My Bargain—A Momentous Question—Tragic Fate of the Bar-keeper—Indian Massacres—" A high-toned Sport "—J. P.'s Visit— The Sale of " Grouse "—J. P. goes under.

I WAS on a return trip with a mule-train, from the Blackfoot country to Fort Leavenworth. We forded the Platte at the Julisburg crossing, and then struck the Denver road. Finding in plenty the three requisites of a good camp— wood, grass, and water—I determined to lay over for a halfday, to graze and rest my mules. Having nothing to do, I strolled down to the road station, about a quarter of a mile off. This station was one of the best on the route. A large square building of adobes (sun-burnt bricks), with a flat Mexican roof of cedar logs, covered with mud-mortar, and with adjacent corrals, stabling and stockades of cedar posts. It was kept by two well-known frontiersmen, who were content to stake their lives against a prospect of quickly " making a pile," which, indeed, they seemed at that time in a fair way to do.

They had plenty of wild-grass hay stacked, for sale ; a large band of horses and a good herd of cattle on the surrounding prairie ; and—*mais cela va sans dire*—the regular quota of squaws and half-breed papooses lying around. My waggon-master was with me, and called my attention to a pointer pup, apparently ten months of age, that was in the bar-room. I at once recognised his form, markings, and style. The stock he came of was quite unmistakable. He was from the best imported pointer dog and bitch in the West. I had killed many a bird over each. The wonder was how the pup had come there. Most probably he had been lost by, or stolen from, some officer *en route*; but that he was going to be owned by me, I instantly determined, and made my approaches to the station-keeper, standing behind the bar, accordingly. Lounging up to the counter, with his and my waggon-master's assistance, "I did the correct thing," and then entered on the usual topics of the place and time, the last news, the price of stock, and the subject which, on the Plains, was then the question of the day, the Indian policy of the Government. This naturally led to remarks on buffalo hunting, on coursing antelopes, on greyhounds, on dogs in general, and finally to my patting the one present, and to the following conversation:

"Who owns this dog? Is he good for anything?"

"I do. Guess he's a good 'coon dorg."

"How do you know that, since there is not a raccoon inside a hundred miles?"

"Wal', frien', yeou see thare ain't nothing in natur' made fur nothing. Neow the purp ain't fast enough fur tew ketch anything, end won't track a deer, end I b'lieve he's a nat'ral born fool; he'll do nothing but stan' the hull day with one leg up, end his tail so yeou kin heng a hat on it, trying tew stare one uv my chickuns or pigeons tew de'th. I've tried him at everything 'cept 'coons, end as he's no 'count fur anything else, I says he's a fus'rate 'coon dorg; end as thare's plenty uv 'em whar' yeou air going tew, yeou kin have him fur a dollar."

Down came the money on the counter, with "He is my dog," and to my waggon-master, "Tie him up."

The station-keeper stared hard at me and said: "I were only a joken 'bout the dollar, I'd have given yeou the purp fur the taking uv him away; he ain't worth his feed, nohow. However, a trade's a trade. But lookee here, stranger, yeou snapped me up so keen, 'pears to me yeou were arter him all the time; neow, no offence, I don't mean tew be personal, but air yeou a d——d fool, or am I?"

With difficulty I repressed a smile, and told him what the dog was good for, his pedigree, and that when "trained"— it was no use to say "broken" to him—he would be worth fifty dollars at least.

The station-keeper brought his fist down on the counter with a bang that made the glasses jump, and exclaimed, "By ——, I'm the d——d fool, and it's my treat round. Boys, what ul yeou pisen yerselves with?"

Poor fellow! it was doubtless the last dog trade ever made by him. Not many days after I left his station the great Sioux and Cheyenne outbreak occurred. In one night, without warning, for a distance of three hundred miles, every road station but two on the Platte and Big Blue rivers were rushed and captured by them, and, except some few almost miraculous escapes, their inmates massacred—men, women, and children, even babes. Why my train was not attacked during that raid I shall never know. Possibly because, as always was the case, whether in hostile country or on friendly soil, my camp was nightly pitched in a good defensive shape on advantageous ground — the waggons parked to make a temporary fort, enclosing the men and mules, and guards properly set; and perhaps because the certain heavy loss of life to any party who attacked me was a higher price than Indians cared to pay for a prospective chance of capturing an *empty* train. But though the trip was made in safety, it became an anxious and melancholy journey. We daily saw the smouldering ruins of burned and gutted stations—busy scenes, when we had last passed that way, of life and motion. Lonely desolation had replaced activity and enterprise. The unfortunates who had occupied them, then so full of confidence and hope, were murdered. All of them had been our acquaintances, some almost our friends. At one place the bodies of a family of sixteen strewed the ground, looking ghastly and horrid in the bright light of day. There they lay, all, from the gray-headed old grandfather to the last infant—the corpses of the sons, their wives and little ones; their sisters, the old man's three marriageable girls; an orphan grandchild—all lay there, stripped, mutilated, partly charred. Decently and reverentially we put them "below' wolf smell." More bitter curses than prayers were said I fear over those graves by the rough and hardy mourners who stood round. "Lo the poor Indian" would have received scant mercy at their hands had a chance for vengeance presented itself. In after years more than once the memory of that scene has flashed through my mind, and, "Sergeant, pass the word quietly amongst he men that we can *not* be troubled with prisoners to-morrow," has been the result.

And what became of the dog? Well, Grouse, for so I named him, proved to be all I had expected, and was so well-bred there was no trouble in breaking him, especially as I had steady, knowing old dogs to hunt him with. But I did not keep him long. I was soon to be engaged in the pursuit of very different game, and could not take dogs with me. I sold him to J. P., a well-known "professional gambler," a typical specimen of, to use one of their own expressions, "a high-toned sport"—a species of gambler unknown I think in Europe. There was no disguise as to J. P.'s calling in life. He kept a bank—a faro bank—and considered himself quite a man of honour. His credit was excellent; there was no lack of confidence as to his paying his debts. No man suggested a doubt of the truth of his word, or questioned the fairness of his "tables," unless he wished for an opportunity to "look down the hole of a shooting-iron." His dress was good style; his manners quiet and courteous; and his bank a very pleasant lounge, where his friends, at his (J. P.'s) expense, smoked the best of Havannahs, imbibed the choicest of drinks, and were waited upon by the most respectful of "coloured boys;" but where the play was very high, and no doubt the percentage in favour of "the game" gave him a handsome income. Certainly it was known to me that J. P. made regular remittances to his old mother "in the East," to be by her invested. Still he *was* a gambler, and therefore not in *society;* and though madame his wife was quite correct, and a pretty, ladylike, well-informed little woman, dressed to the extreme of good taste and expense, she was not called upon by the *ladies* of that frontier neighbourhood.

One evening I dropped into J. P.'s bank, just to look at the play and try a new brand of cigars, of which my opinion had been requested. Before leaving I was asked by him : " Can you spare a thorough good *bird-dog?* " I told J. P. promptly, "Yes," and what the dog would do. That at a whistle he would look round and obey the move of the hand, ranging forward to the right or left, come to heel, or down charge, as the signal might be given; that he quartered the ground with his head up, hunting by the taint in the air, not the trail on the ground; that if the birds took to running he would make a wide circuit, getting them between him and the gun ; that he backed, dropped to shot, and retrieved ; and that it would take seventy-five dollars to buy him.

Seventy-five dollars for a pointer was then and there an awful price, so I wound up by saying : "I do not ask you to take my say-so only for his perfection ; come down to my little place, any time next week, stay over the following day, and we will go and kill some birds to him, and you can judge for yourself." I could do this, notwithstanding J. P. was not invited where there were wives and sisters, because, though, from knowing the helplessness of man, and to make things pleasant about my home, I had secured that first necessity to comfort, a good housekeeper, she did not hold either of those relationships to me, so I could do as I pleased in such matters.

J. P. came down accordingly, and we passed a very

pleasant evening together. He was a good talker, had seen a great deal of life, and descriptions of it from his standpoint, had a newness and originality that were quite interesting.

Next morning, after breakfast, the "gunning waggon" was brought to the door, a hamper of cold collation, another of ice, something to drink, and the dogs and guns placed in it, and, seated behind a couple of "wind-splitters," we started for the prairie. By luncheon-time J. P. and I had bagged thirty or forty "chickens" (grouse) and some wood-ducks (ducks that perch and build their nests in trees), made our way to a prairie "creek," and resting in the shade of a large swamp-maple that overhung a hollow where the stream had widened to a pool, rewarded skill and energy with the C. C., and then made chemical experiments with Angostura bitters, champagne, crushed sugar, pounded ice, and Sp. Vini Gal.—purely, of course, in the interest of science. This led to a discussion on the theory of the formation of clouds, and consequently necessitated some practical illustrations, so that we spent three hours pleasantly and instructively. We then drove to some wild-plum and hazel thickets, where the quail were found in such numbers that for a while the shooting sounded almost like file-firing. I do not recollect the total bag, but remember it was large, even for that country, for the shooting, especially before those chemical experiments, had been very good, and Grouse had highly distinguished himself. Nothing, however, was said by either of us about the dog's purchase until J. P.'s buggy came to the door the next day, when, after asking for pen and ink, my departing visitor took out his bank-book, filled in a cheque for the amount I had named, and handing it to me, made a pretty complimentary speech of thanks for the pleasure, &c. &c.

Poor J. P.! He considered himself a good Conservative, was hot on politics, and, of course, sprang to arms at the first tap of the drum, whose echoes soon after rolled over the land from the Gulf of Mexico to the St. Lawrence. He fell at Table Mountain, in a desperate rally against overwhelming odds, fighting for his "principles and country."

CHAPTER XIII.

"The best Dog in the World"—Nip and Tug—Joe and Laughfy—Their Peculiarities—The Outfit—Traps—Description of Wet-mountain Valley —Sangre de Cristo Pass—The Mosca Pass.

IT has been my fortune to own many good dogs besides Grouse. In my experience every sportsman asserts he once owned "the best dog in the world." This time I am equal to the occasion, and assert I once owned the *two* best. For camp service and the pursuit of large game, they were certainly unsurpassable. It has also been noticed by me that most men, when they think they have possessed unusually good animals, like to talk and write of them, and believe everybody else would like to hear and read about them. I am no exception to the general rule. I should like to say a good deal about those two dogs. They were almost more than dogs to me, for I found them interesting companions as well as efficient aids during a long winter's camp-out in the Rocky Mountains. To write a detailed account of that camp-out would enable me to gratify my inclination, would give an idea of the sports and pleasures, the difficulties and hardships, of life in the wilderness, and would furnish a general notion of the scenery and habitants of the central portion of the Rocky Mountains. So, leaving out everything connected with the trip that would not serve these purposes, I shall proceed to do so, commencing with some description of the *personnel* composing the party, and giving those two dogs the *pas*. Nip and Tug were brothers. Their mother was an extraordinarily large and powerful English greyhound, which had been procured at a long price, and imported at considerable expense, for the purpose of breeding antelope-coursers from. As other wards have been known to do, she eluded her guardian and eloped, going off with a savage bull-mastiff, who from his size and ferocity was a terror to his own neighbourhood, and who had the honour to be father to the subjects of this "first-class notice." Nip and Tug remained the two survivors of a massacre of the innocents, and were "raised" more out of curiosity as to how they would turn out than with any idea of their becoming valuable. Contrary to what might have been presumed, instead of proving clumsy, ill-made, bad-conditioned curs, they were very symmetrical dogs, combining the general greyhound outline of form with prodigious strength of build—adding to the reach and gather of the greyhound, the send and power of the mastiff, and the courage and pertinacity of the bull; and, strange to say, were both higher and heavier than either of their parents; in fact, using the words in their American as well as English sense, they were the "tallest" dogs I have ever seen. In colour and markings they were striped black and tawny brindles, and so much alike that many who were in the habit of seeing them daily could never tell them apart. Four men

—that is to say our two "hired hands," and myself and the partner and companion mentioned in the buffalo hunt already narrated—completed the party. A small one, but sufficiently large; because the ultimate success of the expedition depended, amongst other things, upon the discretion and faithfulness of all concerned; and no danger was to be apprehended of molestation except from Uté Indians, who were at peace with the whites; and as they, being a warlike, well-armed tribe, could, if so inclined, dispose of any force short of a regiment, there would have been no added safety in increasing the party; while, once away from our base, having to depend entirely on the supplies taken along, more men would have been but adding to expense, trouble, and annoyances. The two who accompanied us had long been in our (myself and comrade's) employ, and their courage in danger, readiness in difficulty, and caution in matters of importance were well known to us.

Joe was a big, good-natured, pleasant-looking Missourian, who had received only a slight common-school education, but was one of the best pistol-shots I ever met, and very nearly as good a one with the rifle. He considered that the accomplishments of life were to be an "elegant" axeman, a dead shot; to possess ability, while sitting on the "waggon-box," to flick a fly with a driving-whip off the nigh ear of the off-leader of a six-mule team without hitting the other leader; and, finally, to be a good horseman. Book learning he had great respect for in its way, as a sort of thing that some people ought to know; but he considered there was much humbug about it. Once when in a confidential mood, he told me that at school he had been taught the world was round and went round the sun, which might be all very well to teach town fellows, but was "derned bosh" to tell *him*, who they knew meant to travel and was sure to find out they were lying. Joe had also strong convictions about slavery. His old father, who was a hard-fisted working farmer in a very small way, once owned a nigger, and Joe considered he belonged by birth and position to the slaveocracy. This question was the *great* point of difference between our two "hands," who, when they had nothing to do or talk about, held long and extraordinary arguments on the subject.

Our other man "went to bed with the name" of Lafayette, which of course had been shortened to Laughfy, and by that *sobriquet* he was always called, which, considering he was of a grave and sedate aspect, was sufficiently absurd. Laughfy was a "Yank," from Maine, as tall as Joe but not so burly, and as sallow of complexion as the former was ruddy; an equally expert axeman, very nearly as good a shot and teamster, he yet held proficiency in such things in contempt. He was great on "isms," a spiritualist, a Swedenborgian, a propounder of the "higher law," a (in theory) negro-equalist; but had actually little, if any, more education than Joe, and certainly not the clearest of ideas on any of those difficult subjects. Both were ardent patriots in a restricted way. Joe was firmly persuaded that "Old Missouri" was the finest country in the world. To hear him talk, you would come to the conclusion he had no use for any other country except to furnish places to be disparagingly compared with his "state." I have no doubt if he had not "travelled" his belief would have been that the sun rose and set in Missouri, and that the rest of creation was only favoured with a view of that luminary's back. Laughfy's patriotism took a different turn, he "went" on people, not things, and maintained that Yankees, especially Maine Yankees, were the salt of the earth. They were the discoverers and expounders of all true liberty in religion, politics, and social science — the great inventors and ameliorators of the age; all mankind had their eyes fixed on them in admiration, envy, fear, and astonishment. Laughfy's opinion of the inhabitants of his "section," and Joe's of the natural advantages of his state, were not mutually shared. Indeed, Laughfy's contempt for Missouri was only equalled by Joe's "estimation" of Yankee character; but neither would willingly have hurt the other's feelings by openly avowing their beliefs, for were they not both true frontiersmen and mountaineers, who, as such, held each other in respect, and were bound to one another in the natural freemasonry of manly straightforwardness and kindred pursuits?

"The outfit" consisted of two strong and light waggons —thimbleskins—built expressly for mountain travel; two teams, each composed of four fine well-broken mules, fifteen hands high and very heavy; two extra mules, and two saddle-horses—hunters. The waggons had "tilts"— covers of Russian duck stretched over hickory bows—and were freighted as follows: Nine fifty-pound sacks of flour, two hundred pounds of bacon, three months' rations of coffee, sugar, and salt; some cans of lard, a keg of whisky, a bale of tobacco, a few strings of red peppers, soap, Indian corn for our animals; clothing, blankets, ammunition, arms, traps, cooking utensils; instruments—a diminutive medicine-chest, a small kit of gunsmith's and blacksmith's tools, axes, shovels, picks, pans, ropes, a grindstone, sledges, drills and gads, a keg of blasting-powder, a coil of fuse; "fifth chains" for double teaming over bad places, spare single and double trees; extra waggon-tongues and axle-grease pots, slung alongside; and lastly, but not least in estimation, some currant jelly, and the materials for an old-fashioned English plum-pudding, which, with roast venison, turkey, and all procurable hunters' delicacies, was to make our Christmas dinner.

The traps were twenty in number—beaver-traps—that, with their chains, weighed eight pounds apiece. So, though we had cut down everything necessary to take along to the least prudent amount, our waggons were heavily enough laden, considering the length of the contemplated trip, and the badness, or rather non-existence, of roads in the country we were to travel over before arriving at our ultimate destination—that old centre of trade and mining, the ancient Mexican city of Albuquerque.

Hunting was not only to be our chief recreation to while away time that would otherwise be spent in inactivity, but was calculated upon as a means to provide our daily meat. The beaver-traps were taken because we were keen trappers, thoroughly enjoying that pursuit, and besides that beavers are excellent eating, their fur was then up in the market. Every pelt we might have to dispose of at Albuquerque would bring five dollars, and so be tangible rewards for skill and care; and we were about to travel where beavers were said to abound and had not been trapped for many years; while, being first-rate trappers, we reasonably looked for success.

The locality of our winter camp was a place then known by the few whites who had been there, as Wet-mountain Valley. And we were "laid on to it" by an old mountaineer, who gave us our route, and a good description of the topography of the valley, besides other most important information. He also satisfied us it was just the place to winter in, being full of wood, water, grass and game; and that, excepting for short occasional periods when visited by Uté hunting-parties, it was totally uninhabited. For a mountain valley we were told it had an excellent climate, being, owing to its comparative lowness and the shelter of the mountains that surrounded it, quite warm in winter; that snow rarely fell there, the storms being intercepted by the mountain-peaks, and that when it did, it soon disappeared, melted by the hot sun of a southern latitude, and absorbed by the warm, gravelly soil; that about Christmas there might be heavy snow-storms in the mountains, but it was very unusual for them to be so severe as to close any of the passes. In ordinary winter seasons, our informant added, the valley could be entered or left at any time, and should any of the passes be closed, it would only be for a very short period. And we might count to a certainty on getting out in the course of a spell of fine weather, that always intervened between the middle of February and the storms of the equinox; the snow that would then be in the passes having settled down and got hard enough to travel over.

We found Wet-mountain Valley to be a district covering a space of forty miles by twenty, enclosed by interlocking peaks, belonging to the Rocky Mountain system, some of which were the highest of that range, and to be a congeries of mountain glades, glens, and small valleys, opening into each other, and of dividing ridges, some sharp and rugged, others having small table-lands on their tops; in fact, a basin of intermingled miniature mountains and plains. Down most of the valleys coursed streams, which headed in the inaccessible surrounding summits, and were fed in summer by the melting of the snow which lay upon them. The upper portions of these streams were bordered by osiers and willows, and occasional groves of ghostly-looking, quaking aspens; replaced, lower down, wherever the ground was level, by large bodies of cottonwood-trees, of unusual size, whose trunks, being free from branches for some twenty feet from the ground, permitted the growth of a dense underbrush, which in many places was so matted together with grape and other vines as to be quite impassable for man. These bodies of timber ranged in size from a few acres to several hundred; and in them were places where mountain whirlwinds, in passing through, had thrown every stick of timber down into a chaos of confusion, over which vines, brambles, and creepers of many kinds had grown, making jungles which were the safe retreats and contained the lairs of bears, pumas, and that largest and fiercest of the wolf species—the gray mountain-wolf. The low dividing ridges were covered with dwarf cedars, juniper

trees, piñons—a pine, having large edible seeds, which are stored by Indians for winter use—and by clumps of small oak-trees of many varieties, thousands of which trees lay on the ground, pulled down or twisted and broken off by bears, to enable them to feed at leisure on the acorns. On the flanks of the mountains were hemlocks, spruces, balsams, and pitch-pines, and their slopes were covered to the snow-line with a dense forest of the Mexican piños-real. The open spaces of the valley were covered with grass, which, having cured on the ground by the great heat of the almost rainless summers of that locality, had become a natural hay, and under the timber were patches of long bunch-grass, which there remains green all the year round. The main stream, resulting from the confluence of the others, was about sixty yards in breadth where widest, and very tortuous, being often doubled back upon itself by the protruding points of rocky ridges; and ultimately cutting its way through the eastern boundary range by a deep narrow pass or cañon, several miles long, debouched by a cleft in the rocks—the "Gate of the Plains"—into a large open valley, that led to the "great American prairie." The trail from the outside world to Fort Garland, in the San Luis Valley, came up this cañon, and then, swinging to the south, left Wet-mountain Valley by the Sangre de Cristo Pass into the San Luis Valley—a pass *over*, not *through* the mountains, and practicable for mule trains, which took from three to four days to make the crossing from one valley to the other; the time varying with the amount of pick, shovel, and axe work necessary, and the strength of the train. The old mountaineer had informed us that the

Sangre de Cristo Pass had, in some exceptional seasons, been closed by snow; for the summit valley through which it ran had steep sides and was about six miles long, and had been known to be totally filled up with light drifted snow; but that there was another pass to the San Luis Valley from the Wet-mountain, one leaving its upper end and going towards the north-west, that never was totally closed. Even in the worst winters, men on snow-shoes could always get over. It was called the Mosca Pass, but being very steep and precipitous on both sides, and crossing the summit at a much greater elevation than the Sangre de Cristo, and being besides the direct road to nowhere, the trail had from disuse become long since unperceivable. An Indian trail from the north was, he believed, the only other inlet to Wet-mountain Valley. It was the route of the Utés from Elk Mountains, but was in every respect a bad one, and only available to enter the valley by not being practicable to ascend.

CHAPTER XIV.

The Scenery—Our Winter Quarters—A Lean-to—The Country—White Tails—Black Tails—Spruce Deer—Ashlata, or Bighorn—Antelopes—Bears—Wolves—Foxes—Pumas—Lynx and other Game—The Snow-storm—An empty Larder.

WE entered the valley which, for the time, was to be our home, by the "Gate of the Plains," followed the old Fort Garland trail until we came to an abandoned log-hut and corral, which had been a road-station when Fort Garland was in course of construction, and thence made our way up Wet-mountain Valley as best we could. There was no longer track or trail but those of wild animals.

As we emerged from the head of the cañon, most charming pictures opened out to us, and, what pleased us more, we not only continually crossed the fresh tracks of game of many kinds, but often, on looking up the different side valleys whose mouths we passed, saw the animals who had made them. Streams of clear mountain water were rippling and sparkling down each vale; grass, timber, and game were all round us; every few minutes new and varied scenes of beauty and grandeur presented themselves to our eyes. A warm haze mellowed and blended the thousand tints of autumn, and we seemed to be gazing on Fairyland.

Our progress was necessarily slow; for though, when our course led over open grass-land, we travelled at the regulation pace for loaded mule-trains—three miles an hour—we had many times to cross side streams, and often the main one, on which occasions roads had to be cut through their bordering fringes of timber and jungle, while when crossing the main creek, fords had to be found, for in many places it was deep and turbulent.

In the afternoon of the third day we reached a spot near the upper end of the central or chief valley, which was so well adapted for the site of our winter quarters that we halted, aad at once commenced operations. A "lean-to," for a residence, was thus built. Three forked oak posts were planted firmly in the ground and twelve feet apart. In these forks, at a height of six feet from the ground, were laid two spruce-fir boles forming a "ridgepole;" light poles were placed against it, six inches apart, and extending backward at an angle with the ground of forty degrees, and forming the rafters of a roof sloping from the ridgepole to the earth; against these was placed a layer of cedar boughs, with the leaves pointing downwards and several feet thick, making a shelter impervious to rain, snow, or wind. Twenty feet in front of our lean-to was built our fire—a permanent institution. It was laid for the whole length of our shelter composed of trunks of trees, and was to be kept alight while we remained. Beyond the fire, at a similar distance from it, a "hitching-bar" was put up, to fasten horses and mules to. A high platform was built to keep meat and other things out of wolf or puma reach; a hole sunk in the ground and lined with flat stones as an oven. Our winter quarters were "fixed."

The situation chosen was on the left bank of the main creek, in the angle of a sharp bend formed by its swinging round close to the base of a precipitous spur from the mountains bounding the valley on the southern side, and just above the junction of a considerable stream coming through a narrow, rocky, timbered cañon, which, a little way up, opened to a large valley that was one dense mass of jungle, crossed and re-crossed in all directions by much-used game-paths.

To our right, for about a mile, extended flat, open grass-land, followed by a succession of low parallel ridges and intervening narrow glades, these ridges getting higher and more precipitous, and the glades partaking more and more of the character of mountain gorges as they approached the base of the boundary mountains to the north. This broken country was five miles across. The ridges varied from one hundred to several hundred feet in height, and their tops were small table-lands, sometimes thickly covered with cedars and piñons, at others having but a fringe of those trees around them. Beyond commenced the gradual slope which constituted the base of the mountains that rested on it, a huge natural glacis, of an average width of two miles and ascending a thousand feet. From it rose up the granite range, in a series of precipitous cliffs and grassy alps, to a height of from seven thousand to eight thousand feet, two-thirds of the way clothed with

K

heavy timber, and capped and crowned with snow—the Sierra Vérde. Behind us the principal valley spread into a park-like country, joined by many small valleys from the south and west, and then veered round to the north, and continued with varying width to the base of the mountains.

There being no inducement to our stock to stray—grass, shelter, and water abounding round camp—they were turned loose to rest and fatten; but each night two or three were tied to the hitching-bar, to provide for unforeseen necessity, and because their companions, always remaining near them, were less likely to be attacked by wolves or pumas than if they had spent the night in some neighbouring ravine, to which the bunch-grass might have tempted them.

Our early explorations in Wet-mountain Valley incidentally assured us of two very gratifying facts. We had the whole valley to ourselves, and it was full of game—fur, feather, and fin—the streams being full of trout. The game consisted principally of several kinds of deer. In the low valleys and the timber bordering the creeks were "white-tails," so called because their tails, which, for deer, are very long—fifteen inches—are quite white on the under side, and they have a way of raising and flourishing them as they gallop away which is very noticeable. These deer have very long legs, standing high for their weight, which averages for bucks in good condition eighty pounds net, and for does in equal condition sixty; and are essentially a creek or valley deer, not frequenting the mountain slopes. Nor do they congregate together in large herds. We often found solitary ones, sometimes two or three, and but rarely as many as a dozen together.

"Black-tails," large-bodied, short-legged deer—the bucks dressing a hundred and fifty pounds, the does proportionably heavy—were on the mountain sides, the alps, and the most elevated of the small mountain valleys; being only seen in the plain when crossing from range to range.

Large black-tail bucks we often found alone, but it was not unusual to see twenty or thirty black-tails in a herd. On one occasion thirty-seven were counted.

Last and least, "spruce-deer," of which a few small bands ranged high up the mountains; fat, short-legged little fellows, about the size of goats, very hard to find and kill, but furnishing the best of venison. Above, far up on the rocky snowy peaks, were droves of the ashlata or bighorn—the American equivalent for the argali of Asia—a true sheep in all respects, though their wool does resemble hair, and whose mutton is, so far as I can judge, the best in the world. In the larger valleys were several herds of antelopes, averaging about twenty head, but in the "park" was one of over seventy. They were all very wild and wary, rendered so by being continually chased by packs of wolves.

Quantities of elk antlers lay in some of the most retired valleys, some so large that a pair being set up on its points would form an arch high enough to walk under without stooping; but we saw no elk. The "sign" of bears—black, brown, and cinnamon—was everywhere; but they were "housed for winter." Grislies were *said* to be habitants of the country, but I do not believe they were.

My experience of grisly bears—and I have often made their *personal* acquaintance—is, anybody to the contrary notwithstanding, that they do *not* hibernate. I think the belief that they do has arisen from the cinnamon, or more properly speaking the *cimmarron* (Spanish-American for wild or savage) bears being continually confounded with them by those who write chiefly from hearsay. They are, however, distinct and separate species, one *always* hibernating, the other, I think, never doing so. Certainly the grisly does not hibernate in California, where I have frequently tracked them in the snow in midwinter, and seen their *fresh* tracks every day all winter through; and as we did not do so in Wet-mountain Valley I doubt their existence there.

Wolves were very numerous, and of three species—first and foremost, the gray mountain-wolf, the largest and fiercest of the genus, hunting in packs by day as well as night; next, the timber-wolf, of a dark bluish-gray, a solitary, skulking-night prowler; lastly, the coyóte, a small, cunning fellow, always hunting or sneaking about by day or night singly and in small bands.

Of foxes there were a few silver-grays, whose fur is the most valuable of the fox family; innumerable common American gray foxes, a few specimens of the red fox, and many "swifts"—the last-mentioned a species of fox I have rarely met with, and nowhere as plentifully as in Wet-mountain Valley. He gets his name from his great speed, which is astonishing. I believe he is not only the fastest goer of his size, but absolutely *the* fastest of all animals. He is of a blackish-gray colour on the back, with a handsome silver-gray, white-tipped tail. His ears, neck, upper fore-legs, and hocks are reddish orange, and the edges of his thighs, belly, breast, and throat pure white. He is as pretty as he is fleet, and can catch a rabbit as easily as a collie can a sheep.

The cat genus, from lynx to pumas, was well represented. Raccoons, badgers, mink, otter, and beaver, were plentiful, and " varmints " of all kinds abounded.

Of game birds only wild turkeys were in sufficient numbers to be objects of pursuit. There were a few mountain partridges and some wood-grouse; but wild cats and foxes kept them very scarce, as they also did rabbits and mountain hares. The turkeys differed slightly from those we had been in the habit of shooting farther north and east. They were much lighter and more party-coloured in their plumage, showed much more white and brown markings, but had the same calls and habits. None of the flocks were large. They ranged from a dozen to thirty head to the " drove."

Of predatory birds first mention belongs of right to " the king of the air," the great American white-headed eagle, who in that locality was, for him, numerous. Turkey-buzzards could be always seen wheeling aloft, and occasionally some immense vultures; but we were not able to get a close inspection of any of them, for they kept out of shot. Had we not been so far north of the limits assigned by naturalists to the condor, we should, from their size and flight, have believed these birds to be such. Hawks and owls of many varieties were there, and magpies and jays were more plentiful than welcome, for they were very bold, and great nuisances, pilfering our meat, springing our traps, and alarming game that we were stalking by screaming out at us; in short, by making themselves generally detestable; and small birds, not game, abounded in every wood and thicket—many of familiar kinds, many of strange ones.

Until within two weeks of Christmas we had most charming weather; occasional snow showers were seen to fall amongst the mountain-peaks, but in the valley neither snow nor rain fell, and almost all the time the sky was a clear cloudless blue. The middle of the day was quite hot —we were pretty far south—but owing to our elevation and the time of year, the nights had been sharply cold; our huge log fire had, however, kept us warm and comfortable, and our spare time been well enjoyed in hunting.

One morning we were surprised by finding that snow was falling, and had apparently been doing so all night. Our animals, except those tied up, had run off before the storm, and their tracks were of course snowed over and not visible. The storm lasted until next morning, when the weather cleared up bright and fine, the ground being covered a foot deep with snow. That day was spent seeking in vain for the missing animals, but they were found the following one, in a little nook they had discovered, where there was good shelter and abundance of tall bunch-grass, unburied by snow. They were doing famously, and there we left them. While looking for the animals a very unwelcome fact was revealed. The game had all disappeared. Not a track was to be seen but those of beasts of prey. That they would return, having only gone off temporarily to sheltered places, as our mules had done, we felt confident; but we feared disappointment in the Christmas dinner, which had been long looked forward to, talked about, and provided for, excepting the fresh meat; and the storm had caught our larder in a most unprepared state, and just ere the arrival of the time when we had calculated to lay in our stock of game for the Christmas feast. The remains of a fore-quarter of venison was all the fresh meat on hand. We had a first-class prospect of keeping high festival on fat bacon and plum-pudding, which as a Christmas dinner would not only be a great disappointment to our expectations, but an outrage on our sense of the fitness of things. But, mountaineer-like, we hoped for the best.

CHAPTER XV.

A Drove of Turkeys—A fat Buck—Coming to Grief—Cold Work—The Turkeys again—Skyed—The flowing Bowl—The big Buck "gone for"—Our Bill of Fare complete—How it all happened—Our Christmas Dinner.

On the evening of December 23rd, word was brought into camp by one of the hands who had been looking up the mules, that he had come across the tracks of some twenty-five turkeys, within five or six miles of camp. This was indeed great news. Hope dawned upon us. We should have the fat turkey for Christmas, at all events.

At daylight the next day we started for the spot where the turkey tracks had been seen. The snow was melted off the low ground, but still lay thick on the cedar and piñon ridges, and in patches on the bottoms.

On arriving at the place we took the trail, and soon ran it to a ridge-top, covered with piñon trees, on the nuts of which the turkeys had been feeding. Here the tracks spread in all directions, since the turkeys had wandered about, each on his own hook, searching for nuts; and, to double the chances of finding them, we also separated, one going up, the other down the ridge; going, too, very carefully, for wild turkeys are the most wary of all birds, and require to be hunted with, if possible, more caution than do deer. And we knew not the moment when we might come upon our game, as it was highly probable they were close at hand; for turkeys, if unmolested, daily frequent the same range of feeding-ground until it is exhausted of food. By-and-by I came to where eight of the straggling birds had come together, and started off again in company. The drove had evidently separated into two or more lots, and I followed the eight turkeys for many miles and many hours without seeing fresh sign, until at length I came to the edge of a precipitous cliff overlooking a wide part of the valley, the river flowing just below me, and a large grove of big cotton-wood trees in a bottom not far away. Evidently I was at the place from which the turkeys had flown off the night before to go to roost. I quickly descended, and going under the cotton-wood-trees, searched in the tangle and jungle for sign of their having roosted above, and soon satisfied myself that they had done so. The next step necessary was to discover where the turkeys had alighted in the morning, but this might entail a long search, and as it was already past noon, I sat down to rest, eat the luncheon I had provided myself with, and come to some conclusion as to which direction I had best choose to make my first cast in.

I had not proceeded far on my way again, when I came suddenly upon "sign" that arrested my attention, and raised hope in my breast—the tracks of a big fat buck! He had crossed the river-bottom diagonally, and his trail plainly told me all about him; the great width of, and the distance between his tracks, proclaimed his sex and size, and their depth in the ground his weight. He had been going at an easy trot, the glaze on them was bright, their edges unbroken, not a speck of drifted dust was on them; they were as fresh as new paint. They were not an hour old.

In imagination I smelled roasted venison, and instantly started in pursuit. I followed on the tracks until within an hour of sunset, but never got even a glimpse of the deer; and by that time his trail had brought me to the bank of a stream flowing down one of the side valleys. The buck, browsing here and there, but never stopping long in one place, had led me a wide circuit, through and over valleys and ridges. He had not seen or smelled me, however, since none of his movements showed that he had been alarmed.

The stream, at the place where the deer's track led to it, was unusually wide, consequently slack in current, and therefore frozen over. The snow still lay on the ice, and the buck's tracks, where he had crossed, looked but just made. The ice seemed firm, and I started to cross the creek. About ten feet from shore, bang through I went, waist-deep, into the cold water, and broke and scrambled my way back with great difficulty, and with noise enough to frighten into a gallop any wild animal that might be within a quarter of a mile of me.

It was very disagreeable, very annoying, and *very* cold; and my clothes beginning to freeze on me, I started for camp at a brisk walk.

Just as the sun was going down I passed near to where the turkeys had flown off to roost. It struck me that by watching there a short time I might see them return to the same or a neighbouring roost, knowing they often do so. This, however, was very cold work, my clothes being in a half-dried, half-frozen condition; and I was just going to give it up, when I heard the faint distant report of a rifle. The sound redoubled my attention, since I supposed that game was stirring.

In a few minutes I heard the quick sharp alarm-call of the turkey—the unmistakable *pit-pit*—and saw four of them sail off from the edge of the cliff, at about sixty yards' distance from me, into the top branches of the trees forming one of the groups in the valley below. Drawing gently back, and keeping as much as possible under cover, I made my way down into the valley, and started in the direction of the grove of trees in which the turkeys had settled. It was getting dark, and I had gone but a short way, when, at a distance of about two hundred yards in front, a most extraordinary-looking object presented itself to my view. It looked like a haycock on legs, with the handle of a pitchfork sticking out of it, was steadily advancing through the gloom to where I stood, and arrived quite close to me before I could make out what it was. It proved to be my companion, with two turkeys tied together by the legs and slung over his shoulder across his rifle. The wind coming up the valley and blowing their feathers out in all directions, had given to the turkeys in the gloaming the extraordinary appearance that had astonished me so much. I gave a low whistle, and he joined me. I pointed to the turkeys in the trees. He dropped those he already had, hung them up out of wolf reach, and together we cautiously crept under the four roosting turkeys.

The light was very bad for rifle-shooting, but our front sights were of ivory, and our birds were skyed; so, drawing the best beads we could, we fired simultaneously, and with great success, two fine birds dropping dead at our feet—the others making off.

We congratulated each other, and started for camp with four fat turkeys—and fat indeed they were, for they had been feeding all autumn on walnuts, hickory nuts, grapes, sweet acorns, and piñons, at—or rather I suspect without— discretion.

We had a long trudge home, the turkeys getting apparently heavier every mile. As we tramped along, my companion related his day's experience. About noon, he had come upon the fresh tracks of some turkeys feeding along one of the ridges, and had followed the birds until within about three hours of sunset, when, on peeping into an open glade, he saw fourteen of them scattered over it, picking up seeds and strutting about. As the turkeys seemed to be approaching him he lay quite still, watching them through the thicket which concealed him. Ultimately they got quite close, giving many fair opportunities to shoot one. But he was determined not to fire unless necessary, preferring to wait for an occasion to present itself, enabling him to kill two at one shot—a very rare chance to obtain. He said it was most interesting to lie there at his ease, and watch the motions and movements of the birds as they fed about and spread themselves in fancied security. At last his opportunity came, and firing without a moment's delay, he floored his birds, taking the head of the nearest clean off, and shooting the farther one through the body at the butt of his wings. This was the shot I had heard.

I then told him what I had seen, and what had befallen me, and we got home quite done up, but rejoicing at our good luck.

Supper was waiting, and this meal, a blazing fire, and the pipe of peace, recruited us after our fatigues.

We had been very careful and sparing in the use of our spirits, not knowing how long it might be before we should be able to get a fresh supply, or what necessity might arise for their use; but this was considered an occasion when the flowing bowl ought to be indulged in, so grogs all round were mixed, and our success celebrated. When this interesting ceremony had been concluded, my companion remarked to me: "Our luck has evidently turned, and, as gamblers always do, we ought to press our good fortune while it lasts. We have got our Christmas turkeys; no doubt the buck you followed is destined to grace our Christmas dinner. I am the man to kill it. Daylight shall see me on his track. You will behold my face no more until I return with the haunches of the big buck." Then he turned in, and I quickly followed his example. At the time I had not the remotest idea that my comrade really intended to put his threat into execution; I thought he was "gassing," and put it down to the credit of the flowing bowl.

Next morning I awoke at my usual time—daybreak—got out of my blankets, arose, stirred the fire into a great blaze, and turned my back to it to get a good warm.

I looked for my companion—his blankets were empty; I glanced towards the arms—his rifle and belt were gone; I felt his blankets—they were cold. He had consequently been gone some time.

I made a cast round, and struck his fresh tracks going in the direction of our last day's tramp. He had "gone for" the big buck. For my part, I was too tired to stir that day. Though then as hard as nails, and in first-rate condition and training, I was thoroughly done up and quite stiff—"played out" with the previous day's wetting and walking—so remained in camp, and spent the time in helping to make the plum-pudding, dress and stuff the turkeys, and in resting—principally in resting.

Night came, but not my comrade. I was not exactly uneasy about him, for he was a first-rate hunter and mountaineer; but many are the unexpected accidents that may happen to a lone wanderer in the wilderness.

I piled wood on the fire, and sat waiting for him until near midnight. Then I began to think I was foolish to do so, and had better go to sleep. Just as I was turning in the dogs jumped up and ran out, frisking and capering, into the darkness. I heard the whistle of my comrade, and he strode into the light of the camp-fire. On his back, in a sling extemporised out of the skin of the deer, were the hind-quarters of the big buck. It was not yet twelve, and though a close shave on being Christmas-day, our bill of fare was filled. Some more flowing bowl.

At breakfast the following day my companion narrated

to us the story of his late hunt, as nearly as may be, in the following words:

He said: "By daylight I was where you came to grief by breaking through the ice, with this difference—that I was upon the other side of the creek, having crossed it higher up by means of a beaver-dam. Being a cold trail, I pushed ahead sharply, keeping a good look-out, and in a little over two hours came to where the buck had lain down to pass the dark of the night. There being no morning moon, I knew he had not stirred before sunrise, and might, therefore, be browsing or standing under some tree quite near, so continued my way most cautiously, never following the tracks when they crossed an open unless obliged to do so, but, if possible, making a detour to leeward, and striking the trail farther on in the cover. In places it was very difficult to do so, on account of the ground being frozen hard, so that it often took me a long time to get his trail again after leaving it; but I knew, if the buck once saw or got a sniff of me, he might run ten miles without stopping.

"About eleven o'clock I sighted him. I was peeping cautiously out of a thicket, at whose edge I had just arrived, into a large park-like glade, and saw him under a big, white-oak tree, eating the acorns. There was no cover between me and where the buck stood, so I could not risk trying to get nearer to him except by making a long detour, and the nearest edge of the timber I was in was too far off him to risk a shot from. There was, therefore, nothing for it but to sit down and wait until he pleased to move on or lie down, and so give me a chance to get nearer.

Being hungry, I utilised the time by eating my luncheon, and then fell to smoking. Well, he kept me there over an hour, and then started off in a straight line in a trot. As he took a 'bee-line' for the river, I knew what he was after—he was going to take his 'little drink.' *I*, too, should have liked to indulge in a little drink to wash down my luncheon.

"As soon as the buck was well under weigh I started at the double, on a parallel course, hoping to get a shot at him in the river's bottom. I crossed the open ground of the valley in a bend that was above and out of sight of the course he was taking, got into the cover along the river's bank, and followed it down, but saw nothing of him. By-and-by I came to where the buck had drank. He had there crossed the river and gone straight on at a long easy trot towards the Sierra Vérde.

"Should he intend going up the mountain my chance of seeing him again that day was over; if he was going to feed in the piñon ridges, then careful stalking and the avoiding of all mistakes would make him my meat. I could not afford to lose time by going to a beaver-dam to cross, so at once peeled and waded over.

"After going about two miles, the buck's tracks showed he had subsided into a walk, and then almost immediately turned, to my great satisfaction, into the piñon-ridge country, in which, after about an hour's careful stalking, I sighted him again. He was strolling along, feeding, but it was getting pretty well on towards sunset before I was able to approach close enough to him to care to fire a shot, for I had taken so much trouble that I was determined to incur no risk I could avoid, but have patience until I had a certainty of killing him in his tracks. At last he stopped to browse in a little open, oval table-land, on the summit of a cedar ridge.

"The ridge-top was nowhere over a hundred yards across, and was surrounded with a thick fringe of dwarf cedars. Peeping through one of these dwarf cedars, I could see the deer's broad fat quarters about forty yards in front of me. The buck was slowly walking from where I stood concealed. I put my cap in a fork of the cedar, laid my rifle-barrel on it, brought its stock to my shoulder, and bleated like a doe.

"The big buck stopped, turned his body half-round, his head wholly so, and looked straight towards me with his head down.

"I drew a careful bead between his eyes, and dropped him—stone dead!

"I ran up to bleed him, feeling quite relieved and glad at so successful a termination of ten hours' difficult hunting. I had not noticed it while engrossed by the interest of pursuit, but now found I was very hungry, and so lit a fire at once, that there might be roasting-coals ready by the time I had skinned my deer.

"I was soon enjoying a jolly rib-roast, making a tremendous meal, and recruiting myself for the tramp of from twelve to fifteen miles lying between me and the camp."

So after all, we had our Christmas dinner according to programme, and a capital one it was, too.

The turkeys were *à merveille*, the venison delicious!

for the big buck—he was nearly as big as a Mexican burro-deer—was very fat indeed. It is only the man who has eaten *really* fat wild venison who knows what good venison *really* is. The kidneys were completely covered with tallow, and my companion assured us that the buck cut nearly an inch of fat on the brisket. The quarters had been hung out to freeze all night, and were thawed in melted snow-water before being cooked, and so were quite tender.

The plum-pudding was over a foot in diameter; we could hardly pull it out of the pot. It was as good as possible, and followed by a bowl of punch, our punch-bowl being for the nonce a tin bucket; not to mince matters, it was our horses' watering-bucket, which, though not elegant, was capacious, and the only utensil we had capable of holding the amount of punch the occasion called for.

No holly grew in the country, but the bright red berries of the Indian arrow-wood and of the bearberry-bush made beautiful substitutes, and there were more evergreens in sight than entire Christendom could have made use of, so our camp was profusely and gaily decorated. Altogether the day was well and duly celebrated, and it is marked with a white stone in the calendar of my memory.

CHAPTER XVI.

The Beaver—Trappers and Ex-trappers—Captain John Connor—Beaver-houses: their Construction and Position—Breeding in-and-in—Food—Aquatic Romps—Attempt to "out-smart" a Beaver—Beaver-dams: how built—Traps—Beaver Medicine: its manipulation—The "Setting Ground"—Beaver-trapping—How he is caught—Disappointment—The Pursuit of the Beaver as a Sport—Frost.

THE fur on the beaver had by this time arrived at its perfection, and we therefore turned our attention exclusively to trapping that animal, for though we had been assured the streams in Wet-mountain Valley always remained sufficiently open during winter to permit of this pursuit being followed all through that season, it was becoming so cold we feared an exceptionally sharp "nip" would close them, and consequently trapping might be stopped.

To know the nature of a beast is the first step towards becoming a successful hunter of it.—*John Connor.*

The habits of that most interesting animal, the beaver, and the mode of his capture, have not, that I am aware of, been ever written about by anyone who has had practical experience in the matter. Trappers are almost without exception illiterate men, totally incapable of writing upon any subject; and their extreme jealousy in regard to everything connected with what they consider the mysteries of their vocation has nearly invariably prevented them talking openly on the subject to an uninitiate.

This I have myself often experienced. I have met with but few trappers following their vocation, but with a great many ex-trappers; and knowing them, from reliable information, to be such, have not scrupled to broach the subject to them. In every instance, until they had satisfied themselves by cunning examination I too was really and truly a trapper, they would never talk freely to me on the subject.

It was the highest possible mark of personal regard for our master in the art—Captain John Connor—to teach us by precept and practice how to trap; before doing which he impressed upon us it was only for our own pleasure and profit he did so, and that we were to keep our knowledge from anyone who would make use of it to his people's disadvantage, or impart it to others who might. As regarded the ingredients of the different "beaver medicines," we were to tell them to none.

In all descriptions of the habits of the beaver that I have met with, mention has been made of their houses, and descriptions given of how they were *built*. Such descriptions have, in the main, tallied with what I have been told by northern trappers; but although I have trapped a range of wild country extending, in round numbers, eight hundred miles east and west by four hundred north and south, I have never seen such houses. Differences of climate and locality, or more probably in the nature of the waters, may be the cause of this change in habit.

I have dug up many beaver-houses, both to recover traps and to obtain a knowledge of their construction. It has always been a work of considerable labour to do so, on account of osier, willow, and other trees growing on the banks of the streams, and of the rocks and stones in the ground. Their construction I have invariably found to be the same in all essential particulars; their locality, the banks of the pool made by their dam, and for a very good reason. It is essential to the comfort of the beavers that the water in their houses should be always at about the same level. To ensure this during an unusual flood, they partially but sufficiently break the dam.

The entrance to these houses is about a foot under water, and is a round hole in the bank of the stream. This hole is about nine or ten inches across, and runs back into the bank from four to ten feet, according to the soil and other circumstances. At its termination is a circular basin, generally about four feet across and as many deep, and having a vaulted roof a foot or so above the level at which the water stands. This is the beaver's winter bath-room, its depth below the surface of the ground (the bank of the river being any number of feet high), and its distance back ensuring that the water in it will remain unfrozen. Radiating from this vaulted chamber as a centre, and sloping upwards, often for many feet if the stream is liable to great floods, are passages leading to dwelling, breeding, and store-rooms. How ventilation is secured in these subterranean dwellings I do not know, for I have never found any outlet opening from them to the air, nor do I think their architects make any, as to do so would, in countries infested with predatory vermin, be opening a door to enemies, while by having the only entrances to them under water they are quite safe. These houses are each inhabited by only one pair of beavers, and, when they have a family, their two pairs of young ones, which, when old enough to breed, are driven out by their parents, who, however, assist each pair of young beavers to make a new house for themselves.

Curious, that the brute whose reasoning powers are nearest to those of civilised man, who is both a good theoretical and practical engineer, who cuts down trees larger in proportion to his size than the greatest forest mammoths are to us—choosing them with great judgment, felling them to the exact spot required; building dams capable of resisting mountain-torrents, constructing dwellings showing some knowledge of hydrostatics, and not doing all these things invariably and always alike, as if instinctively only, but changing and adapting his ways and modes of proceeding according to the circumstances of each particular case—curious, I repeat, that the course of continuation of species such animals follow, *ab initio ad infinitum*, is the very one we are taught to consider the surest to induce mental and physical degeneracy. Here is a stubborn fact for our learned "physicists."

During the autumn the beavers are busy laying in the supply of food that is to last them all winter. It consists of the tops of withes, small twigs of osiers, and the inner bark of cottonwood-trees, swamp maples, alders, and willows. I have seen large beds of osiers cut down by them, to be stowed away for winter provisions, as cleanly as if done by a sharp briar scythe. Protected from frost and kept moist by being in a damp place, these twigs remain fresh and tender until spring.

The beaver is, in his way, a frolicsome and playful creature. I have often, from a secure ambush where they could neither see nor smell me, watched them by the light of the moon for hours as they chased one another, climbing out on the bank and taking headers off it, splashing the water with their broad flat tails, in fact, having a regular aquatic romp.

I will here give a little anecdote *àpropos* of beavers, for the truth of which I can vouch.

A party of miners, working placer-diggings, brought a ditch on their ground for sluicing purposes. As the placer lay pretty high up, they had to take the water out of the river some five miles above their works, and give it as little fall as would bring down a good ground-sluice head. The ditch took the water from a pool pre-emptied by beavers, and lowered it a few inches. This they evidently highly disapproved of, for the second night after the water was let into the ditch they had most effectually dammed it. And not content with one demonstration of their opposition, they continued to re-dam the head of the ditch as fast as it was re-opened. As it took a man above an hour to walk up to the head of the ditch, and two hours and a half for the water to come down it, a guard had to be placed there, to keep the beavers from shutting off the water, and so stopping the work. A man's time being, then and there, worth half an ounce of gold per diem, this was quite a consideration, and all interested tried to hit upon some plan that would prevent the beavers from stopping up the ditch-head during the day-time.

At length, one of them, wise in his own conceit—there is no fear of *my* giving offence to the individual—announced he could "out-smart" any beaver, and would engage to make the ditch-head safe during daylight, without a guard. He consequently made up a little bundle, took it up to the ditch-head, sent back the man on watch there to his work and commenced operations. Producing from the bundle an old pair of overalls, an ancient red flannel shirt, a "demoralised" flour-sack, a condemned hat, and a ball of twine, he, with grass and leaves for stuffing, constructed a dummy-man. Two heavy stones served for its feet, and propped by a stake, it stood astride of the ditch-head, holding aloft, in a menacing manner, a great club. Giving his handiwork a glance of satisfaction and a nod of approval, this ingenious "iconotect" took himself off back to camp.

At night the dummy was removed, for fear that during darkness familiarity might breed the proverbial contempt. Early the following morning, the beavers' usual night-work across the ditch-head was destroyed, and the dummy-man replaced in another new and striking attitude. By the time breakfast was over the water had got down to the diggings, and work commenced and continued without interruption. After dinner everything was still going on all right, and the man who could "out-smart any beaver" commenced putting on airs. All at once the water stopped! "Mr. Smarty" mounted his horse and rode off to see what *accident* had happened, because it could not be the beavers this time.

This was the "accident:" Dummy had been ignominiously pulled down, his club taken from him, his stone feet cut off. Then he had been floated down the ditch some little way to where there was a short flume, and stuffed into it, middle first, while his head and legs had been neatly tucked into the corners, and all crevices plastered up with river-mud. Mr. Beaver was *not* out-smarted, but somebody else was— badly.

The conduct of the beavers on this occasion was unique in my experience, for when trapping them, I had invariably found that the slightest human taint near the trap, or on the banks in its vicinity, prevented any beaver approaching. Their unusual boldness on this occasion may have arisen from the fact that the occurrence happened at the height of the breeding season, when of course they were unusually anxious to keep their pool full, and they may also have had a more than commonly sagacious leader; or possibly the place had never been trapped, for it was in a wild and unexplored region, quite out of any recorded trapping-ground, and so the beaver's instinctive fear of the scent of man had not been increased by sad experience.

The way in which the beavers build their dams has been the subject of much speculation. They have been watched while engaged in the construction of that portion of them which is near the surface of the water. I have often, indeed, watched them myself, by moonlight; but their dams are always built upwards from the bed of the stream, where of course their movements cannot be observed, and often thrown across rapid watercourses, several feet deep at their lowest stage; while, to add to the difficulty, they are composed of wood that floats. I will attempt a description of these structures, being very familiar with the subject, it having several times been incumbent on me to superintend the destruction of them, on account of their interfering with mining and irrigation works. Their height varies with the rapidity of the streams they are built across, and where the current is fast the fall of the watercourse is great; and then they require to be high, otherwise the water would not be backed sufficiently far to make a pool of adequate size. In mountain streams about eight feet is their average height. For instance, suppose you stood below one, regarding it, then the dam would stretch across in your front, from bank to bank, eight feet high, and present a perpendicular face of branches, with their butt-ends towards you; these ends varying in size from half-an-inch to two inches in diameter. This is undoubtedly the right way for the sticks to lie, as is well-known by all engineers who have had occasion to make "brush-dams;" and the reason is obvious, for as the smaller twigs and forks on each branch, when laid in such a manner, face the stream, they catch all sediment coming down with the water, which, lodging, helps to make and keep the dam water-tight.

The edge of the dam is the smooth trunk of some tree that grew on the bank of the stream, which has been felled across it, and its branches all cut off. No water is allowed to pass *under* this, a tight calking of small twigs and mud-mortar preventing the passage of a singe drop.

The trunk of the tree takes all the scour of the water passing over it, and the friction from the *débris* that comes down in freshets. The means possessed by beavers of estimating the height of a standing tree, is quite incomprehensible to me, since they are not able to climb one; but it is most rare to find an instance where they have taken the trouble to cut down a larger tree than would suffice to reach across from bank to bank of the stream, excepting where they could get no other; and as to their cutting down too short a tree, I do not think they are ever guilty of such a folly. I have sought for the stumps that would show where they had made this mistake, but sought in vain. That there is both skill and judgment required to fell a tree of forty or fifty feet high, and a foot or more through at its base, so that it shall fall just where it is wanted, is obvious; and that the perpendicular wall of branches forming the dam, and the felled tree trunk should come together, requires both calculation and ingenuity. On the upper side the dam slopes gradually downwards, and where the stream is liable to heavy freshets this slope is very long, making an angle with the perpendicular side of the dam of nearly sixty degrees; but where no freshets of consesequence are to be apprehended, the angle is sometimes quite sudden.

Nature has provided the beaver with a natural flexible trowel, his tail, and he uses it as such, making a mortar by puddling the earth of the banks of the stream, carrying it on his tail to where it is required, and then with it spreading and plastering the prepared mud just as a mason would apply his mortar with his trowel. Authority, worthy of high respect, says this is not so, is physically impossible; but many times I have *seen* the unmistakable *print* of the beaver's tail on his mud-mortar.

Probably the beaver commences the construction of his dam by loading branches with mud until they sink, conveying them in his mouth to their assigned place, and there plastering them down with his tail. But however he may proceed, the building of a beaver-dam is an undertaking necessitating great forethought, patience, and labour, and must require the combined industry of many animals all the summer to complete it.

Dam-building is not the result of an irresistible impulse or instinct in the beaver, for in waters frequented by that animal, which are naturally both sufficiently extensive and unfluctuating in level to serve their purposes, they do not make any dams; and there is also a great range of ability shown in their construction, as it is quite common to find on the same stream dams of first-class workmanship, and some that are far otherwise.

The trap used for catching the beaver is made on the same principle as the ordinary gin, but has two springs. These springs have to be of the best steel, and very well tempered, as they cannot be too quick, and are, besides, required to be so strong that great knack and power is necessary to set the trap. Their jaws are about six inches across and three high, forming, when open—that is to say when the trap is set—a six-inch square. To the trap is attached about twelve feet of chain (trace chain is what we always used), and at the end of the chain a strong piece of twine is fastened.

As it is necessary to go into the water to trap, you must be clothed accordingly; I have no doubt but that waterproof trousers (the stockings would not come high enough), such as are used for fishing, would be admirable for the purpose ; but we trapped in a country where such things were ̇not, and so equipped ourselves as follows : Thick woollen trousers, woollen socks, blucher boots, two thick woollen shirts, and a felt hat. Thus dressed, we waded in and out of the water, regardless of wet and cold ; and as the streams were melted snow-water, often with a skin of ice over, or blocks of it floating down them, it was bitterly cold. A belt round the waist with a long-handled tomahawk and sheath-knife stuck in it, and the " medicine " bottle slung therefrom, completed the " rig."

The " beaver medicine," for so the bait is called, requires extraordinary care in its preparation. The great danger in compounding it is that of its acquiring a human taint.

The medicine is not something to eat; it is its smell alone that attracts the beaver, and he is an animal endowed with extreme acuteness of the olfactory organs, carefully avoiding any place or thing giving the least scent associated in his mind with danger.

The first thing is to procure your materials, principally roots, and sappy branches of several different aromatic plants and herbs. These, though I know them well by sight, I am not a sufficiently good botanist to . be acquainted with the names of, except the Indian ones ; nor, were I so, could I give them here, having received the information as a confidential communication. Besides these vegetable matters, there have to be in addition some animal substances, to be procured by hunting. The vehicle used is pure grease, simple cerate is the best; but lacking that, deer's tallow melted, strained, and then re-melted, thrown hot into cold water, and potted, will do well enough, if it has not acquired any smell of man. The materials, as obtained, should be bagged in strong white paper bags.

We kept ours, together with a broad butcher-knife, never used but for making beaver medicine, safely locked up in a close-fitting tin box, made for the special purpose of containing them.

When getting the materials, leather gloves should be worn. A pair of thick kid or thin buckskin are the best; they should be used for no other purpose, and freshly smoked in pitch-pine or greasewood smoke immediately before using them.

The way to make up your medicine is as follows: You select a convenient-sized flat stone, carry it to the water, submerge and wash it thoroughly, pitch it ashore, put on the gloves, approach the stone from the *lee* side, carry it against the wind to where you intend compounding, and place it on the ground. When the sun has dried the stone, you macerate your roots, &c., on it, incorporate the expressed juices with your grease, facing the wind all the time; and your bait, or beaver medicine, is prepared. When made it is to be immediately put into bait-bottles, and well corked up. These bait-bottles are simply vials about three inches long, with wide mouths of not less than an inch in opening. We knew many different receipts for beaver medicine, but only used three of them, being those we found we were most successful with.

Having made all preparations, operations would be commenced as follows: In the middle of the day, that being the time when it is least probable for any stray beaver to be stirring, a preliminary survey of the stream would be taken, to decide where the traps were to be set, great care being observed to approach the stream no oftener than absolutely necessary; only the salient points of its banks would be visited—those where a view up and down the stream for some distance could be obtained; from them the places where the traps were to be fixed would be determined on, the best way of approaching the respective spots noticed, and you would return to camp for your traps.

The number of traps an experienced man can handle is eight, but only a first-rate trapper can nightly set so many, even on the best of trapping-grounds, without making so much "sign" as to spoil the stream; besides, the proper skinning and stretching of eight beaver-pelts is a day's work for his assistant.

Eight equipped beaver-traps will weigh about sixty-four pounds; so, if the ground is practicable for a horse, you will take one to carry them for you, especially if your "setting-ground" is far from your camp; and if not pressed for time, you will wait until the day following the one on which you have made your reconnaissance to set your traps, so as to be able to get them all down before evening approaches. On arriving near the place where your farthest one is to be put, you will tie up your horse at a moderate distance from the stream; then you will cut a willow-pole, about the size of a large clothes-line prop, and a dozen or two slender osier twigs, each about two feet long—these latter you will insert in your waistbelt; then you will set your trap, tie the end of its chain to your pole, about a foot above its bottom end, which you have sharpened to a point, and, with the pole in your right hand and the open trap in your left, enter the river at the place you had previously decided upon as the best for so doing. You will then wade up or down the stream, as the case may be, to where you intend to plant your trap, remembering that the farther the place where you leave the bank to enter the river is from where your trap is to be left the better; for should a beaver get a sniff suggesting human presence on the bank, he will keep the middle of the stream for a considerable distance, and no "medicine" will allure him to its edge. When opposite to where the trap is to be placed, you will temporarily thrust your pole into the bottom of the river, and leave it standing upright. Then you will completely submerge both your hands, and, keeping them and the trap under water all the time, place it firmly on the ground, close to the edge of the stream, and at from four to ten inches under water, according to whether you wish to catch your beaver by a front or hind leg. If the water is there deeper than that, then you must make a foundation for your trap; if shallower, you must "set" at some other place. You will then select a twig from those under your belt for a "bait-stick," cut it a proper length, split one end several times so as to make a sort of brush of it, turn your face to the wind, rinse your bait-stick well in the water, open your medicine-bottle—if an Indian, say an incantation—put the brush end of the bait-stick into the medicine, give it a twist round, take it out, and cork your bottle.

But if you have inadvertently allowed a single drop of water to trickle off your hand into your medicine bottle, throw it away—you will never catch a beaver with the medicine in it again. On this point I speak not only from my own experience, but on the authority of old white-headed professional trappers, men who have trapped for their living ever since they were old enough to do so.

Having "medicined" your bait-stick, you will sink the hand holding it under water, draw it down until *only* that part of the bait-stick which has medicine on it is unsubmerged, and raising it only as high as necessary; your hand being kept carefully under water, plant it inside the jaws of the set trap, leaving about eight inches above the surface, and leaning well back towards the bank. Taking some more of the twigs from under your belt, you will pass them under water too, and stick them in the river-bed, some above, some below the trap, making a sort of avenue leading to it in the shape of a very broad letter V. Then you will take up the pole, wade out a bit, push it as far out into deep water as the chain will permit, plant it as firmly as possible in the river-bed, wade back to where you went in, splash a lot of water over the bank to wash any taint away, go ashore, and, rejoining your horse, start for the next place.

Night brings the beaver on the scene. As he paddles along the centre of the stream, he sniffs the—to him—alluring fragrance of the medicine. He turns towards it, and swims carefully in its direction. He detects nothing alarming, he gets into the avenue of twigs, and guided by them, arrives close to the bait-stick. He raises his nose towards its scented top—it is just above his reach; he gives a quick paddle or two in the water to raise himself, one of his feet strikes the pan of the trap. Quick as a lightning-flash he is fast. Immediately he turns, and strikes for deep water. The chain, fastened to the pole, brings him up out of his depth, and in mid current; its weight keeps him under water. He is drowned, and he is yours.

My readers will now see why a heavy chain and trap are requisite? A light weight would never drown a beaver; and should one ever get ashore after being caught he would have all night to try and get away in.

It very frequently happens the bottom of a stream is so rocky or gravelly, that a pole cannot be driven into it; in that case a big stone anchor may be substituted for the pole; but the most usual objectionable circumstance is for the stream to be shallow so far out from the bank where you have "set," that the chain will not reach out to deep water: in which case, there is small chance of a caught beaver being drowned, and should he get ashore he will lunge and pull on the chain with all his might, and with great perseverance, and may eventually pull up the stake. Should the beaver succeed in getting the stake loose, he will drag it to shore, cut the chain from it, take to shallow water, swim and paddle along until he arrives at some hole in the river's bank, and as he will not have left any track in the running water, both trap and beaver will most probably be lost. Should, however, your stake hold fast, until daylight, you must, to secure the captive, be on the spot by that time; otherwise he will infallibly, unless quite young, amputate his leg and escape.

The beaver is the only animal that I am acquainted with who does this, and once I had most mortifying proofs of such trait of determined resolution.

I had discovered a new pool. It was a very large one, and full of beavers; but very shallow, and about five miles from camp. Taking my eight traps thereto, and setting them with great care, I hoped to catch eight beavers in one night, an achievement which neither of us had, that season, accomplished.

It was only possible to set two traps near deep water, so I determined to be at the side of the pool before light the next morning. When I arose to prepare for starting, it was snowing and freezing hard. My companion—a better trapper than I—was certain that no beaver had stirred in such weather, and gave it as his private opinion, then made public, that only an imbecile or lunatic would start off without a hot breakfast inside him, to go five miles before day, and wade about in the ice-cold water for an hour; so I put off going until after I had cooked and eaten a hasty meal.

When I arrived at the pool it was broad daylight. In one of the traps set near to deep water there was a fine dead beaver—the other was unsprung, being frozen over—in each of the remaining six traps was a beaver's foot!

I was disgusted! In the first place, I had lost my time and trouble; then I had lost some six pounds at least in money's worth; and, worst of all, had spoiled the trapping of the largest and best-stocked beaver-pool on our range. We gave it a week's rest, and then tried it again thoroughly, but never once took any fur out of it.

How beavers can communicate with each other I, of course, do not know, but that they can, no trapper doubts; certainly if a beaver gets away in any pool from a trap, it is not worth while to waste time by setting any more in it that season.

I fear this account of beavers, and the trapping of them, has been much less interesting to my readers than the recollections it has brought to my mind have been to me; and I feel sure that many of them will think any man who would voluntarily go through the exposure and hardship necessary for successful beaver-trapping, and call it an amusement, is an unreasonable fanatic; but I can assure them the love of beaver-trapping grows upon him who has once tasted its pleasures until it becomes a most interesting and fascinating pursuit.

To a great extent it compares to nearly every other field sport as chess does to most indoor games, combining the maximum of skill with the minimum of chance. For in undisturbed and inhabited beaver-pools, if the trapper is unsuccessful, it is his own fault; while at the same time the most apparently trifling carelessness, lack of judgment, or ignorance of some particular in the nature or habits of his quest, will entail on him a complete failure.

Beaver-trapping is a contest of acquired skill and

knowledge ; of patient, unremitting care and attention ; of energy and of endurance, *versus* the natural instinct—if we may not call it reason—of the most sagacious, acute, and wary of all the brute creation. It stands at one end of that scale of sports of which the "battue" is the other.

Hard frost closing the streams at last stopped the catching of beaver. The same traps, however, serving admirably for the capture of coyotés, lynxes, foxes, and other land fur animals, we turned our attention to doing so, and found it great amusement to "run the traps," each morning ; for notwithstanding we were much bothered by the blue jays and magpies occasionally springing our traps in trying to get a share of the bait, we generally had a "take" of about a dozen animals every morning.

CHAPTER XVII.

A white World—The Animals gone—A Gale—Snowed-up—A Chance of Starvation—Disagreeable Alternatives—The Party determines to divide—A Substitute for Starvation—Adieu—Nip and Tug "strike a Lead"—Wild-cat as Food—A Fairy Godmother—Go after her with a Rifle—Joe on the Watch—Death of the Doe—The missing Stock come into view.

THERE had been several light snow-storms, each succeeded by bright, warm, sunny days; the season for severe snow was over. The spell of fine settled weather promised to us in the early spring seemed at hand, and our stock of provisions having got very low, it was decided, one evening, that the time to be off had arrived.

And indeed there was no reason why we should tarry any longer. So it was arranged to take two or three days, during which to procure, by diligent hunting, fresh meat for our journey, for our men to pack up, and then to make a start.

The next day we were not at all successful, game seemed unaccountably scarce, and towards evening the sky commenced to be overcast. About 11 o'clock that night I was awakened by my companion. My eyes opened upon a white world, and snow was coming steadily down. After debating the matter, we came to the conclusion it was only a last parting adieu of Old Winter's—that the coming morning would be clear and fine; and so we went quietly off to sleep again.

Morning came. It was still snowing, more determinedly than ever. The loose animals had run off as before. The three mules tied up to the hitching bar, stood with their backs arched and their tails turned to the wind. All day it snowed, all night, all next day. A thick, ceaseless, steady, downfall of large flakes. Then came the wind—a furious gale; and with the wind, a blinding, driving storm of fine, hard-frozen snow—so thick, so close, you could not see a dozen yards before you. Soon the already fallen snow began to drift with the wind. Then we knew what was up. We were snowed in, hard and fast. It would not take many hours, at the rate the snow was drifting and falling, to fill the passes and render them impracticable. An ugly prospect, with an empty locker, an exhausted larder, and no game to be procured.

The fourth morning cleared up still and cold, with a cloudless sky, but with nearly three feet of snow upon the ground, where it had not drifted.

We took stock of our provisions, and called a council of war. It was a case where our hired men had as much right to be consulted and to advise as we had to come to any determination—for it was a case of possible starvation.

The position, when looked squarely in the face, was this: Our stock of provisions was nearly exhausted; the game had gone, for their instinct had forewarned them of the storm, and they had hid themselves in sheltered places —perhaps crossed the range of mountains and migrated to some lower-lying valleys; and all but three of our animals were missing.

Except on snow shoes, there was no possibility of our getting immediately out of the valley. To make and start out on them, or, after waiting awhile for the snow to settle, to try and get away with our three remaining animals, would be an abandonment, and consequently total loss, of the remainder of our stock and outfit, which would not only be a great pecuniary sacrifice, but tantamount to a postponement, *sine die*, of the further prosecution of the enterprise we were engaged in, since we were several hundred miles from where we could replace equipment necessary thereto, and which in such case we should lose.

Such a move was only to be contemplated as a last alternative. With a continuation of the most favourable weather it would be at least a month, perhaps two, before we could expect to get our waggons out of the valley, even should we make sleigh runners to put them on to cross the snow with. To kill and live upon some of our animals was, if possible, to be avoided, as so doing would cripple our means of transport. But the great fact stared us in the face—we had only about four days' rations of flour left, and not much more of anything else, except a sack of old corn (maize) for our animals. Hence *something* had to be done, and that soon.

It was at last decided to divide the party. Two would remain, and the other two take the animals and try and cross the mountains by the Mósca Pass, strike the Rio

Grande del Nórte in the San Luis valley, follow it down to
the military post there, get as much provisions as the three
animals could carry, and return as soon as possible. The
contemplated undertaking was a hazardous one. None of us
had any knowledge of the route, all we knew being that the
fort in question lay about thirty or forty miles south-west of
the place where we were, and that the Mósca Pass was, to
its summit, somewhere between twenty and forty miles to
the north, that it was a very high pass, and reputed difficult
to find at the best of times. However, the Sangre de
Cristo Pass was manifestly impracticable and out of the
question.

Prudence demanded that a delay of at least three days
should be incurred, so as to have some assurance that the
weather had definitely settled, and to allow the newly-fallen
snow to become solid enough to permit travelling. Four
days half-rations of our mules' corn was put to one side for
the animals to eat on the journey—a most inadequate
supply for such a trip, as they would have no chance to
forage; and the remainder, some twenty pounds weight,
was *appropriated* by us for our own immediate subsistence,
as we wished to save as much of our flour as possible for the
two who were to go over the range to take with them in the
shape of bread. To make the corn go as far as possible, it
was boiled in water, with a little salt, to a coarse porridge,
thus making a food that might be described as an indifferent
substitute for starvation; assuredly that is the highest praise
I can give it.

There was not much choice between going and staying—
both parties would be in pretty equal danger, for the safety

of those who remained, would, to a great extent be dependent on that of those who went. The chief fear was that another fall of snow might catch the relief party *en route.* Should such a misfortune happen, they would most probably be drifted-up and perish; while the two who remained in the valley would, if they did not have the good fortune to find the strayed animals or get some game, have only the two dogs between them and starvation.

Should the provisions of the relief party become exhausted before they got to where they could obtain a supply, they were to kill an animal and pack his flesh on the others, replacing him, if possible, at the military post; but whatever they did, they were in the first place to consult their own safety.

My comrade, being the best mountaineer of the party, insisted that the dangers and hazards of attempting to find a way over the mountain-range should fall on him. The two hired men settled between themselves who should go and who stay, deciding the question by a game of "seven-up," which fated that Joe should remain in camp and Laughfy depart with my companion.

Three days of uninterrupted sunshine greatly encouraged us, and although it froze hard each night, the middle of the days were warm and pleasant; and all preparations being made, the adventurers started out upon their dangerous trip.

The commissary supplies were miserably scanty for such an expedition: a few pounds of bread, half the remainder of the cooked maize strained from the water it had been boiled in, all the sugar and coffee in camp—some three days' rations—and about half-a-dozen pounds of deer-meat were all the available provisions; their weapons, two tin cups and a fryingpan, a couple of blankets each, to sleep in, and a light axe completed their equipment. Very light marching order for men starting out on a journey so full of uncertainties, and with so many prospective perils; its direction vague, its distance unknown, a path over the mountains to find of which our only information was its name and that it was to the north of us; chances of being snowed-up, of being lost, of being frozen, of sinking in some immense snowdrift and being smothered! We bid one another adieu, therefore, with a solemn feeling that the chances were against our *all* meeting again; and though everyone spoke cheerfully and tried to be jolly, the attempt was a manifest and miserable failure. I know that when I and my then sole companion returned to camp—we had gone a short way with the others to start them off—we felt very downhearted and forlorn. Perhaps our recent diet had something to answer for in this respect. Boiled maize may be a very virtuous regimen, but it is emphatically not one conducive to high spirits and a feeling of gaiety.

The afternoon we spent setting every trap we had to catch rabbits, but without much hope of success, as we knew that, thanks to the foxes and wild-cats, they were very scarce.

For some days our occupation was seeking the runaway stock, and at the same time keeping a good look-out for signs of game, for rabbit-catching, as we feared it would prove to be a myth.

Those two redoubtable dogs, Nip and Tug, managed, however, to keep fat, for they "struck a lead." We had caught a great many lynxes, and, after skinning, had thrown their carcases away, at some little distance from the camp, in a heap, and most of them being frozen were not the worse for keeping. One of these hidden delicacies the dogs dug out of the snow, whenever they were hungry, and seemed to relish well enough. *Experto crede*, we would follow the example set us by sagacity, and see how lynxes "went;" so, picking out a promising-looking one, we tried a stew; then another, and tried a roast; then a barbecue. No go! "Lynx was no good no ways; no how you could fix him," as Joe said. Now we had no squeamishness about eating a lynx, for we were *very* hungry for meat of any kind; but lynx-meat would not stop eaten, so we had to abandon the experiment.

The fifth morning succeeding the departure of our companions, fortune smiled upon us, just as soon after daylight we sat cooking our last handful of corn. We should not even have had that to cook had we not pinched ourselves lately in our allowance.

Joe was a good man and true, brave, honest, and reliable; but he was a big hearty fellow, with a fine appetite, and could *not* stand short-commons, and so had become full of dismal forebodings. He was for killing the dogs that afternoon, flaying them, salting the meat, making snow-shoes, and taking the trail of the relief party. He was sure *they* would be lost and *we* should starve. Joe had been already singing "The very same words to the very same tune" for two days, so I only made fun of him.

While he was croaking and I chaffing, we saw a vision. A fairy godmother appeared on the scene—as, indeed, it was time she should, the period of our extremity having arrived.

She appeared about three hundred yards off, drinking at an air-hole in the river-ice, and in the shape of a doe.

We looked at one another, but did not stir; except that Joe grinned the grin of satisfaction until I thought he would "grin his head off." When the deer had drunk her fill she started off at a gentle trot, and crossing a low ridge, disappeared from view. We jumped at once to our feet, buckled our ammunition-belts on, snatched up our rifles, chained up the dogs, and started in pursuit.

Taking a line of direction which would cut diagonally the course the deer had gone on, and keeping as much as possible abreast, and about two hundred yards apart, we pushed eagerly forward.

After going about a mile, I was fortunate enough to get a shot, though not under favourable circumstances. I came suddenly in sight of the deer long before I expected to strike her trail—she had loitered to feed.

I was on the run when we came in view of each other, and she instantly dashed off at full speed; as she did so I pulled up, threw my rifle to the shoulder, and taking a rapid aim—well forward and low—fired at her. Excepting that the doe hunched herself together at the instant of my firing, she showed no signs of being hit, for she went on, without checking her speed, or apparently shortening her stride, and was soon out of sight.

On hearing the report of my rifle, Joe ran up an

eminence to my left, hoping to get a shot too, but not doing so, joined me, and together we went to where the deer had been passing when I fired, to see if there was any blood drawn. And there it was — not much, but enough to be plainly visible; and an occasional drop of it, at intervals, was unmistakable evidence the doe was hit somewhere.

The nature of the ground had prevented our marking the course the deer had taken for any great distance. If hard hit, she might be laid down in the next hollow; she might run until she dropped. We thought the safest thing was for one of us to mount the nearest high ground, and from it keep a good look-out in the direction in which the deer had disappeared, and for the other to go back to camp and bring up the dogs on a leash.

When Joe returned with Nip and Tug, I took the trail, he leading the dogs well to windward of it, in order that they should not smell the scent, for, had they done so, holding them would have become out of the question.

The tracks told me that the doe, after galloping nearly half-a-mile, had changed her pace into a trot and then a walk. For a considerable distance there had been no more blood visible on her track, and we came to the conclusion she had been shot through the hollow of her body, and was bleeding internally.

We had gone about a mile, when the deer jumped up some hundred and fifty yards in front of us. Nip and Tug saw her immediately, and sprang forward with such a jerk as to throw poor Joe flat on his face. Fortunately the leash slipped right, set the dogs at liberty; and away they went, we after them at our best pace. The run was evidently to be soon over, for while the doe was going with a very short stride and slow gather, the dogs were covering the ground like quarter-horses; in fact, before we had run ourselves out of breath, the faster of the two, Nip, had ranged up even with the doe, Tug being about three lengths behind. For a distance Nip kept alongside, gathering himself together for his spring and then with a sudden bound caught the doe by the hock and threw her; as she struck the ground Tug had her by the throat, and in a few moments she received the *coup de grace*. The doe proved to be a large blacktailed deer, not fat, but in fair condition, weighing in the neighbourhood of eighty pounds—ten days' rations. We felt safe. Long before the expiration of that time we hoped to be rejoined by the absentees; and, besides, there was a probability of our getting more game. It was hardly likely that the deer we had just killed was the *only* head in the neighbourhood; indeed the fact of seeing a blacktail in the *valley* showed that the deer had commenced travelling, and were returning to their old haunts.

Let no one think ten days would be a short time for two men, circumstanced as we then were, to eat up an eighty-pound deer—we could have done it in half the time; we were very hungry, we had been living for nearly a week on boiled maize and salt only, nothing else.

A man can do very well, for a time, without bread and vegetables, or without tea, coffee, sugar, grease, or meat, to say nothing of milk, butter, eggs, and fish; but when he goes without *all* those things, and subsists for a while on half-a-handful of boiled maize only per diem, and that, too, while living day and night in the open air—a keen, bracing, appetising mountain air—he accumulates a most voracious appetite. Certainly no men ever enjoyed venison more than we enjoyed our first meal off that deer.

Next day more good luck still. The absent stock came into view, walking leisurely up the valley. Like the game, they were coming back to their accustomed haunts, and possibly to look for their old companions. There was plenty of feed for them close to camp, the snow, which had never been deep along the centre of the valley, on account of the wind's full sweep down it, having been entirely melted on large patches of ground by the preceding eight days' sunshine; and so, catching and tying up one of the animals to be sure of a mount, we allowed the rest to remain grazing at liberty, the "hitched" animal being changed every four hours during the day-time, and a different one tied up each night, so that all of the stock should have an equal chance to feed.

CHAPTER XVIII.

Gray Mountain-wolves—The Traps again—Caught—A Trap missing—On a Wolf-trail—Sagacious rather—A Jump for Life—Fagged-out—An uncarthly Scene—A Night's Rest—Nip and Tug take the Track—The Wolf before us—The Fight—A Pause—Death of the Wolf—Joe and the Ashlata—a happy Return.

ONE night, at about ten o'clock, our stock astonished us by trotting into camp and taking up a position close to the fire, remaining there all night. In the morning we discovered the reason why they had done so. On making the round of the uniformly empty rabbit-traps, the tracks in the snow of three gray mountain-wolves showed that evil-disposed neighbours had been prowling around; no doubt the mules had smelt them, and sought the camp fire for safety.

Knowing what large, well-furred pelts these animals had, and having long wished for some to make a carriage-robe with, I determined to set as many of the beaver-traps for them as I could find good places for, it being necessary to trust to concealing the traps in the "runs" made by the different wild animals through the thickets of jungle, instead of using bait; for it was quite possible we might want every morsel of deer-meat we had to bait ourselves with. I therefore smoked myself and my gloves thoroughly in pitch-pine smoke to kill the human smell, swept the dead leaves away where each trap was to be placed, set it there, fastening it by passing its chain round the bole of the nearest tree or bush with a clove hitch, covered all carefully with leaves again, and, retreating backwards as I left, brushed snow over all with a long cedarbough, and trusted to fortune for the result.

In almost the first trap I came to on "running" them the next morning, there was a big dog-wolf. Perceiving me approaching, he commenced lunging and pulling on the chain, making frantic efforts to get away; but finding he could not get loose, when I got quite near he made a most savage and determined rush at me, and when brought up by the chain snapped his teeth together with a sharp clack, and growled and snarled like a savage watch-dog, his green eyes glaring fiercely at me, the long hair round his neck and on his shoulders standing out, turned all the wrong way.

Laying down my rifle, taking my tomahawk in my hand, and getting as near as possible to the wolf to be out of his reach, with a quick and sudden blow I buried its sharp edge in his forehead, killing him instantly. I was well pleased with my prize, and leaving it, continued my round.

None of the remaining traps had been disturbed excepting one, and it was—gone. It had evidently caught a fine large wolf, who had smashed, torn, and bit everything within his reach, and ended by gnawing in two the stump round which the chain of the trap had been fastened, and going off with it.

Thinking that before the wolf could have gone far the long chain would have caught or become entangled in the thicket, and that I should soon find him fast to something, I followed on his tracks. However, he was, apparently, aware of the danger travelling through the jungle entailed, for I soon found he had left the cover for the open, and there being a good tracking snow on the ground, I followed him at a steady dog-trot. Before I had gone very far I sighted him. He had, no doubt, seen me first, for he was hopping along on three legs at a very decent pace, considering how he was impeded by the trap, which was fast to his off fore-leg, and by the long chain dragging through the snow and grass. Thinking he was going his fastest, I got into a sharp run, expecting to close on him directly.

Then the wolf, changing his hop into a long swinging canter, in spite of trap and chain, kept his distance in front of me.

Half-a-mile's run pretty well pumped me, and the wolf being out of sight over a roll in the ground, I gave up the chase for the time being, and returned to camp for my breakfast, my horse, and the dogs.

I found camp deserted, and a little note pegged to a tree to inform me that Joe having seen a small drove of antelopes had gone in their pursuit, taking with him the dogs. My breakfast was soon eaten, the dead wolf dragged into camp, my horse caught, saddled and bridled, and the pursuit of the escaped wolf recommenced.

Having my good horse under me, I expected to get back to camp with the wolf's skin and the beaver-trap, long before night; nevertheless, out of consideration for Joe, and on the improbable chance of the absentees returning that day, I had written a statement of my movements across Joe's note; and, out of consideration for myself, pocketed a good hunch of cold venison before starting.

By about ten o'clock I was on the wolf's trail again, following on it at a canter, and before I had gone far came to a place where he had sat down. Thence his tracks ceased to show the drag of the chain; either it had got wrapped round and round the trap by the continual jerk caused by the wolf's galloping—an improbable conjecture— or he had had the sagacity to wrap it round on purpose; certainly he had sagacity enough to keep in the deepest and lightest snow, and, when necessary, to change his course so as to enable him to do so; the advantage to him being that while his three unencumbered feet sank at every stride in the snow, the trap with the chain wound round it acting like a snow-shoe on his other one, prevented its sinking, thus practically enabling him to go on four legs instead of three; and it gave him another advantage over me. My horse, burdened with my weight, broke through the light crust on the surface of the snow and sunk deeply in it at every step, and the soft snow balling in his hoofs, compelled him to go slowly.

After some hours, during which time I frequently caught sight of the wolf, he, finding that I still continued to pursue him, tried a new line, and, abandoning the edge of the valley, made for the roughest and most rocky of the cedar ridges. On them the tracking became extremely difficult.

In many places the snow had entirely disappeared from the ground, and the surface being hard, naked rock, on which no trace, excepting an occasional chip or scratch made by the trap was discernible, I frequently completely lost the trail, and had to make wide circuits in order to strike it again, where a softer surface or the presence of snow gave me a chance of so doing.

The close unremitting attention requisite to follow the wolf had so preoccupied me, that I had hardly noticed the flight of time, and was surprised by finding that sunset was close at hand, but by then I was entirely under the dominion of "the spirit of the chase." The ardour of pursuit had been so heightened and intensified by the difficulties encountered that to turn back never once occurred to me; and my self-respect as a hunter forbade my abandoning a trail when it was going to become more difficult. The moon, nearly a full one, had been up some time, and gave sufficient light for a practised eye to follow a track by; so, availing myself of every stretch of good ground to put my horse to his best gait, in order to close as soon as possible on the nearly tired-out wolf, I still pushed on.

Soon the wolf again changed his course, and leaving the ridges headed straight for the large open valley below our camp. I feared he was going to take to the cover—indeed that was what I had been apprehensive of his doing for some time—but he did not. His last night's experience had no doubt destroyed his confidence in jungle-paths. He probably feared a trap in each of them.

As I emerged into the level valley the wolf was in full view about a quarter of a mile in front of me, going very slowly towards the river-bank in a direction that I knew would lead him to a place where it was high and precipitous. He was still some distance from the edge, and it seemed quite possible to come up with him before he could reach it. There was no need for me to call upon my horse. He saw the object of our pursuit as soon as I did, and like the gallant hunter he was, laying back his ears and giving a toss of his head, he dashed after him.

If the wolf had had a couple of hundred yards farther to go the chase would have ended then and there; as it was he disappeared over the edge of the river's bank about fifty yards in front of me. When I arrived at the spot and looked down, I found there was a perpendicular descent there of about twenty feet, with a mass of matted brushwood and grape-vines drifted full of snow at the foot of it. On this the wolf had boldly thrown himself down, and was doubtlessly resting and getting his wind beneath it. It had been a jump for his life.

It became necessary for me to go half-a-mile up stream to where, the river bending, the steep bank would be on its other side, and the side on which I was, sloping enough to permit me to descend with my horse into the creek-bottom. I was satisfied that what the wolf had just done had been an act of strategy, that he knew no horse could follow him straight down the bank; and I was also tolerably sure he would not stir for some time, most likely not until he should again discover me approaching, so I dismounted and walked, leading my horse, not only to rest him but to warm myself, for since the sun had set the temperature had become excessively cold.

When I arrived at the thicket into which the wolf had dropped, I made a cast round and struck his trail, leaving it in a direction leading diagonally down the river, remounted, and followed ; but the nature of the ground prevented my riding with much rapidity. By-and-by I caught a ghostly glimpse of the wolf in the moonlight as he scrambled up the right bank of the river and disappeared. Undoubtedly he had also seen me, and finding I was not to be shaken off, his heart failed him, for he uttered a prolonged and mournful howl. Where the wolf had scrambled up the bluff of the creek's bottom it was too steep to follow. I was again thrown out, and compelled to lose more time, seeking for a place where I could get up from out of the bottom and on the plain again.

Though the course the wolf had run had been very zig-zag, and made many sharp turns and doubles, it had in the main been a big semicircle ; and I was very glad to find, when I got on it again, that it bore more and more to the right, and so was taking me almost in the direction of camp. To confess the truth, I and my horse were beginning to fag. But I was encouraged by the signs of distress the wolf commenced to show by often stopping and lying down, and began to hope I should run into him every minute ; he, however, still managed to keep ahead, and at last the moon went down and tracking became impossible.

It was late—about eleven o'clock—and the interest of pursuit being over, I realised how tired both I and my horse were, and how cold it had become, and so dismounted, unsaddled, lit a fire to warm myself at, and then rubbed my good steed down to refresh him. That done, I replaced the saddle, fastening it loosely on, and started for camp on foot, leading my horse by the bridle-rein. Though the moon was no longer up, the night being clear, the stars shining brightly, and the snow reflecting considerable diffused light, travelling was not difficult; and being only about eight miles from home, I hoped to arrive there without delay or difficulty.

I was in a portion of the valley I had only been in once or twice before, and then it had been daylight, with no snow on the ground; but these circumstances were now reversed, and the changed aspect of the country was quite bewildering.

The uncertain light, the confusion of outlines caused by the pervading mantle of white, the strange exaggerations that the strong white lights and deep black shadows gave to every crest and peak of the surrounding mountains, made the scene look not only quite new and strange, but as unearthly and unreal as it was unfamiliar.

More than once I had to reason myself into the belief that I was still in the Wet-mountain Valley, and not in some, to me, unknown region, or in Dreamland. Had I allowed myself to become in the least confused or bewildered as to my course I should infallibly have lost my way, perhaps my life.

At last, tired, hungry, and cold, I arrived in camp.

Several times as I trudged along had I been obliged to rub my face with snow, to keep it from being frost-bitten, and found the operation extremely painful; and for the preceding half-hour my feet had been so completely benumbed that I greatly feared they had become frozen, hence they were my first care on arrival; so, removing their covering with great caution, I got the faithful Joe to rub them briskly with snow. Soon my feet began to hurt me horribly, feeling as though they were being grilled; but I bore the pain gladly, for then I knew that they were safe. When the pain in my feet began to abate I put them into luke-warm water, and gradually making it hotter and hotter by dropping heated stones into it, they were soon warm and comfortable.

Joe had failed in getting any game. He had fired one long shot, but without effect, and I suppose his want of success had disposed him to see everything in an unfavourable light; for, although he did not express the sentiment in so many words, it was evident his private opinion was I had played the fool in spending nearly thirteen hours in the saddle chasing a wolf, and only succeeding in nearly freezing my feet; and, indeed, he probably thought rightly. Certainly, had I not expected to overtake the wolf, encumbered as he was with the beaver-trap, in a few miles, I should have deferred starting after him until I could have had the assistance of the dogs; but I had been unaware how slight an encumbrance a beaver-trap would prove to a powerful gray mountain-wolf when travelling over snow; nor had I calculated on the generalship displayed by the one I had been following, and, having once committed myself to the ardour of pursuit, was irresistibly compelled to follow on until success or darkness terminated the chase.

Naturally we are all beasts of prey. The old latent tiger instinct, once thoroughly aroused in a man, will prove the strongest passion of his breast; and, unless he be also naturally a duffer or a coward, be it a head of game, a fellow man, or only some special object of social ambition—let anything once become the object of that instinct, and the savage nature long civilisation has smothered—not extinguished—will blaze up again, and, *coûte que coûte*, he will follow like a bloodhound to the end.

The next morning, after breakfasting on venison "straight" —not an elaborate meal, but far ahead of boiled corn— I tied Nip and Tug to the end of my *reáta*, caught up and saddled the best riding-mule we had, and taking the heel of my last night's trail, started for where I had left off the chase. In my heart I was glad of the distraction afforded by this hunt. I had tried hard not to allow myself to become uneasy at my old comrades not having returned—in fact, it was hardly time for them to be expected; but I could not keep my mind from continually dwelling upon and thinking of the dangers and uncertainties of their path, and feeling depressed in spirit by so doing.

As I rode along I consoled myself for my last night's failure by the reflection that I should now have an opportunity of giving the dogs a chance of having their first combat with so formidable an antagonist as a gray mountain wolf, under great advantages, and therefore with a probability of success. Should they obtain a victory without getting crippled or injured, it would ever after give them such confidence and courage in any future conflict with one as would go far to ensure success.

The dogs had, both together and singly, killed in the most dashing manner many a coyoté and timber-wolf; but doing so was child's play compared to tackling a gray mountain-wolf. Had they been ordinary dogs, I would not have risked the almost certainty of their being killed by such a combat; but they were extraordinary dogs; not only most powerful and savage, but in the habit of hunting and attacking their game together, and had always shown great judgment and sagacity in supporting and seconding each other on such occasions.

On arriving at the place where I had left the trail, I dismounted and liberated Nip and Tug, having first scolded and menaced the dogs to bring them into a sufficient state of subjection to be likely to mind me when they should get excited by taking the track. Even after such precaution I had great difficulty in keeping them from galloping on the trail, which I was anxious they should not do, as I wished to be well up when the wolf was started, and also to save my mule as much as possible for the final rush.

In a mile we came to where the wolf had lain down to rest, and I have no doubt he had but just started from his lair, for the two dogs gave a sniff and whimper, and were off like rockets.

We were on the comb of a piñon ridge, along which the

course continued for a couple of hundred yards, and then turned abruptly down the steep side of it, which was thickly covered with scrub trees and brush, rising to a height of about twelve feet. Making myself as small as possible, and shutting my eyes to keep from being blinded, I headed my mule straight down the steep descent. Then giving him the steel, and trusting to luck, I tore my way down through the thicket.

Had I been clothed in any other material than buck-skin I should have emerged an animated bundle of rags; as it was, a severe switching was all the damage sustained.

When I opened my eyes again the chase was in full view. On the plain, about a quarter of a mile off, was the wolf, doing his "level best." Behind him, within a couple of hundred yards, were the two dogs, flying over the ground, Nip as usual beginning to draw slightly ahead.

I indulged myself with a yell, and got the last inch to the hour out of my mule. I was a hundred yards behind when the dogs closed with the wolf. Seeing they "had the heels of him," he had turned suddenly at bay. The dogs, making no effort to check themselves, struck him one after the other like battering-rams, and wolf and dogs rolled over together, enveloped in a cloud of snow-dust.

As I pulled up all three recovered themselves and jumped to their feet, and the high-couraged dogs, nothing daunted by the superior size and strength of their antagonist, sprang at and seized him by the neck just behind his ears; then, laying themselves back close to his sides, they, bulldog-like, shut their eyes and held on, trying their best to shake him. Braced on outstretched legs, planted as firmly as possible, the wolf made determined but vain efforts to bite first one then the other of the dogs, but was totally unable to turn his head to either side sufficiently to do so.

The wolf looked like an incarnation of the spirit of savagery. His long hair was all turned the wrong way. His eyes glared and glowed; like opals, they turned all colours —green, red, purple. They seemed literally to blaze with ire. When he gnashed his great jaws, their fangs clacked together with a sharp, vicious snap, like the report of a pocket Derrenger.

What a subject for the painter or sculptor who could have done justice to that group!

I dismounted, threw the bridle-reins over my arm, and encouraged the dogs with my voice.

The wolf, inspired to desperation by the sight of another enemy, made a furious lunge, flung both dogs off, and then, reckless of odds, rushed open-mouthed at me. As he passed Nip, that gallant dog sprang forward, legged him by his near hock, and with a clever twist threw him on his back. As he fell, Tug rushed in and pinned him by the throat, receiving as he did so a bite from the wolf, who snapped him through one of his ears, fortunately only getting hold of the tip of it, for he took the piece right out. Again all three rolled over and over in the snow, by that time stained and flecked with blood; the wolf bleeding freely at the neck, and Tug at the ear.

Soon the savage monster shook himself free once more of his assailants. Again the three sprung to their feet for another round. But by this time the combatants seemed quite blown, and after regarding each other for a second or two, wolf and dogs lay down panting, with their tongues hanging out, watching each other.

I could easily have shot the wolf, and in fact did draw my revolver with a half idea of doing so, but put it back, thinking it would be a great pity to spoil so pretty a fight ; and besides, I was curious to see if the dogs would prove able to kill so large a wolf without assistance, for his neck was covered with such a mane of hair, and the thick skin upon it was so loose, that it seemed an impossibility for them to choke him.

I determined to remain a passive spectator, unless my interference became requisite to save a dog from being killed or badly injured ; so, feeling hungry for a smoke, I filled my pipe and struck a match to light it by.

It was like an electric spark to a battery. The scrape of the match seemed to simultaneously arouse the resting combatants, and wolf and dogs sprang from their position of repose. But instead of again closing with their adversary, both Nip and Tug commenced dodging round him, making feints as if going to rush in, and then jumping back just out of reach of his vicious snap.

The wolf, on his part, kept making short rushes, first at one, then at the other, of the dogs ; but each time he sprang at either of them, the other would get a bite at one of his hind legs or his loins, and jerk him half round.

At first I thought the dogs were sagaciously trying to hamstring him ; but it soon appeared they were only intent upon worrying and tiring him out.

By-and-by both dogs got opposite the wolf's head, one on

each side of it; they gave a bound or two backwards and forwards, and then, apparently with one accord, rushed in upon him and got the same hold they first had.

The poor wolf could no longer shake them off. He was too weak. The tactics that Nip and Tug had been practising upon him had told upon his strength. He was *very* groggy on his pins, and the dogs shook him to and fro as though he was drunk.

Soon the blood commenced to ooze from his nostrils, his eyes turned a dull greenish-white, his tongue a grayish-purple, his legs gave way under him, and he fell—dead!

The dogs let go their hold of the wolf and lay down panting and licking their hurts. I looked them over, and was glad to find that, excepting Tug's ear, they were not much the worse for the fight. A few bruises from the steel trap received in the tussles, and some gashes but skin deep being the extent of their wounds.

They had killed their formidable adversary within twenty minutes of running into him.

My mule had also conducted himself uncommonly well; certainly he was accustomed to the smell of blood, as also to that of the skins of wild beasts, having packed into camp many a dead coyoté, wild-cat, and deer, still it would not have surprised me had he manifested considerable terror at having a live wolf fighting almost under his nose; but, on the contrary, he had stood perfectly still, regarding the scene with that look of contemplative wisdom which is common to owls, mules, and learned judges.

I had brought a lump of cold roasted venison with me,

and shared it with Nip and Tug, at the same time caressing and making much of them. The dogs seemed quite proud of their prowess, and would every once and again take a walk round and a sniff at the dead wolf.

Having refreshed myself, I soon skinned the coveted pelt off, and tied it and the recovered trap to my saddle.

The skin was a splendid one. Before and since then I have seen several hundred gray mountain-wolf skins, but never such a large one as that was.

On my return I found that Joe had gone after more meat, so busied myself with stretching and staking-out my trophy.

Towards evening the hunter returned, bringing with him a fine ashlata.

The ashlata has immense spiral horns, and short coarse wool, closely approaching to hair in appearance, and his flesh tastes very much like that of the original breed of Welsh mountain-sheep; but he is quite double their size.

The specimen Joe brought to camp was the first animal of the kind that had been killed by any of us that season. We had frequently seen small flocks of them upon the uppermost peaks and highest alps of the mountains encircling the valley, but always in places so nearly, if not quite, inaccessible, that we had been discouraged attempting to obtain any of them. The flock out of which Joe had at last got one had no doubt been driven down to the comparatively speaking low ground in which he had found them by the snow on the mountains, which near their tops was lying so thick and deep that all feed was buried completely out of reach. The ashlata was a fat young ewe, and a most welcome change and addition to our supply of meat, then rapidly diminishing.

Since the departure of our companions the weather had remained uniformly clear and still, a slight wind however playing most of the time around the mountain peaks, and blowing the light snow off them in white fleecy clouds, which, when illuminated by the sun's rays passing through them, were gorgeous with rainbow tints, and at night in the bright moonlight looked like cloud-wreaths of glittering diamond dust.

The days had been really hot from eleven to three, but the evenings, nights, and early mornings frightfully cold; so cold, indeed, that a cupful of water thrown up in the air would congeal into morsels of ice before reaching the ground, making a miniature hail-storm; and our traps had often been prevented from springing, from the leaves and snow by which they were concealed being frozen over them in a solid cake.

Game was returning to the valley, and we daily had some success in hunting; a small band of spruce-deer in the side valley to the left of the camp affording us our chief sport.

As day succeeded day without the return of the relief party, we could no longer repress our anxiety, and gave vent to our feelings by discussing the possible misfortunes which might have overtaken them. Indeed we could talk of nothing else.

On the fifteenth day of their absence the objects of our solicitude, to our great delight, walked into camp. They drove before them the three animals well laden with camp

o

supplies, and looked, men and beasts, none the worse for their expedition.

Our pleasure was no greater than theirs at finding us alive and in such a flourishing condition, for they had feared their long absence might have brought us to much extremity.

We all felt a pleasure only to be experienced under such circumstances.

CHAPTER XIX.

The Start—Unsatisfactory Travelling—The Camping ground—A wakeful Night—Fagged-out and short Commons--The Mósca Pass in sight—An Ocean of Air—The Gap—Danger—A cold Camp—The Fuel lost.

MY comrade's report of his late trip was given, as nearly as can be remembered, in the following words :

" When I parted from you my calculation was to make a long day's march, and so, if possible, get more than two thirds of the way to the summit before camping—my object being to be able to get well down on the other side by the following night, and so avoid the necessity of having to camp near the top of the range, where I knew that it would be intensely cold, the snow very deep, no pickings for the animals, and probably a total absence of the fuel necessary to keep us from freezing.

" As we travelled along I studied carefully the sky-line of the mountains, seeking to determine which was the gap through which the pass might be sought with the greatest probability of finding it. Having at length, after many changes of opinion, decided, my next difficulty was to form some mental map of the country between the distant gap

I had fixed upon and where we were, and impress it well on my mind, for I knew so soon as I should begin to wind about among the foot-hills and lower ranges of mountains before me the distant summit-line would be hidden from my view.

"We made very good headway until nearly 2 o'clock in the afternoon, but the depth of the snow had by that time greatly increased, and the animals were beginning to fag; so I thought it advisable to give them a short rest, and chose a spot for that purpose where some tall bunch-grass, sticking up through the snow, would also give them something to eat. An hour was all the time I thought I could afford, so we were soon pushing on again. We shortly got into a regular jumble of small rugged mountains and transverse valleys, ravines, and gulches; seldom able to see half-a-mile ahead, and obliged to make sudden and unexpected turns in directions totally different from the one in which we wished to proceed. It was most unsatisfactory and provoking travelling. Only by stopping on the top of each rise as we crossed it, and turning round and contemplating the country below, could we come to any definite conclusion as to our whereabouts, or decide on the best way to proceed. But that we were gradually getting very high up was plainly perceivable on looking down in the direction we had come from.

"Knowing that there would be a bright moon, that it and the reflection from the snow would afford sufficient light to permit of travelling after nightfall, I determined to push on for a couple of hours after the sun should have set; but about 4 o'clock it commenced to freeze very hard, and in less than an hour the surface of the snow, which had become softened during the day by the sun's rays, had a stiff crust frozen upon it, through which the unfortunate animals continually broke, cutting their legs, and distressing themselves by plunging.

"We struggled on until about 5 o'clock, when I gave in and camped for the night.

"Our camping ground was a sheltered little nook in a cañon, strewn with big loose rocks, and surrounded with a fringe of quaking aspens, the site, undoubtedly, of a spring —now frozen, for a little thicket of dwarf willows testified to the fact; to these the animals were tied, and after devouring their small and insufficient feeds of corn they gnawed the branches within reach in a hungry manner quite distressing to see, occasionally taking a munch at the snow by way of a drink.

"We found difficulty in collecting fuel, and had to content ourselves with small sticks; we therefore made only a little fire, and lay down to pass the night one on each side of it, each with a pile of sticks within his reach to feed the fire from whenever he should awake; and awake one or both of us continually did, since we could not keep warm for long at a time.

"I started very early in the morning, hoping the crust on the snow would remain for some hours sufficiently hard frozen to support the weight of the animals, and as we relieved them of our burden by walking, they got along tolerably well, seldom breaking through.

"I was very doubtful of my way, but the cañon we were in was gradually getting wider and flatter, the elevations on each side more steep and continuous, and the general direction of it north-west, so I felt encouraged to think I was in a true pass; still, the knowledge that we might at any time be brought up standing by a precipice at our feet, or an unscaleable ascent before our face, and so be compelled to retrace our weary way and try another opening, with possibly a like result, was very depressing.

"By the middle of the day we were, both men and beasts, quite fagged, and gladly stopped to rest and eat; but alas! there was but the shortest commons for any of us.

"The character of the cañon had changed. It had been for some time rising very rapidly, and getting so broken, narrow, and full of boulders and large rocks, as to have many times compelled us to leave it and scramble for considerable distances on one or other of its steep sides, before we could resume our course along it again.

"After eating, I therefore left Laughfy and the animals resting, and started for the highest neighbouring summit, to try and get a glimpse of the main divide, and view out and decide upon our course.

"Half-an-hour's steep climbing took me there, and I obtained a better view than I had anticipated.

"Looking back I saw that we had attained a great elevation, quite as high a one, in fact, as I had supposed the summit of the range to be at. Before me I obtained a view of what was probably the rim of the dividing ridge. Miles away, but apparently quite close, rose a white, inaccessible wall, whose sharp edge cut clear against the blue sky eight hundred or one thousand feet above me. But far off to my left it was broken with a deep gap, looking wonderfully like the one I had pitched upon the day before as being the Mósca Pass. I was *certainly* on the flank of the summit ridge.

"Whence I stood I could perceive that the cañon we had been so long following became but a rugged furrow up the face of the mountain, and that to retrace our way to a branch of it leading towards the south-west, whose mouth we had passed about a mile back, and try such branch, offered the most promising prospect of success.

"At 2 o'clock we started, and were soon in the deep narrow ravine I had noticed, and which we travelled toilsomely up for a couple of hours; its wall to our right getting higher and higher, while the one on our left continued to lessen until it ultimately terminated, and we found ourselves, at last, standing on the steep face of a mountain-summit, which to our right rose with a bold, nearly perpendicular sweep towards the sky, and to our left, after extending forty or fifty feet with a slight downward inclination, suddenly curved out of sight.

"Then came an ocean of air. Its boundary, the sharply serrated horizon line formed by the twin Picachos de España and the snowy peaks extending in a semicircle to their right and left. Its bottom, the lesser mountains, foot-hills, and valleys which lay between us and them, far, far below us, and which the trifling width of the narrow ledge on which we stood sufficed to conceal from our sight.

"The slight joggle or break along the face of the mountain, which formed the natural ramp we were standing on, seemed to be practicable as far as we could see it; but that was only for a short distance, as a hundred yards in front the mountain-side rounded away to our right, revealing the sky, which, cut by the dazzling white of the snow, seemed of the brightest deepest blue.

"We pushed eagerly forward through the deep heavy snow to ascertain what was beyond the curve. When we got round the shoulder, the gap which had so long been our objective point came into full view, right in front of us.

"It was apparently five or six miles away, at a slightly lower level than we stood at, and showed an opening of perhaps a couple of miles in width, which looked like a huge bite out of the upper edge of the rim that had come into full view, and of which the mountain we stood on was a huge spur.

"Our position was not pleasant. Should the way get any steeper, it would become impracticable. Should our moving weight start the snow sliding, we might be precipitated with an avalanche of it into the valley below.

"The question, Where can we pass the night? forced itself upon my consideration. Not where we then were—*that* was impossible. To go back to the ravine we had left was the safest thing to do, and if I had had plenty of food for ourselves and animals, I should certainly have done so; but being in a state bordering on destitution, I was very loth to lose either time or any portion of our hard-earned advance.

"To make the gap that night was equally an impossibility. The snow had become very deep, the air greatly rarefied, and our animals already showed signs of distress. Besides, the gap might be only a sharp comb quite perpendicular on its other side. But beyond us, where the spur we stood on joined the main chain, there appeared to be a few scattered pine-trees growing a little way down in the angle formed by the junction, and I decided to push on to them, hoping to find a dead one that would serve for firing, and there to wait for morning.

"Our chief danger was the chance of a wind rising, for the snow around us was at too great an elevation to have been affected by the warmth of the sun, and having never been melted, had of course never frozen together, but lay so loose and light that the slightest puff of wind whirled it about; should therefore a mountain gust once set it going, our peril would be extreme.

"I thought we should never arrive at those pine-trees. The snow got deeper and looser, and the altitude affected our respiration. We were weak from insufficiency of food. Our tired animals could hardly be dragged and beaten along. It was hours after sunset when we arrived.

"The cold had become intense, and it was so long before we could find a down-tree, that we were almost in despair. At last we spied the tips of some dead branches of a prostrate pine sticking out of the deep snow some distance below us, but to where it lay the descent was so steep as to be quite dangerous to attempt. A fire was however a necessity to existence, and though the animals instinctively pulled back, we hauled and pushed them to the place.

"The pine proved to be a big old tree some three feet through at the butt, and was lying head down the incline. Some storm had torn it up by the roots long ago, since it had evidently been dead many years. We chopped off some few of its lower branches, cleared away the snow from its roots for a couple of feet in depth, and soon had a roaring fire, which the horse and mules seemed to enjoy as much as we did.

"There was nothing to tie the animals to, and the mules were turned loose, but the horse was hobbled—the mules would be sure to stop with him. It was probably unnecessary to have done this, but the pangs of hunger might have driven the tired-out beasts to stray.

"Long before daylight we were roused up by the cold, and saw with amazement there was no fire—not only that, not a vestige of the pine-tree was to be seen; no doubt, the fire having consumed its anchorage, it had slid bodily down the side of the mountain into the abyss below. It was too dark to travel, the moon had gone down some time, and to keep still was to freeze, so we stamped up and down, and beat our arms across our chests, until the first streak of dawn.

CHAPTER XX.

A Table-land—A dreary View—Breaking the Way—The San Luis Valley—
Rio Grande-del-Norté—*Facilis descensus Averno* —"Away down souf"—
The Third Night—The weak Point—A Stone Rabbit—A Rest—Mexican
Hospitality—The Zazal's Music—Arrival at the Fort —Captain B.—A
Road Party—Return to Camp.

"Two hours of wading and plunging through the snow along the steep mountain-side brought us to the gap, when to our great surprise, instead of looking down on a large valley far below, in front of us was a short gradual descent of a few yards in the hundred, leading to an undulating table-land. A wide, shallow, broken summit valley, bordered with a rim of peaked ridges, lay immediately before us. The top of the range where we were, instead of being a comb, was miles across. Doubtlessly the peaks showing on the opposite side of the table-land were the rim rocks of the range on that side, and through one of the openings between them ran the head of the passage leading down to the San Luis Valley.

"The view we gazed on was dreary, lonely, and forlorn as the eye of man had ever seen.

"There were a few groves and fringes of stunted and

dwarfed pines in the hollows and depressions in the ground; but though they were practically a redeeming feature in the scene, as furnishing fuel, they gave neither relief nor variety to the landscape, being so laden with snow as to be scarcely distinguishable.

"A wide desolate expanse of whitest snow, unbroken by a single track of beast or bird, unrelieved by one bare spot of rock or ground, cold, monotonous, and uniform, lay like a gigantic winding-sheet spread ready to receive us.

"Soon the snow became so loose and deep that the animals, sinking up to their bellies, could proceed no farther, and it was with difficulty even we could do so. There was but one course to pursue. Leaving the animals with Laughfy to hold and prevent them lying down, I broke the way in front, trampling and stamping the snow until I made a narrow path firm enough to support them. Along this they were led; then he, taking his turn, worked a short road, while I held the stock and rested. This was not only a very fatiguing but a very slow way of progressing; and it was late in the afternoon before we got to the gap opposite the one through which we had arrived on the summit valley. It was a narrow V-shaped opening; its sides, being two peaks of the rim of the valley, rising several hundred feet above its level. Looking through this opening—an opening like a prodigious hind-sight of a rifle—a magnificent panorama presented itself.

"The San Luis Valley lay revealed to our gaze. A huge oval, nearly twenty miles in width by more than double that distance in length, entirely surrounded by immense mountains terminating in a multitude of fantastic peaks.

"A lovely, smiling plain, with a wild chaos of white glistening domes and pinnacles, and dark intervening shadows, enclosing it on every side.

"The few scattered patches of snow in the valley heightened, by contrast, the bright green of its broad border of junipers and dwarf cedars, and the olive-gray of the masses of sage-brush dotted over it.

"Down its centre flowed, in many a broad sweep and graceful curve, the gleaming waters of the Rio Grande-del-Norté; there a broad and rapid river, though twelve hundred miles from where it pours its flood into the Gulf of Mexico. And on either side considerable streams, issuing out of the rocky cañons and dark gorges of the mountains, wound their silvery way over the plain to join its majestic course.

"We stood on the very brink and edge of the mountain plateau. From our feet the mountain's side, a bare smooth wall of granite, sunk sheer down a thousand feet—perhaps two thousand—perhaps several thousand. How could we tell?

"The foot-hills below, upon whose tops we looked, seemed to be but inconsiderable hillocks. The minute scattered points, and hardly perceptible patches of green upon them, were giant pines and groups of forest timber.

"We gazed down through such a thickness of air that a faint bluish tint pervaded everything, as though seen through clearest of pale violet glasses. Involuntarily the mind realised the reason why the sky is blue.

"It was a grand sight, but it was a great disappointment; evidently we had to seek further to find a way to descend in safety; and so the wearisome work of alternately trampling a path for the animals was recommenced.

"Our point of destination was south of us, so southward we turned our steps; and before we had gone very far I noticed in a depression to our left a few osier switches; farther on, where the depression became more considerable and clearer defined, there was a solitary and gnarled dwarfed willow; still farther, some more; then the depression, becoming wider and deeper, swung round to the right behind a knoll which hid its further course from our sight. The inference was unmistakable. The hollow was but the commencement of one of the outlets of the drainage of the plateau, and most probably one of the sources of the first confluent which joined to the south of us the river below.

"That this was so, I soon felt convinced; the hollow descending with increasing steepness, and at length a turn brought us to a wide opening through which the San Luis Valley and distant mountains were again visible, and the depression in the ground we were in changed to a steep rocky groove, gradually enlarging in its descent until it became a winding cañon which joined the plain below. The place was probably the continuation of the Mósca Pass; at any rate, I determined to there attempt the descent of the mountain. The lower part of the cañon appeared to be thickly wooded, the timber extending far up the side of the mountains, and, but a short way below where we were, groves of quaking aspens appeared.

"For the first few miles of our way the declivity was a very sharp one indeed; but that rendered travelling through the deep snow much easier, and as the steeper it became the quicker we descended, we did not care how precipitous it was so that it remained practicable, and our progress did not become a case of *facilis descensus Averno.*

"Half-an-hour brought us to the first growth of 'mountain quakers;' and an hour more to the commencement of the pine forest clothing the slope of the mountains.

"Under these trees the ground was much more level, and the snow less deep, and we therefore still made good progress. We found, indeed, descending a mountain mantled with snow to be a very different affair, from climbing one.

"By dark we had made such good headway that we had got down among the upper breaks of the highest of the foothills, we were surrounded with timber, the snow was no longer deep, and the climate had sensibly moderated.

"Then the spirits of my companion, who had been very despondent, rose, and he commenced as loud as he could bawl, and in a tune with wooden turns, to inform all creation, in the words of a popular Western parody, that,

<blockquote>Away down souf in de Arkinsaw timber, &c., &c.,</blockquote>

until the wolves and coyotés in the vicinity howled again.

"We halted for our third night out under the spreading boughs of the pines, at the very first place we came to where there was any picking for the animals, and at once went to work to make ourselves comfortable for the night.

"We soon found lying on the ground a sound seasoned pitch-pine, lopped off its branches, logged up its trunk, and built and lit a huge bonfire.

"A cold air was beginning to draw down the cañon from the range, so we felled some small pine-trees, and with their leafy branches built a semicircular wall on the upper side of our fire, and between wall and fire made our beds, first laying a good foundation for them of pine boughs a couple of feet thick, to keep our blankets from the snow. This accomplished, we considered ourselves sumptuously lodged.

"Our weak point was the commissariat. Our bread, our coffee, our sugar, our boiled corn, was eaten; only a few pounds of raw maize in grain were left. This we divided with the animals, for scanty picking grew around the spot, and their gaunt and famished appearance called for pity.

"Melting some snow in our fryingpan, we boiled our share of maize in it, with a little salt. Turning our empty coffee and sugar bags inside out, we put one in each of our tin-cups with some snow, boiled them well, took them out, mixed the liquid in the two cups together, divided it, and called it—coffee! The decoction could not be truthfully described as delicious, but it was hot and wet, and warmed us up and quenched our thirst. Then we ate our frugal meal, and after enjoying a smoke, lay down and slept, warmly, soundly, and comfortably, until broad daylight.

"Our breakfast did not delay us long. It was *not* an elaborate affair. We simply tightened our waistbelts to the last hole, lit our pipes, and were ready to saddle up and push on. As nearly as possible we followed the general course of the stream along which we were travelling; but it often cañoned, when the rugged steepness of its banks and neighbouring 'breaks' often compelled us to make long and wide detours. We rode along in perfect silence, hoping to get a shot at something eatable; but although we began to see occasional tracks of deer, we saw no game. At noon we rested the animals for a couple of hours where the feed was tolerably good, and spent the time hunting for something with which to appease our hunger, but without success. Towards evening we got down amongst the lower foot-hills. The pine forest was already beginning to be replaced by growths of balsams, spruces, cedars, and piñons, and the tracks of foxes, wild-cats, coyotés, and rabbits became numerous. Shortly before sunset we had the good fortune to see and kill a coney, or 'stone-rabbit.' Now the stone-rabbit, though, as his name implies, a dweller in stony places, is almost invariably very fat, certainly the best eating of the genus, but the most diminutive of all the rabbit family. The one we shot was plump and tender, and well-flavoured. Alas! he was also extremely small. There was only just enough of him to mock the appetite of two starving men; however, we soon forgot our hunger in sleep, and in dreams dined *à la carte*.

"Early morning found us stirring. A cast round camp failed to furnish anything for breakfast. The tightened belt and well-filled pipe had again to be resorted to as a substitute for that meal, and we pushed along at a sharp walk, occasionally trotting where the ground admitted it; for the animals, having pretty well filled themselves the previous night, were stronger and more lively than hitherto. Before midday the cañon, whose general course we had been following, opened out into a continually widening vale, with a considerable stream bordered with deciduous trees winding along its centre. Towards the middle of the afternoon we debouched into the main valley, and found it an almost level plain with an extremely sandy soil, covered principally with different varieties of artemisia, some attaining a height of twelve to fifteen feet, with many kinds of cacti, and a general growth of sand and gáyata grasses. Our appetites were tantalised by the sight of a distant herd of antelopes wheeling and galloping about the plain; and by seeing many hares, who jumped up and ran away at a distance that was quite out of shot. It was evident such game as there might be in the San Luis Valley was very wild; probably as a consequence of being often disturbed and chased; for besides its being a regular hunting ground of the Uté tribe, and of the professional hunters employed for the military post we were journeying to, there are several small Mexican settlements in the valley of San Luis.

"A little before sunset we crossed the tracks of a large flock of sheep going towards a side valley full of timber, and soon after heard their distant bleating, and observed the smoke of their shepherd's camp curling up above the tree-tops. This was suggestive of cooking, and I immediately altered our course towards it. We had only had the stone-rabbit to eat, between the two of us, for the last fifty-eight hours, and were quite famished—the strong exercise and mountain air having given a keen edge to our appetites.

"We put our animals to a canter and were soon in the sheep camp. It consisted of a large brush corral, in which were enclosed for the night about two thousand Mexican sheep, and of a small A tent, barely big enough for a man to sleep under. One Mexican shepherd and some half-dozen rough sheep-dogs—who, by-the-bye, furiously invited us to—keep at a distance—were in charge.

"The *zazal* received us with that hospitality which is the most pleasing characteristic of the Mexican race; a virtue alike common to those who claim to be *Castelláno*, to the descendants of the Indigenes, and to the mixture of the two races. Hospitality is *Cosa de Mejico*. The usual salutation to any stranger entering one of their *casas*—'You are welcome! This is your home! All that you see is yours!'—though only a form of speech, does *really* mean that you are heartily welcome to his best hospitality; and the poorer and more primitive your host is, the more sincere, as a general thing, is this reception.

"The shepherd not only placed his little all at our disposal, but gave us his personal service, replenished the fire, brought water from the stream, made us some coffee, fried in tallow some slices of mutton with *chíle-colorádo*, and then set himself diligently to work, making and cooking *tortillas* for us; these last we devoured as fast as he could furnish them. I am sure we kept him cooking nearly an hour, and though we were making a heavy pull upon his little store of flour, he seemed quite pleased at seeing us devour so much of his supply, although he well knew that what *we* ate, *he* would have to lack, ere his next month's rations would be issued to him.

"When our hunger was fully appeased and pipes lit,

we did our best endeavour to give an account of ourselves, and obtain news and directions for our next day's journey; but, unfortunately, our kind host spoke such an awful mixture of Hispano-Mexican and a, to us, strange Indian dialect, as to be almost, sometimes quite, unintelligible; while what we said seemed nearly as incomprehensible to him. The sign-language he knew not, and the conversation was for awhile more animated than instructive. After a time our entertainer made us understand that, conversation being too difficult, he would indulge us with a little music, being very fond of it, and informed us that he was *grande musico*. Then he produced with a flourish a flute; exhibiting it with evident pride, and giving us to understand that he had made it himself. The flute was a large hollow reed, the joints of which had been bored out, and it was bound in places with sheep sinew and raw hide. It had two keys of hardwood, and emitted a feeble, melancholy, droning sound. The *grande musico* apparently knew but one tune—I call it a tune, because I do not know what else to call it, although, frankly, *I* could not discover any tune in the sounds made by him. Perhaps he played classical music. Perhaps 'the music of the future!' The melody (?) he indulged in always seemed as if it was going to end, and never did. This performance was occasionally enlivened by an appropriate accompaniment from an outraged wolf, or the bleatings of some restless sheep. We, however, did not appreciate it. So, after expressing in impressive pantomime the sentiments proper to the occasion, we went to sleep, leaving the Minstrel of the Mountain still apparently seeking for the turn in that tune which would bring it to a conclusion.

"We were wakened next morning to find breakfast ready for us, were pressed to, and did, eat heartily, and started on the way, with our direction pointed out, and a luncheon of tortillas in our pockets.

"I had, before leaving, tried hard to make the poor shepherd accept some money, but he had stoutly refused to take any; an offering of tobacco and powder was, however, quite irresistible. That night we slept in sight of the smoke of the Fort's chimneys, and early next morning arrived at our destination.

"I found Captain B. in command. He was most kind and friendly, delighted to have someone to talk to, and take little 'go-downs' with, and insisted that I should consider myself his guest for so long as I could remain. Laughfy was commended to the good offices and hospitality of the Post Quartermaster-Sergeant. My animals were ordered into the government corral to be well taken care of, and I informed that I had but to fill up the requisition forms that the Q.-M. and C. Clerk would lay before me with a statement of what things I required, and, if in store, I should have them.

"After a substantial eleven o'clock *déjeûner à la four-chette*, to which, having fasted since lunching the day before, I did ample justice, I gave Captain B. a concise account of the trip just made, he expressing the utmost astonishment that I should have succeeded in accomplishing it. Laughfy, too, told his version of the story to his host the Post Quartermaster-Sergeant. The yarns made the round of the quarters, and the two hunters and guides professionally employed with the command—oracles in such matters—on hearing them, gave as their opinion and verdict that 'Airy a man' who would undertake to find and cross the Mósca Pass in such a season had 'a derned sight more grit' or was an 'all-fired bigger fool' than they were. And one of them further added, in 'Pike' vernacular: 'Wal ! see here, boys ! the cuss who cud fine his way over them air mountings, with all that air snow on 'em, cud fine his way eout of H—— blindfole—shure ! yeow bet !' I had achieved a reputation !

"The captain insisted I should abandon all thoughts of retracing my steps, pointing out that no man had a right to expect more than average luck, and that I had recently had such a good and long run in my favour, by the absence of wind and storms, I was not warranted in expecting its continuance, certainly not in acting on any such assumption; and further, that he considered it more than questionable if loaded animals would be able to cross the summit snows; whereas, if I would stop a few days with him, he would ensure my getting safely back by the Sangre-de-Cristo Pass. He then told me he was anxious to open his communications, and had already given orders that preparations should be made for the start of a road-party of forty men, with all necessary transport, stores, and tools, including a snow-plough, on which the Post blacksmith and Post carpenter were already at work, and that in about a couple of days they would start out. If I would take his advice and stop, he would do his best to entertain me until word should come back that the road was opened. By that time my animals would be recruited,

and myself and man rested and refreshed. If, between then and the time when the road-party should start out, I would see to having my packs made up, they should be sent on in one of the waggons, so that when I left him I could travel light until I overtook and passed the pioneer party.

"Of course I accepted his kind offers, and there was no doubt he was right about the summit snows.

"Late at night on the sixth day after the departure of the road-party a messenger from it arrived, to bring word that the route through the pass was practicable, and that it had taken four days to make it so, the drifted snow lying from twenty to thirty feet deep for the entire length of the gorge through the crest of the range. Then I bade adieu to my kind friend Captain B., and pushing over the ground at forced marches, and without experiencing any great hardship or difficulty, arrived as you see in safety."

So ended my comrade's account of his adventurous expedition.

Among the stores brought back was a small but welcome keg of "old Bourbon," and a packet of choice tobacco—presents, with his compliments, from the kind-hearted commander of the Post—long may he wave!—and, with their assistance, our reunion was properly celebrated.

Having again a good supply of all things needful, it was decided to remain in our once more "happy hunting-ground" until the spring should fairly open and the roads become good, unless the Uté Indians, whose appearance was then to be expected at any time, should so comport themselves as to render departure advisable.

CHAPTER XXI.

The Utés—A Deer Hunt—Nip and the Indian—Peace—" My Name is Norval "—A Visit from the Uté Warriors—A Pow-wow—A Surprise—Diplomacy—" All do some Swop "—The Indians take their Departure."

NOT long after the reunion of our little party the expected Utés appeared on the scene. Our first encounter with one of them was full of incident, and happened in this wise. I had started out on horseback, intending to visit a distant deer-haunt, and taken the dog Nip with me. Some two miles from camp, while riding along a bench of high ground parallel to the river, I saw a deer emerge at a gallop from the timbered edge of a side valley to my right, about half-a-mile off. It was heading for the river, and going in a course diagonal to mine, which would eventually bring it to a thicket at the edge of the stream of about that distance in front of where I was. Nip saw the deer and started instantly, taking, with his usual sagacity, the cut-off. I tried to call him back, knowing he could not catch an unhurt deer, but, to my astonishment, the dog seemed to be going at the quicker pace of the two, so I desisted hallooing, and put my horse into a gallop. I had hardly done this when, from the spot whence the deer had come into sight, there appeared a horseman—a Uté! The Indian was well mounted, and his steed was going his best pace—*ventre à terre*. Whether he observed me or not I could not tell; probably he did not, for while he was in full view in the open ground I was riding through a growth of dwarf cedars reaching up a little above my head. It was a race between us, but the Indian had greatly the advantage in the ground, and the fact was immediately apparent I should be distanced.

The deer and dog disappeared into the thicket simultaneously. They seemed to tumble headlong into it, as if the dog had seized the deer as they did so. Crossing a rough hollow I lost sight for a while of the place; and when I again came in view of it, the Uté's horse was standing at the edge of the thicket tied to a tree; the Indian having doubtlessly followed deer and dog into the jungle. Fastening my steed near that of the Indian, I forced my way through the underbrush in a direction from which came a most extraordinary duet, and was soon in sight of the performers.

Astride the dead body of the deer stood the redoubtable Nip, his hair turned the wrong way, his lips drawn back exhibiting his long fangs, and giving utterance to deep growls and making savage snaps. Scarce twenty feet from him stood the Uté hunter on the defensive; his drawn bow was in one hand, the other held the arrow, and he was violently remonstrating with the dog. The Indian spoke in Uté, throwing in a liberal allowance of such English as he could manage on the chance of its duly impressing the dog. All the English, however, he appeared to know was not much; and what there was of it was certainly more expressive than elegant. It consisted of a short word commencing with a D, and a description of the dog's descent on the maternal side — expressions he had doubtlessly picked up round some frontier camps. It was an animated and expressive scene; but, fearing my appearance would encourage Nip into taking the initiative, and so bring about a catastrophe, I terminated the "situation" by ordering him to down-charge. I then stacked my rifle against a bush, and held up in the air my open right hand with its palm towards the Uté (the well-recognised Indian sign for peace). Relaxing his bow the Uté Indian laid it and the arrow down, and, keeping a sharp eye on the dog — who was watching him with an expression of countenance *not* encouraging—advanced and shook hands with me.

We soon discovered we could only exchange ideas through the Indian sign-language; but he had no difficulty in making me comprehend—what, indeed, I had already suspected—that he had wounded the deer, and was following it when captured and pulled down by my dog. The Uté then made some further signs which I confess I did not comprehend in the least; but I made the sign of acquiescence, on general principles, and then, for it was cold, lit a fire to warm my hands at and as an excuse to loiter and see what the Indian meant and what he was going to do. Drawing his knife he quickly skinned and cut up the deer in a most workmanlike manner. Then he tied the fore-half of it up in the skin and placed it to one side. The other half he laid at my feet, pointed to Nip, and delivered himself of a speech in the Uté language, and of which I did not understand a single word. But I then knew what he had meant by his signs. He and the dog had jointly killed the deer; I, as owner of the dog, was entitled to a share.

I answered with a speech!

I did not know exactly what to say; but what did it matter? He could not comprehend me; still, Indian etiquette demanded a reply at least as long as his address had been. So I gave him "My name is Norval"—in full, with appropriate gestures as taught at school by the master of elocution. It was a *great* success. He was impressed and gratified. We shook hands with effusion and parted.

Taking each our respective share of venison, and mounting our steeds, we rode off on our separate ways; I making for camp at a gallop to take the news there that the Utés were in the valley, for it was impossible to know what course of conduct towards us they would adopt. That if friendly disposed they would shortly pay us a visit of ceremony was most likely, and we made our preparations accordingly. Our dogs were securely chained; our weapons stacked in the centre of our shelter—making quite a display of offensive and defensive armament; all our deer-skins, the bulk of our provisions, our tools and instruments, and all other articles likely to be tempting to Indian acquisitiveness, were carefully concealed in the waggons; and our waistbelts, each with a brace of Colt's dragoon-revolvers and bowie-knife in it, we buckled on *under* our hunting-shirts. These arrangements made, we were ready to receive our wild visitors; but it was not until the following morning about ten o'clock that the looked-for callers appeared. A dozen Uté warriors galloped up to our hitching-bar and dismounted. They walked into camp in a frank friendly way, as if quite sure of their welcome, without making àny preliminary sign of peace, as if indeed to do so would be unnecessary and superfluous. They were in full Indian bravery, got up regardless of expense, in paint and feathers, armed to the teeth, and admirably horsed. My acquaintance of the previous day's making was of the party; and, after we had shaken hands all round, he called the attention of his companions to the dogs, and we could see by his expressive gestures he was giving them an account of Nip's late performance. We invited our guests to sit down and smoke, and they squatted accordingly, placing themselves so as to form three parts of a circle, and we, following their example, completed the round. We were evidently in for a regular "Pow-wow."

Our largest pipe was filled, lit, and the regular puffs made, one towards each of the four cardinal points, and one straight up. Then it was passed round in silence, each in his turn going through the same ceremony. The meeting being thus opened in due form, a speech followed as a matter of course. A big stout Indian, who looked some sixty years of age, "took the floor." To our surprise, after speaking a short time in the Uté language, that his comrades might know what he was about to say to us, he gave, what we supposed to be, a translation. Although delivered in very bad and broken English, plentifully eked out with Hispano-Mexican, and an occasional word of Uté, the substance of what he said was quite intelligible to us. The old savage commenced by stating that we were in their country; all that we could see belonged to them (*i.e.* we were trespassers). He then told us that he and his braves were brothers to the white man, therefore his country was theirs (rhetorical flourish). He had been to the great council-camp of the whites, and talked with their big chief. Our big chief was his friend, and years ago had given him his picture in silver; on saying this he exhibited a medal suspended by a string round his neck. It was a medal, with an effigy of James Buchanan on one side, and a representation of the Capitol at Washington on the other. Then he enlarged upon the benefits we were receiving from them. Our animals were eating their grass. We were cutting down and burning their timber, and killing and eating their game (evident foundation-laying for bucksheesh). Then he demanded our reason for being in the valley, and asked when we were going to leave it; winding up with an eulogium on the wealth and generosity of all whites, who never allowed themselves to be outdone in giving (broad hint to shell-out handsomely). Then the old bilk sat down. Solemn pause. "My name is Norval" evidently no go on this occasion. So one of us rose and replied to the following effect: We had heard that a *very* brave Uté chief (initiatory compliment) had been to see our great father, and that they had agreed together that the Uté and whites should be friends and brothers (never heard of it before). We were very glad to see that chief face to face, and to have shaken hands and smoked the pipe of peace with him and his friends (wished them all beyond Jordan). That we were far from our homes, going a long journey, and were obliged to cross their country because it was so big we could not go round it (oh!). That we had been trapped by the snow, and detained until we had eaten our provisions, and feeling we were their brothers (hadn't recognised the feeling before) we had not hesitated at killing their game and using their wood and grass. Should they ever come to our country, they must consider it theirs and do the same (foundation for bucksheesh knocked into a cocked-hat). When the roads became good we should leave. We were going into a country full of bad Indians at war with them and us—the Comanches, and we wanted more powder and lead (a head-off, we had plenty); we were sure that if their store of ammunition was as big as their hearts (figurative, *very*) they would give us some (knew they wouldn't). We had very little salt, matches, or anything else, but we would divide with our brothers because we knew they would do so with us (euphemism of "How are you on for a trade?")

Our spokesman subsided. Awfully long pause.

His silver medalship on his legs again! Rejoining: He was very sorry we were so badly off for everything — especially powder and lead, as they, too, wanted some more —very much (knew they would)—but that if we would come to his camp, and bring such things as we could spare, everybody would be glad, and we could "all do some swop" (straight talk at last). Then he sat down.

After a few moments' silence, one of us announced we wished to show our friendship by a small present of tobacco; so two plugs of cavendish were produced, divided among the Utés, and the "pow-wow" was over.

Our visitors remained half-an-hour longer, looking at and examining our weapons and everything else in sight, and carrying on as much conversation with us as mutual ignorance of each other's language permitted, and, shaking hands again all round, departed.

CHAPTER XXII.

A Return Visit—Indian Dogs—Uté Coquettes—Their "Get-up"—The Children—Indian Bucks—Trading—Glimpses of Indian Social Life—Married Women,

LEAVING our men to take care of camp, we returned the visit paid us by our new neighbours the Utés; and found there was quite a large party of them—fifteen tents. As we approached we could see the women running from all directions into their tepees just like so many rabbits scudding for their burrows on the appearance in their warren of a dog. At the edge of the Indian encampment we dismounted, were met by our newly-made acquaintances, surrounded with a crowd of bucks and papooses, and yelped and snapped at by a pack of Indian dogs.

The Indian dog, of which the half-starved wild-looking brutes "yapping" at us were specimens, is, I believe, the only indigenous North American dog. In appearance he looks like what might be expected from a cross between a Scotch collie and the small European wolf. He is generally of a whitish colour, clouded with patches of intermixed blackish-ash and brown; with sharp cock ears, slender legs, sharp muzzle, thick bushy tail, and slightly oblique eyes; and is always gaunt and hungry-looking, a realisation to me of the idea of the dog-fiend of German legends that I have "evolved out of my inner consciousness."

After a time we were conducted into the tepee of our friend of the silver medal. It was a large buffalo-skin tent, with a good fire of hard wood in the centre, which, being a mass of red-hot charcoal, gave out great heat and no annoying smoke. There was an old squaw and four young ones seated inside, and from the tent poles hung some little flat wickerwork cradles, each with a baby in it. We only stayed a few moments in this tent, and then started on a tour round the encampment. We found little groups of women and children seated on the ground in front of every tent. The women were all painted and dressed to the last agony, and we then understood why they had bolted on first sight of us. It had not been, as in our guilelessness we had supposed, because they were frightened or shy, but because they had been *en déshabillé !* In fact, we found they were by no manner of means shy. *Au contraire*, they appeared quite pleased to attract attention, and the way they used their eyes was quite wonderful. I declare those untutored savage females made eyes in exactly the same way that I have seen some *very* civilised ladies do. Verily human nature is great and will prevail.

Taking these Indians as a lot, they were an unusually well-to-do set of savages. They had good tents, were well dressed in buckskins and blankets, had plenty of meat hanging up, a drove of about two hundred horses, and all well armed.

The women were dressed as follows.. Firstly, braided buckskin moccasins, with raw hide soles. Then, buckskin leggings, mostly very handsome; being fringed, stained with a variety of colours in different devices, beaded, and embroidered. Evidently they were considered the most killing portion of the costume. And, finally, long buckskin garments, which ought, I suppose, to be called chemises, because that is what they really looked like. These last-mentioned articles of apparel were very narrow, cut straight all the way down, reached to the calf of the leg, were very low in the neck and large in the arm-holes, and without sleeves; and they were all, more or less, covered with extraordinary designs, executed with different coloured dyes; some very pretty and tasteful, others verging on the grotesque and hideous. This was the *fashionable* way of wearing the hair: parted down the centre of the head and across; front hair, hanging in two long straight locks, one on each side of the face; back hair hanging down behind like a massive black mane. The side locks reached, generally, to a little below the women's waists, and were bound round for six inches from their ends upwards with strips of fur. Their back hair was also bound with fur in the same manner, and in most cases reached down to below their knees, in some almost to the ground; and was still further ornamented with stained and dyed feathers attached to it at intervals. These belles were painted, of course; and the prevailing mode was the following: the partings of the hair were coloured bright red; the edges of the eyelids dark brown or black, and the cheeks heavily rouged with native red oxide of iron, and the married ladies were distinguished from the maids by five narrow parallel blue bars, tattooed in straight lines from the under lip to the chin; while all of them, married and single, wore armlets, bracelets, anklets, and necklaces in profusion. I had nearly forgotten to mention, the young women's hands were very pretty and well shaped, and the most elaborately got up among them had their finger-nails coloured red.

The children were dressed principally in—well, next to nothing! That primitive arrangement, invariably and always worn by all American savages, irrespective of tribe, age, or sex, consisting of a string round the waist, met at right angles by a very narrow strip of cotton-cloth, softly-dressed skin, or inner bark of a tree, which is called by the whites "the breech-clout," being all they had on.

The bucks were arrayed in good hunting moccasins, fringed leggings extending half-way up their thighs, buck-skin hunting-shirts reaching down nearly to the tops of their leggings, and *serapés*, or Mexican striped blankets. Their hair was dressed like the women's, except that the side locks were looped up, and the back hair twisted into what our grandmothers called a Grecian knot. They each wore on their left wrist a wide guard-bracelet of ornamented raw hide, to serve as a protection from the jar of the bowstring; and some of them had on robes of dressed puma or bear skins. Necklaces of the claws of those animals were not rare. One of the braves sported a necklet of human teeth; and another, one made of the dried tips of human fingers with the nails on.

They were a well-armed party, nearly every man having his Hawkins' rifle, Colt's revolver, knife, tomahawk, bow and arrows, and lasso. And all were hideously painted.

One of them had the most beautiful lasso I have ever seen. It was a plaited one, made with thirty-two fine strands of picked buckskin, and sixty feet long. It was soft and supple as a silk cord, strong enough to hold a bull, and worth a horse.

We went from tepee to tepee trading for trifles, not with any view to profit, but to make our visit more interesting to the Utés, to obtain objects of curiosity—examples of Indian handiwork and skill—and for the fun of the thing. We were accompanied on our round by an ever-increasing crowd, all in a high state of merriment. Judging by the numbers talking at a time, their laughter and expressive gestures, their glances, signs, and grimaces, it was very evident no end of chaffing was going on. Our trading was only done with the women. The slight value of the articles dealt in, and the smallness of the transactions, rendered the traffic quite beneath the dignity of warriors, and unworthy of their serious attention. But the women were delighted at a chance to achieve at the same time two ends, each dear to the (savage) female breast—making good bargains, and attracting attention. The fact of our seriously bargaining for such toys, and the eager emulation of the women, seemed to be considered great fun by all. Even Old Deportment, alias Old Silver

Medal, nodded his head and grinned continually. Certainly we succeeded in attaining our chief object, that of establishing a friendly feeling towards us on the part of the Utés, and at the same time avoided the making of presents, which Indians would to a certainty have considered tribute, and a proof we were afraid of them, and only required to be "crowded" to give them all we had.

We saw a good deal of these Indians while we remained in the valley, continually exchanging visits and joining, by invitation, in several of their game-drives. My intercourse with them served to strengthen an opinion I had previously formed, and since abundantly confirmed, viz., that to represent the American *indigène* as an unimpassioned, mirthless, solemn being is incorrect. I have had many and unusual opportunities of studying the social life of several tribes—I do not here allude to the border Indians, who have acquired most of the vices and few, if any, of the virtues of civilisation, but to the unmitigated savage—and am satisfied that such an appearance on his part is only a mask. It is the Indian's idea of manifesting the dignity and politeness *necessary* to be observed before adversaries or strangers, and with each other on official or important occasions. Amongst themselves, in ordinary social intercourse, I have, when sufficiently known for my presence to have ceased to be a cause of restraint, always found them to be more like a pack of children than grownup people. I have often seen a lot of as cruel and bloodthirsty savages as ever "raised hair" laughing, talking, squabbling, and joking, over one of their queer round games, with as great animation, and making as much noise, as a party of English children would when enjoying a Twelfth-night frolic. And no man has a keener relish for a practical joke, at some one else's expense, than the Indian. As to the women, they almost invariably sing over their work. And they quarrel about their lovers too. I have seen more than one fight between two jealous maids—regular pull-hair, slap-face, clinch-and-roll-over fights—fights inflicting great mutual damage to personal ornaments, and during which not a little involuntary undressing was done.

And I have seen more than one Indian woman sit down and regularly cry herself into hysterics, because her personal charms had not been sufficiently appreciated, because she had been contumaciously treated by some other woman, or because she could not have her own way about something or other, acting, in fact, in a most natural and unstoical manner.

Another misapprehension is that Indian wives are cruelly treated by their husbands. It is positively not the case. I grant Indian women do all the work, but what does *all* the work amount to? None of it is laborious, and if they did not dawdle, sing, or gossip over it and take as long as possible to do as little as may be, their time would hang quite wearily on their hands. What does all their bead-work, quill-work, and embroidery testify? That they have had to invent ways to kill time. The buck does all the hunting, fighting, and stealing. His share of the burden of life is the one entailing toil, hardship, privation, and endurance. And as to an Indian striking his wife, let alone kicking her, I never heard of such a thing.

Amongst the thousands of squaws that I have seen I never yet saw one with the mark of a man's hand on her. I most sincerely wish I could say the same regarding my countrywomen. To the scandal of religion, to civilisation's dishonour, to the disgrace of manhood, and to England's shame—*I cannot!*

I verily believe there are more wives struck or kicked by their husbands each and every night in the metropolis of London, than there have been squaws struck by their savage husbands since the landing of Columbus to the present time. I make this statement with shame and reluctance. But I *do* make it, because I wish to denounce such a crying evil. It is only by bringing it as prominently before *society* as he can, that any individual can hope to do something towards wiping *such* a stain from his country's escutcheon.

The testimony I have given in favour of Indian character is not that of a partial witness. There is no love lost between me and the American savage. Some of my best friends have been foully murdered by them with every instance of aggravated treachery and cruelty. Many of my old comrades and companions have fallen before their rifles and arrows. I have myself once been utterly and completely ruined by them. I retired to rest a well-to-do man, worth considerable property, considered to be on the high-road to speedy wealth. In a few short hours, thanks to them, I was worth nothing in the wide world except the clothes I stood in, and the arms in my hands; my prospects gone, and heavy odds against my getting away with life. But I will give the devils their due.

CHAPTER XXIII.

Game Drives—Old Silver Medal—A Uté Diana—Turkey-roosting—A strange
Scene by Moonlight—A bold Puma—A Robbery.

THE Uté mode of hunting the deer—"driving"—is good lively sport. You turn out, well mounted, some hundred strong, have small parties posted in possession of every little mountain pass through which there are deer runs for a circle of some miles in diameter; and then, by a rapid drive, start running every deer and antelope in the surrounded space, each man shooting at them whenever he gets a chance. Where game is plentiful such hunting is full of excitement and incident, but it is the ruin of a hunting ground; for after a few drives not a fresh deer or antelope track is to be seen for miles, and the game becomes so wild as to be totally unapproachable by stalking or fair hunting.

Old Silver Medal generally took the management of the driving party, and on such occasions was usually accompanied by his only daughter. This young lady, out of all the women in the Uté camp, appeared to be the sole huntress. The old man had no sons living, and she was like one to him. Quite an old girl to be still unmarried (for an Indian), being eighteen or nineteen years of age, she was nevertheless unquestionably the belle of the band; a woman who would everywhere have been considered pretty, and to have a magnificent figure. This Indian Diana sat her horse *à califourchon*, as the French call it, handled a rifle very fairly, and rode as well as any man. She was as vain as a peacock, and as coquettish as the most accomplished civilised flirt.

Before very long, neither deer, antelope, nor ashlata were to be had; they had been literally *driven* away, and so we made a raid upon the turkeys. These birds had been unmolested by the Utés; the reason given by Old Silver Medal being that the turkey was a "totem-bird" of his tribe, and so they never killed him. We believed it was because the turkeys were too wary for them. Driving these birds is impracticable, stalking them on a disturbed range only vexation and loss of time, while "turkey-roosting" is a method unknown to Indian woodcraft.

The diversion of turkey-roosting, as it is called, is not without its attractions for the sportsman; and being a mode of killing turkeys only practicable in few places and at certain times, can be but occasionally indulged in, and so possesses the added charm of rarity.

The full of the moon is the opportunity for turkey-roosting, and the first necessity is to "roost your turkeys." This is done by watching, from a little before to some time after sunset, on an eminence commanding a view of some range of timber in which turkeys are likely to roost. Even in a country abounding with these birds it may require many evenings' watching before a roost is discovered: when it is, word is brought into camp, and the preparations made. Sufficiently long before midnight to allow of getting to the roost by that time, the hunters are awakened. A steaming can of hot strong *café noir* is ready for each of them, and a snack of refreshment. This is quickly despatched, and they sally forth. On arriving at the roost the hunters scatter out under the tall trees, in the upper boughs of which the game is sleeping, and each picks out his turkey. The first object of the hunter is then to "moon his turkey"—that is to say, to get a partial turkey-eclipse of the moon by bringing his eyes and that bird and luminary in line; this being accomplished, he brings his rifle to his shoulder, pointing it horizontally in a direction which would meet at right angles a perpendicular from the ground to the bird. In this position the moonlight falls full on the barrel of his rifle and lights up its sights. The hunter draws the front sight well down in the notch of the hind one until he gets his "bead," then he carefully raises his weapon until the shadow of the turkey falls upon it. As the rifle-sights darken, the hair-trigger is touched, and if the sportsman's nerve is steady, his eye and finger true, and his rifle what it ought to be, a prize well worth the exercise of his skill will drop, with a heavy thud, at his feet.

The amount of sport necessarily depends on many circumstances, which will suggest themselves to the reader; but I will give the result of my last day's—or rather night's—turkey-roosting in Wet-mountain Valley because it is as nearly an average night's sport of the kind as any I have had. There were two guns at work—my own and Joe's—and the bag was thirteen fine fat wild turkeys within twenty-five minutes after firing our first shot. The flock numbered thirty, more or less, the birds that escaped, flying away by ones and twos, as they were started off by the fall through the branches of those killed above them; for, strange to say, neither the crack of a rifle nor the blaze from the powder seems to frighten, but rather to stupefy, or make the wild turkey fear to move.

It was on returning from the night's sport just mentioned that I beheld the interesting sight I will now describe. We arrived at the crest of a hill overlooking a wide vale while it was yet illuminated by the full semi-tropical moon, by whose light we had been shooting, and, casting a glance over it, observed a pack of gray-wolves surrounding a herd of feeding antelopes. We paused to watch their proceedings. About fifty wolves were spread out in a great semicircle, crawling and sneaking along, their gray coats hardly visible in the silvery light. As the horns of the semicircle commenced to close round the herd of antelopes, some among them got the wind of the wolves, and giving the alarm, the whole herd immediately closed up and stood looking about them, hesitating which way to fly. Simultaneously the wolves rushed in, and the antelopes scattered in all directions, the bulk of them breaking through the line of their assailants, but some half-dozen being pulled down, torn to pieces, and devoured instantly. Then the wolves packed, and started in a long swinging gallop on the tracks of the flying herd, giving tongue as they ran, like a pack of hounds.

During our stay in Wet-mountain Valley we neither got bear nor puma. The bears had housed up for the season shortly before our arrival; and although they reappeared before we left, being then quite unfit to be eaten, their pelts totally worthless, while from hunger they were very dangerous, though we daily saw signs of their being about, we did not make them objects of pursuit. Still, had we *seen* one, we should certainly have risked a shot. Pumas we were anxious to get; we wanted their skins, and we wanted their claws; but pumas we could not get. We often heard them roar. Any time we could see their footprints; on some rare occasions we saw them! But they proved too fly for us; and they saved their skins, and they saved their claws. We tried to track them up; we watched the bodies of dead deer; we set guns for them. All to no purpose. Their haunts were in such thick impenetrable jungle we could not follow them, and our set guns were sprung by the lesser beasts of prey. Neither were they sufficiently numerous or hungry to afford a prospect of success in watching for them near a dead decoy deer.

The pumas made some few night attempts to steal the meat hanging up round camp, and once successfully. The first time one of them made a raid upon us, the dogs attacked him furiously, and got well mauled; they were very lucky not to have been torn to pieces, having no chance whatever against such a terrible opponent. It was a lesson to Nip and Tug which they did not forget, for though on every occasion thereafter when a puma approached camp, they charged out upon him, those knowing dogs took very good care never to turn a demonstration into a real attack, and were always ready to make a "masterly advance to the rear."

The puma, although nocturnal in his habits, frequently prowls about in the daytime; and notwithstanding his being a feline, is sometimes bold in action. A notable instance, illustrative of this statement, happened before we left Wet-mountain Valley. One afternoon my comrade successfully stalked a buck and a doe, who were feeding together; upon his firing, the buck dropped—killed in his tracks—and the doe ran off a short distance, stopped and looked back. Not having seen or smelt anyone, she seemed uncertain which way to go, and waited for her mate to get up and join her. My comrade rapidly reloaded, tried a long shot, and knocked her down; but she immediately recovered herself, and bounded off through a dense but narrow strip of chapparel, he following at a run, charging his rifle as he went. A hundred yards beyond the thicket she had traversed the doe fell again, that time to rise no more. My companion, when he reached the prostrate deer, bled her, and turned back to perform that necessary operation on the victim to his first shot.

I had heard the two reports, and having gone in the direction whence the sounds had come, joined my comrade just as, returning from where his doe lay, he emerged from the chapparel and stood in sight of the place where the buck had fallen. He pointed to the spot, but no buck was to be seen. We hastened up. No mistake had been made as to the place; there, where the deer had fallen, was the impression of his body, his blood on the grass. There were his tracks. But there were other tracks, too—the tracks of an unusually large puma, coming from a neighbouring jungle and returning to it again ; the return tracks being accompanied by a drag on the ground, made by the body of the dead buck. It was a bold thing for a puma to do, in broad daylight ; especially as he had no doubt seen the deer shot, and knew that there was a hunter with a gun close by. We instantly took the trail, and soon found the dead buck's body, dragged under a thick bush and covered over with leaves. Leaving it there, we tried our best to have a shot at the puma ; once catching a glimpse of him, as he bounded across a small opening in the brush ; but his tracks soon disappeared in a jungle which we could not penetrate, and we had to abandon all hopes of getting a robe off him.

Mention of the above occurrence serves also to give an idea of the great strength of the puma, for the deer that was dragged away by this one was an eight-point buck, in fat condition, and his gross weight could not have been much less than a hundred and fifty pounds.

I have related such incidents connected with the wintering of myself and party in Wet-mountain Valley as I think likely to interest the general reader, and be appropriate to and within the scope of my somewhat rambling collection of disjointed reminiscences. To enter into an account of our serious business in that valley—why we went and what we did there—further than what has already been told in the foregoing chapters, would prove interesting to but very few, and certainly be most inappropriate and out of place in these pages.

CHAPTER XXIV.

A Desert View—Salt Grass—The Caves—A Desert Valley—An improbable Tradition—Soda Lake—A medicinal Spring—Beelzebubs—Snipe.

"IT's a far cry to Loch Awe," and many hundred miles lie between Wet-mountain Valley and Fort Mojave, on the Colorado River. The connection between these statements is not obvious, neither will it be apparent that there is any such linking this chapter with the last. There is indeed none whatever. In it the scene was laid in the Rocky Mountains. Now I purpose to write about the Mojaves of the Colorado, their country, and their ways; and anything else that may come to my recollection, which is likely to be interesting to the reader. In this book no attempt has been made at a general sequence in the relation of facts; so if I am entertaining, as I always endeavour to be, why need I care for the unities?

Fort Mojave is generally first approached by the military road from Southern California; and as this route is over a very remarkable country, whose features are totally unlike anything European, and have been seldom described, I will try and give some idea of it by—in fancy—travelling it again, in the good company of my reader.

We have left "The land of the orange and vine," by the Cajon Pass—one of the mountain gateways of the Sierra Nevada—and stand at an altitude of something over five thousand feet in the Summit Gap. Behind is a charming scene of luxurious verdure, bounded by the blue Pacific. Before us all this is changed. Coming quite up to the base of the mountains, among whose crests we stand, and extending far as eye can see, is a vast panorama, whose essential features are those of a howling desert. Our eyes roam over a dreary expanse of sand, spreading out in immense unequal rolls and undulations to the horizon, broken through in many places, by low detached masses, ranges, and solitary peaks of bare, black, volcanic rocks. Through this forbidding country winds the Mojave river—or rather its course does. Only at long intervals of years does the Mojave river wind to anywhere.

The desert stretched before us is not totally devoid of vegetation ; some green things are there. The sandy plain, glaring and shimmering in the roasting heat, is in places dotted with the grotesque, weird forms of gigantic cerei candelari; the tall, dull green columns of the opuntas, and those vegetable hedgehogs, the globe cacti ; and patches of Spanish lances, greenwood, and other desert growths are sparingly scattered around. Every plant has thorns; none seem to have true leaves. Their forms are all eccentric, strange, and fantastic. What plants are there, are nightmares.

A long day's march, during which no drinking place for man or beast is passed, brings us to the Mojave river, down to an altitude of only three thousand feet, and by a short sharp descent of the sandy rim of the river's "bottoms," to our camp ground—a flat meadow of "salt grass." This salt grass is short, tough, and wiry; will cut like a knife the hand that incautiously pulls it; and is covered with an incrustation of fine salt. In some places so thick is this efflorescence, as to give the ground the appearance of being covered with white frost; and everywhere the grass is quite salt to the taste. Horses and cattle will eat salt grass, when they can get nothing else; but it is not good food, being very weakening, and making them thirsty, in a land where the water is always more or less poisonous. A hundred yards in front of our camp is a long, almost still pool of clear but greenish water, around which grow beds of rushes and thickets of willows. At its upper end this pool is fed by a stream, which is the head-water of the Mojave river; and from the salt-grass meadow whereon our camp has been just pitched, it receives the trickling flow from several springs of alkaline water. At its lower end this lagoon becomes a sharply running narrow stream— the river. The water runs merrily along for a few hundred yards, and then sinks in the thirsty soil, not to appear again for many a long mile. A solitary white stork, a few blue cranes, serve to give point and emphasis to the lonely dreariness of the scene. A succession of very similar camps, at places where the river rises to the surface in pools and short reaches of water, and then sinks—at an average distance of twenty miles apart—and we find our-

R

selves at "The Caves," distant from the Cajon Pass a hundred and ten miles, and nearly fifteen hundred feet above the sea-level.

The Caves is probably a contraction for the Pass of the Caves; that name being the one by which a pass through the range of mountains lying across our road is known, and in the middle of which some caves are situated.

It is truly a pass, in the strictest sense of the term. It is a passage through, not over, a mountain range. The mountains, cleft by the pass called The Caves, are a short but steep chain of basaltic and red-sandstone peaks, high, rugged, and bare, loosely connected with each other by obtruding masses of lava-rock, the whole rising abruptly from the general level of the desert. The pass is about eight miles long, and the entrance to it quite narrow; but we soon find ourselves in a small, long, winding valley, in which beds of tulés, immense rushes and bamboo reeds, and thickets of willows and osiers alternate with pools of green alkaline water, strongly impregnated with arsenic and medicinal salts —the Mojave river, risen again to the surface.

This valley has been the chosen place for several Indian massacres, the reeds and thickets affording admirable ambushes, and the unscalable sides of the pass preventing defensive flank movement. Not a few small cairns of stones, each surmounted with a rude cross, mark the spots where wayfarers, who have gone this road before, have "gone under;" and, impressively if silently, admonish us to " keep our eyes peeled."

Three miles farther on the pass cañons again, becoming

quite narrow. The walls on each side of us rise to a great height, and the intervening space is a level floor of fine silvery sand. Not a speck of verdure is to be seen; but, in compensation, the cliffs, which are variegated green and red sandstone, have had their faces fluted and columned by the rain-wash of ages into most extraordinary and beautiful architectural designs. And so nature, like time, brings all things even. This portion of the pass is about a mile long, and in its middle we come to the caves, which have given to it its name.

These caves are insignificant in size and few in number, only three being as large as ordinary-sized rooms; but we find them most welcome resting-places. It is midday, and they afford the only escape from the heat and glare of the sun's rays, which, reflected from the hot dazzling sand, and from side to side of the cañon, is just frightful. Their appearance suggests the idea that they have been made artificially, and their construction has been credited both to mine-hunters and to the ancient inhabitants of the country. In my own opinion their existence is due to the scooping action, on soft portions of the rock, of the immense floods of water which have, from time to time, swept through the pass.

After a short rest we push on, and, arriving at the mouth of the cañon, see before us a large desert valley. I can tell you its width; I have crossed it often. It is forty miles. I cannot tell its length, for I have *not* travelled it. No man has. It extends northward to—none knoweth exactly whither—and southward to the Gulf of California, two hundred miles distant.

It has been stoutly maintained by geologists of repute that, in comparatively recent times, the valley before us was a prolongation of that gulf; and a tradition exists among the Mission Indians and monks of Lower California, that somewhere in it lies the wreck of an ancient Spanish galleon, freighted with gold from Arazona—the Spanish El Dorado. So firmly is this improbable story believed by them, that, to my knowledge, two well-equipped searching parties have gone out in quest of the mythical old tub, both of which suffered great hardship, and nearly perished of thirst. In one case one of the adventurers *did* "sun his moccasins." In each, the expedition returned with several of its members delirious from the heat and want of water.

The side of the valley opposite to us—that is, its eastern side—is bounded by a high barren range of mountains, that, owing to the absence in them of water and grass, have never been prospected for minerals, but which have all the characteristic appearances of being rich in metal. Midway between us and the mountains lies Soda Lake, on whose shore our next camp will be made.

Soda Lake is ten hundred and seventy-five feet above the level of the Pacific, so that, if it was ever a portion of the old Vermilion Sea, it has had a pretty good hoist since then; however, nearly half way between it and the head of the gulf, at a place called Dos Palmas, to which the descent is so gradual as not to be noticeable, the level of the valley is twenty-three feet below that of the ocean; so a gradual rise thence of one in five hundred, or an average one of an inch in every thousand for the entire distance, would suffice to give the elevation.

Soda Lake is a monstrous natural fraud, a grim practical joke of old Dame Nature's.

As we stand in the mouth of the pass of The Caves, we see the lake spread out before us at a distance of some twenty-two miles. It looks like a lovely oval sheet of clear glistening water, miles across and miles in length, with strips and patches of verdure dotted around it. We stand parched with thirst; for the more of that liquid abomination, the water of The Caves, we have drunk, the thirstier we have become. We are scorched and blistered by the heat, we are half blind and choked, and wholly begrimed by the all-prevailing alkaline dust and fine sand. There arise in our minds—I mean in your mind, I have been there before — pleasant anticipations of copious draughts of pure water—a wash, perhaps a delightful swim! We almost feel that to be drowned would be a pleasure, so parched with thirst, so scorched with heat are we.

And it is all—a sell! A lizard could not be drowned in Soda Lake in the dry season—that is to say nearly all the time. If we march across it without canteens of water we shall suffer thirst. If we do so with thin boots on, the soles of our feet will be scorched; and in the wet season, when there is one, Soda Lake is a mass of bottomless mud; a spread blanket or a mosquito would mire down out of sight in it.

It is late at night and quite dark when we arrive at the lake. We made but a short morning drive; but we have since come twenty-three miles, which, though down-grade all the way, has been through very heavy sand, and we are as tired as the animals. Not only from humanity's sake, but from a motive of prudence, we have walked most of the way, well knowing that our horses have yet many days of hard travelling and short commons before them. Fatigue and darkness render us disinclined to make elaborate ablution or much improvement to our toilet, and we are glad to eat our supper, roll ourselves in a thin blanket, and go to sleep. And we make a long night of it, too, for to-morrow we shall " lay over." Men and animals are in need of rest, waggons have to be greased, harness must be mended, whip-lashes braided, and a general wash of clothes and persons has been decreed.

We spend the day in making ourselves as comfortable as circumstances permit—looking round, and, generally speaking, recruiting and repairing.

The deceptive appearance presented by Soda Lake, when viewed from a distance, we find to be caused by the fact that the level expanse of baked mud forming the Lake is thickly covered with efflorescent salts, in many places indeed it could be shovelled up with a spade. The "charming verdure" is, in reality, stretches of sand grass and compact beds of tulés—a marsh-grass looking like a cross between a reed and a bulrush. Where these tulés grow round the lake there is water, but it is not visible; were it not in the shadow of the tulés it would be dried up by the blazing sun. This water, though clear, is bitter, salt, and abominable, impossible to drink, and acrid to the skin. It has been known to take the hair off the pasterns of mules who have stood long in it to crop the tops of the tulés.

The "camp water" is furnished by an extraordinary spring rising only a few yards distant from where the waggons have stopped, and about twenty from the edge of the lake. A small stream of water wells up among a group of rocks projecting through the sand. It has apparently made for itself a circular basin fifteen feet across, and seemingly a foot deep, but really over five, so clear, bright, and transparent is the water. Running over the edge of this basin, at the side nearest the lake, it flows a short way and sinks into the sand.

This water has strong medicinal and remedial qualities, but requires to be drunk very carefully, at first, by both man and beast, or very serious results may ensue. It has one quality in common with The Caves water—the more you drink of it the more you want to do so. It is slightly saline in flavour, and decidedly sweet. When first taken from the spring it is too hot to drink; in fact, the water in the basin is so warm that the hand cannot be long held in it. I have used the water in July, and I have used it in January, and it was of just the same temperature. It is the most delightful water to wash with ever used, has a soft velvety touch to the skin that is delicious, and leaves it in beautiful condition, pure and white like that of Venus Aphrodite, smooth and fine as the coat of a race-horse in high training. But it makes the vilest coffee, and the nastiest tea conceivable.

The place where we are has some minor annoyances; rattlesnakes, tarantulas, scorpions, centipedes, horned-toads, lizards, immense ants, are everywhere. They all evince a most friendly and confiding disposition, and are not at all difficult to become acquainted with. But the greatest pest of the place is a huge horse-fly. I do not suppose this fly is restricted to the shores of Soda Lake; I hope he is. I have only seen him there, and certainly do not want to see him anywhere else. His body is about an inch and a half long, and his wings much longer. He is a black, hairy, large-eyed, vicious-looking fly, and I hate him. Indeed these Beelzebubs are no joke. I have seen a white mule literally covered with blood from their bites, and though I never lost any animals by them, not having on any occasion stopped more than one day at Soda Lake, I know of several cases of cavalry horses having died of weakness from loss of blood caused by their pertinacious attacks.

I was once at this place in early February and made quite a little discovery, a very pleasing one. I flushed a snipe—a regular old-fashioned English snipe. Leaving what I was about to do undone, I had my double-barrel quickly disinterred from the ambulance-waggon; and, although my shot was altogether too large for such *very* small game, I had an hour's fair sport, bagging over a dozen of the little brown beauties. They were the fattest, best-flavoured, biggest snipe I ever saw, or, still better, ate; and, as I devoured them, Soda Lake spring as a camp ground rose quickly and rapidly in my estimation.

CHAPTER XXV.

The Pinch of the Journey—Marl Springs—The Pied Quail—Rock Springs—
Silver Mine—Pah-Uté Hill—The Great Moss Lode—The Colorado—
An extensive View—A Mountaineer's Opinion.

OUR next *jornáda* constitutes the pinch of the journey, and an early start is essential. We breakfast by the light of the camp fires and the morning star. At the first streak of dawn our waggon-master sings out, "Break corrál;" and our teamsters being old hands and "smart," and the mules docile, in three minutes' time we are "hitched-up." As our train-master throws his leg over his horse, he gives the phrase of the occasion, "Roll out, boys, roll out." The drivers' whips "pop" with a noise like the report of so many pistols. The well-trained mules come down to a steady pull. Swing haw! then gee! straighten out! And, one after the other, the heavy waggons, whose wheels have sunk some inches in the loose sand, yield to the strain. The train moves. We have taken up our line of march again, and we are *en route* for Marl Springs, our next stopping-place.

We have a forty-five miles tramp before us, most of

the way a steady ascent, and all the way over, or rather through, deep sand; much of it fine, hot, running quicksand. In this the wheels of our supply waggons will sink half way to their hubs, and it will close behind them like water. Other portions of it we shall find full of loose stones of all sizes, which will sometimes give way and slip from under out feet, at others suddenly arrest our steps; so we shall flounder along with unequal strides, now twisting an ankle, anon stubbing a toe, and all this under a brazen sky and a blazing sun. Were it possible, this *jornáda* ought to be made during the night; but there is an insuperable objection—those infernal flies.

To make such a severe march it is necessary to start with rested animals, and mules and horses will not, and cannot, rest in the daytime at Soda Lake. So, thanks to those winged torments, we and the poor brutes have to endure a blast-furnace heat from soon after the rising of the sun until the going down thereof; indeed, the sand will radiate heat for some hours longer.

We have been rising steadily all day. We have made very good time, all things considered. We have only been eighteen hours on the go, and we arrive at Marl Springs before eleven o'clock, nearly four thousand feet above where we breakfasted. *We* are are all right, only tired and dirty, but the poor animals are nearly "give out" from thirst, and as soon as they have cooled off, the task of watering them begins—and task indeed it is.

The supply of water at this camp ground is very limited, but it is not as limited as it is nasty.

The "springs," forsooth! are a shallow puddle, and two

deep narrow holes in the ground. To get water out of them, the men let buckets down with ropes, and haul them up hand over hand. The first half-bucketful—no ingenuity or cunning of hand will bring a bucket up full—is covered with a thick slime, the next is muddy, then it gets worse until it is half mud, and it will take thirty minutes for the water to collect again. To water a large party is impossible; to water a small one, laborious and tiresome.

This water is said to be very wholesome. It is most certainly nasty. It is tepid, slightly bitter, and, even after standing all night in a vessel to settle, thick and discoloured. I cannot say what its washing qualities are—it is too scarce to be wasted for such a purpose; but, if so used, would probably make a man slightly more dirty than he was before.

On going to the water-holes in the morning we see flocks of the pied or desert quail coming to the puddles to drink— a rare and beautiful game-bird, well worthy to have a few words said about him.

Pied quails are strictly confined in range to deserts, and in them only found in a few places; though, wherever met with, these birds are generally numerous. They weigh, in their feathers, three to the pound; and, as far as comparison by memory is to be relied on, seem identical with the common Mexican quail, except in plumage. The desert quails are of a general sandy hue, mottled and splashed all over with irregular gray-brown and reddish spots. When in open view, a little distance off and quite still, they are practically invisible, looking exactly like a lot of scattered stones. But the most remarkable thing about them is that, unlike all other wild birds I am acquainted with, not only are no two of them exactly alike in their markings, but the variations are excessive, both in the colouring, shape, and size of the spots.

At Marl Springs I have invariably been successful in making a decent bag of these birds, but I must confess to having sinned against the sporting code on those occasions, and taken an unfair advantage of them; but it must be remembered I was shooting, not for sport, but for breakfast, and wanted to get a sufficient number of birds in time to be cooked for that meal. I used, therefore, to *cache* myself behind some rocks within easy distance of the puddles, and wait for the flocks coming to drink at daylight, and, on their arrival, take a rake at them. On the last occasion of my camping at Marl Springs I murdered—that is the proper name for it—twenty-nine of these beautiful and delicious birds in three shots. First shot, thirteen; the next, nine; and lastly, seven.

We turn our backs on Marl Springs gladly—almost as gladly as we arrived there. In such a place there is no inducement to remain. It is an excellent place for only one thing—to leave. Its one redeeming feature, the pied quails, have no longer any charms for us. We have eaten our fill of them, and on no account would we wish to remain long enough to get hungry again; and though we have fared sumptuously, our animals have not, for the grass in the neighbourhood is only remarkable for its absence. Twenty miles of alternate barren rocky ridges and desert valleys, of steep hills and abrupt declivities, bring us to our next halting-place—Rock Springs. Here we find the only really good water on the entire route; and it is good water—pure, limpid, and cool, and, above all, plentiful. We find it in a succession of natural rock tanks, running in a sharpish stream from one to the other of them, but sinking into the sand, directly it is reached, on escaping from the last tank.

Near Rock Springs is a silver mine, which was found and opened by some adventurous prospectors, and into which they drove a tunnel forty-five feet. Then they were murdered by the Pah-Utés. The charred and smoke-stained ruins of their burned cabin, a heap of ore, and the tunnel, remain mementoes of their hardy enterprise.

The close of the next day brings us to the summit of Pah-Uté hill, which we attain without making any great ascent, for it is the edge of the table-land, or *mesa*, on which we have been travelling all the afternoon; but had we been coming the other way, we should have found it to be indeed a hill, an acclivity of two thousand eight hundred feet, most of the way so steep as to render it necessary to "double team" to get the waggons up. We find an abundance of good grass all round us, but no wood and no water. The nearest water is some miles down-hill, and the mules and horses are driven loose to it by the herders, and then back to feed round our camp all night, under good and sufficient guard.

Our efficient train-master has taken care that liberal rations for all of that necessary but not inspiring fluid, water, has been hauled in the waggons from Rock Springs, and " bois de vache " has been collected by the teamsters for fuel.

We are within a day's march of our destination—down-hill! The hardships of the trip are over.

Standing on the edge of Pah-Uté hill, where the descent begins, we are at an elevation of nearly three thousand nine hundred feet above the sea-level, and, to reach the valley below, shall have to wind and twist about for eighteen miles of short abrupt rises, and long curving descents; some of the latter so precipitous, indeed, as to require the hind-wheels of every waggon to be rough-locked and chained to the waggon-beds.

Only one sentence—only one word can adequately describe the view.

The Colorado and its valley are before us!

Magnificent!

Far below where we stand flows the river; two hundred and fifty miles from its mouth at the top of the Gulf of California; sixty miles below the termination of its wonderful cañon, the Cañon Grande of the Colorado—profoundest, most stupendous, longest chasm in the world; and seven hundred miles from its sources in the Rocky Mountains.

Looking across, our view is limited by the crests of what appears to be a range of mountains bounding the Colorado Valley on the other side of the river, but which really is the scarp and glacis to the table-lands of Central Arizona, and piercing through it for several miles, the "croppings" of the Great Moss Lode are traceable.

The Great Moss Lode is a gold-bearing quartz vein, and its outcroppings are larger, and have been traced farther, than those of any other lode yet discovered. It has been mined in many places, both by American and Mexican companies; sometimes to great loss and disappointment; at others, yielding to the adventurers large quantities of gold, from rich chimneys and pockets. But the difficulty, almost amounting to impossibility, of keeping a working party in such a country supplied with food and other necessaries; the scarcity of water near the lode; the total absence of timber; the uncertainty and cost of labour; and, worse than all these obstacles taken together, the "Indian difficulty," have caused all mining operations on it to be suspended *sine die*.

Looking up the Colorado, our view thereof is quite limited, for but a few miles off, the heights bounding the valley on each side encroach entirely on the level ground, and come quite to the edge of the river, which winding suddenly round a rocky point to the right, disappears from sight. Raising our eyes, a succession—range after range, tier upon tier—of lofty mountains, interlocking with and backing each other, tower higher and higher toward the sky; all ragged and treeless, and having the sharp serrated outlines peculiar to the mountain-ranges of almost rainless climates.

*Looking straight down, we behold beneath us a broad semicircular sweep of the Colorado—a huge horse-shoe of burnished steel; and in the centre of the "bottom" embraced within the curve, we see embosomed in groves of acacias a beautiful little sheet of water—the Beaver Pond. In any other country it would be a lake. It is about the size of our own Derwentwater.

We gaze in the direction of the river's course. The view is boundless. The whole country slopes gradually away in a bird's-eye panorama of mountain-chains and intervening valleys; the mountains lessening, and the valleys widening, as they succeed each other in endless rotation. Through the centre of the picture flows the stately river itself; its flanking heights receding farther and farther from its banks; its "bottoms" widening and enlarging into plains, it winds its way along in many a glistening coil, like some gigantic, endless, silvery anaconda gliding into immensity. Our gaze follows its course until at last mountains and valleys, "bottoms" and river, are merged together in one misty gray, and then blend with the blue of heaven. The horizon is too far off for man's unaided vision to detect its line.

The actual extent of the view, the distance to where a straight line from our eyes to the horizon would touch the earth, I have no means of estimating. I have been told by persons upon whose statements I habitually relied, that smoke from the funnel of the steamer which occasionally brings supplies to Fort Mojave from the Gulf of California, has been seen here, while she was yet sixty miles off. A hard statement to credit, but the air is wonderfully clear in this excessively dry climate, and I have no doubt that the line of horizon is much farther off than that. I know, on approaching the Rocky Mountains from the east, crossing the so-called Great American Plain, the summits of those mountains first appear above your horizon, looking like the tops of thunder-clouds, when you are yet at a distance of a hundred and eighty miles from the base of the range, while, from such base, those summits are forty to fifty miles still further back. I can vouch for this, since I have seen them from there often, and that too with sufficient clearness to recognise and point out, by name, to accompanying strangers the well-known peaks; and I am certain of the distance, having myself measured it. And now I have brought you from fair California to the Colorado. We have travelled together a rough and rugged road, but not beset with danger, for an old hand has led the party, and a gallant escort protected it. Had it been otherwise, we might have left our bones to bleach, as many an honest miner, many a venturesome "tenderfoot," good man and true, has done. There are more graves and more charred ruins on the route than attention has been drawn to. Why should we have made ourselves sad?

We have been broiled, grilled, and bedevilled for two hundred and fifty miles, over which we have toiled at a tediously slow pace. You cannot trot mules on that trip. Alkali dust, hot sand, prickly cacti, poisonous water, hard marching, have done their worst to us. The *jornáda* from Soda Lake to Marl Springs we shall not soon forget: we were very tired. We have seen a queer country. I heard once a quaint description of it from an old mountaineer as I sat at breakfast at Marl Springs. It bordered on the irreverent, but not intentionally. He said: "I guess wen this hear old foot-stool was abeout finished, thar weare *some* cartloads uv brickbats uv mountings, end shavings uv vegitation, end en all-fired-sight uv waste sand, end mortar, on hend; end the Great Arch-e-tect didend kneow zakly what tew dew with it, so he jest dumped it, all of a heap, promiscus; end this hears the place."

Certes we have had a hard trip; but at its end, I have

shown you a superb view—so transcendently superb, that as we stand and gaze upon it, we feel amply recompensed for what we have gone through.

"See Naples and die." Bah! See the Colorado Valley from the summit of Pah-Uté Hill—and you will not want to die.

Buén Camaráda á díos.

CHAPTER XXVI.

The Colorado Bottoms — Coal — Climate — Gum — The Mojave Indians — A thoroughbred Look — Their Diet — Mojave Costumes — "Fixed to Kill" — Chá-Cha — Divinity of the Human Form.

THE Colorado "bottoms" merit some attention, principally because they are far from the beaten highways of travel. They are remote—very. Murray treateth not of them. There Cook's great name is all unknown. His ticket availeth not. His coupon serveth but to light a pipe! The beglassed, bestrapped, beguided, and bewildered tourist, veiled, umbrella'd, alpenstocked, knickerbockered, flasked, and sandwichboxed, infesteth not the land. The tax-gatherer doth not vex. The undertaker's hammer is not heard. And no man weareth a box-hat.

The "bottoms" are a succession of valleys, or rather one valley of ever-varying width, and of an almost dead level. The gradual downward slope amounts only to a descent of eleven hundred feet in nearly two hundred and fifty miles. The soil is a sandy alluvial deposit of irregular depth, an accumulation during past ages of deposit from the river; for the Colorado has its regular annual flood. Early in June an immense volume of pent-up water surges and raves along through the deep cañons of its upper portion, and widening out as it leaves its last rocky portal, floods the bottoms for miles in width. And then, assuming a steady and equal flow, commences to deposit a sediment from the sand and soil, with which a thousand tributary mountain-streams have charged it. This sediment is very fertile, and no sooner has the river subsided—which it generally does in a week or ten days—than a tropical vegetation starts up; and growing with magical rapidity, soon covers the face of the valley.

This country, now a wilderness sparsely inhabited by scattered bands of Indians, has a great future before it. Its intense heat—excepting during the winter months—the regularity and certainty of its being periodically overflown, its almost total immunity from rainfall, its fertility and the facility with which it can be irrigated, render it admirably adapted for the production of all such tropical lowland plants as are either annuals, or able to endure occasional slight frosts in January. The navigation of the river, though intricate, is always practicable for fair-sized steamers as far as the mouth of the Cañon Grande; sand-bars being the only obstacles, and grounding on these involves no danger, only at most a short detention. The sand forming the bars is of a loose shifting nature, readily allowing a steamer to be warped through or backed off, and a deeper channel can always be found by seeking it. There are many extensive belts of large cottonwood trees along the Colorado, sufficient to furnish steam-boat fuel for many years. Coal will be found—I have myself seen numberless pieces of drift-coal scattered along the river's course—and the mountains on each side are full of minerals.

One thing is lacking—a *reliable* working population, racially adapted to its climate. Not that it is unhealthy. Contrary to what would naturally be expected, the bottoms are unusually exempt from malarious fevers ; the sick-roll of the garrisons at Fort Mojave, and other posts in them averaging very light. Indeed, as a residence for sufferers from pulmonary disease, the valley of the Colorado has proved itself to be admirably adapted. To account for such a general healthfulness in so hot and occasionally humid a situation, several theories have been from time to time propounded by medical officers stationed there; but which, as a general thing, were more matters of conjecture than capable of demonstration. The climatic obstacle to white labour is the heat. I can, of my own knowledge, give data by which the reader may judge of its intensity. One night in August, when *en route* from Southern California to Arizona, I found a Government survey party encamped in the bottoms, and paid my respects to them. It was not an unusually hot night for that locality. I had spent many as hot, several much hotter there. It was 11 o'clock, and the thermometer at the camp was suspended in the current of what little air was drawing down from the mountains. When I looked at the instrument, the column of mercury in *that* thermometer was up to 112 degrees of Fahrenheit ! In the daytime, when the sun's rays pour down between the mountainous sides of the valley, and the direct, reflected, and radiated heat accumulates and concentrates, the temperature becomes scorching·

An egg quickly cooks in the sand, and even the salamander lizards seek the shade. It is the heat absorbed during the daytime by the rocky walls of the upper bottoms and the sandy soil, that, by radiation, keeps up the temperature of the air during the night; early morning being always the coolest time of the twenty-four hours. A Dutch recruit once remarked: "Dis blace ist but von littel half mile, unt you bees in das höllesche feure."

I know of one natural product of its soil, waiting there for the brain of enterprise and hand of industry. Large areas in the bottoms are covered with a gum-bearing acacia, which in the proper season exudes plentifully a sap that, hardening on exposure, becomes masses of excellent gum. Once, many years ago, on leaving Fort Mojave for San Francisco, I got some Mojave Indians to collect a quantity of this gum; and, taking it with me, submitted portions to different wholesale importing chemists in that city for their opinion. They were, one and all, very inquisitive to know where, or from whom, I had obtained it. I did not tell them. Each assured me it was fully equal to the best oriental gum-arabic, and offered to take any quantity at the full market price of that article. A title to the tracts of land on which these growths are could have been readily obtained, by going properly to work, at an almost nominal sum per acre, but the labour difficulty was then insurmountable.

The upper bottoms of the Colorado river are the land of the Mojaves—an Indian race which, inhabiting a continuous strip of river valley, enclosed with mountain walls up which they never venture, are practically isolated, and consequently not without many peculiarities. At eternal war with the tribes from which these mountainous ascents separate them, their long isolation has either developed differences of customs, language, and looks, or they have preserved ancient forms and appearances with greater purity than the roving, marauding bands on either side of them. Certainly they have a more thoroughbred look than have any other tribe of American *indigènes* with which I am personally acquainted, excepting the Zunians.

When I say a thoroughbred look, I fear I shall hardly be understood except by showing what I mean by its reverse. If a reader who is an artist will station himself for half-an-hour on London Bridge, and for that time attentively regard the several individuals of the passing crowd; and then, turning to one side, attempt to produce a form and face embodying and showing forth the general impression or image they have created in his mind, he will find that, instead of a general impression, he has a chaos of conflicting ones. He has seen some few handsome faces, many plain, and examples of every variety of ugliness have passed before him; but a prevailing type he has *not* seen.

He has seen every variety of nose, from the long hooked to the short snub, bottle-noses, snipe-noses; eyes, varying from the large blue Norse eye, or oriental dark one, to watery, fishy eyes, pigs' eyes, eyes like burnt holes in a blanket; mouths and chins as various; foreheads, from the hydrocephalic to the monkey's; some finely-formed and well-balanced figures, but many and various disproportions and contortions, only hidden by clothing from the undiscerning eye; tall heavy men; tall thin men; the high-shouldered; men who are neck to their elbows; the podgy, the bandy-legged, and the knock-kneed; all complexions, from the carroty, sandy, and dust-coloured, to the almost black; curly and straight, coarse and fine hair; and all these varying descriptions mixed.

He is inevitably driven to the conclusion that, physically speaking, the crowd that has passed before him is a mongrel one. Fortunately for its members, they are results of the innumerable crosses of the higher races of mankind with little or no infusion of inferior blood; but, though containing many specimens of the highest forms of beauty, when taken *en masse*, failing to satisfy critical judgment as does the classical look which depends on typical regularity.

The whole cast of countenance of the Mojave Indians, every feature of every one of them, is out of the same typical mould; and the mould is in every respect an American and a good one. While many, if not the majority, of the American-Indian tribes are very ugly, as compared with the European ideal of good looks, the Mojave tribe is decidedly a handsome one.

Unlike all other wild tribes with whom I have had intercourse, the Mojaves do not allege that they have come from anywhere; on the contrary, they maintain they have always been where they now are. Though in appearance a superior kind of Apache, they claim to be of other stock, and their language is certainly very different from any of the Apache dialects; all of which, indeed, the Mojave affects to regard with contempt, contending that they are not languages, but only "crooked talk."

The country they inhabit being almost destitute of game, these aborigines live principally on maize, frijoles or Mexican beans, and fish; of which latter there is an abundance in the Colorado, principally sturgeon, and a fish locally known as white-fish. In their season, pumpkins and other indigenous vegetables, which they cultivate in little garden-patches, furnish them also with food.

They are a very intelligent people, and had their lot been cast in a country where clothes were a necessity, where tillage was beset with difficulties, and, above all, where the inclemency of the seasons had compelled them to make the first steps in architecture—that science which has been the mother of geometry, mathematics, mechanics, and the arts—they might possibly have developed from being naked savages to a high state of civilisation.

That they are nearly naked savages, a description of the national lack of costume will amply demonstrate; excepting the breech-clout, they are, from the ground under their feet upwards, entirely unclothed; neither do the men affect paint, feathers, or ornaments; this, however, cannot be charged to want of appreciation of the beautiful, since their weapons and implements are carved in the usual Indian fashion, and with more than usual Indian taste.

They wear their hair—which, like that of the Apache, is very long, and of the usual colour and texture of American aborigines—exactly as the Tangierean Jews do, and have done since the time of David. It is combed down on their foreheads, cut straight across the middle of it, from side to side, and gathered together in a mass behind.

The costume of the women is more elaborate. I mean of the young women. The old ones, putting aside the vanities of the world—you see they are *not* civilised—abandon the ornamentations of youth, and are dressed just like the men. (Triumph of the Woman's Rights movement. Hooray!) The general effect, however, is in their case unfortunate, to put it mildly; since, as they get old they get very fat, and then become one entire network of wrinkles. These old women always reminded me of nutmeg-melons. But to return to the Hiloes: these are, when "fixed to be killing," dressed in a sort of kilt, made with strips, two inches wide, of the inner bark of cottonwood-trees, dyed and stained different colours, fastened to a narrow buckskin waistbelt, and hanging down to within a little of reaching their knees. In front, the strips forming this fringe are placed just near enough to touch each other, and hang close to the figure. Behind—why, when I was first amongst the Mojave savages many years ago, the belles of the tribe were, in one respect, ages ahead of fashion as set by Paris—behind, the particoloured strips are put on one over the other until a result is obtained like, yet far exceeding, that achieved by a most prodigious "dress-improver," but having a much more artistic effect. Their hair is worn "Gainsborough style" in front, "rivulet style" behind, and reaches down to the middle of their calves. The Hiloes rouge with red clay powder, with calcined mussel-shells, kohl, with charcoal and grease, and wear all the necklaces, armlets, bracelets, and leglets they can get hold of. Between the ages of thirteen and thirty these women have unquestionably most perfect figures; certainly I did not observe an ill-made woman amongst them, and, having often witnessed crowds of from twenty to a hundred bathing in the river, I have had my chances to form a judgment, especially as on such occasions they are not bashful; on the contrary, if you are acquainted with any of them, these unsophisticated maids and matrons, innocent of the requirements of propriety, will expect you to join the group on the bank and admire such extra touches in the diving and swimming performances as any of the nymphs may like to indulge in. And a water frolic being one of the chief diversions of the Hiloes, they generally spend, from their childhood up, a couple of hours of each day enjoying one, becoming most expert and intrepid swimmers.

The belle of the nation, Chá-cha by name, had a face undeniably handsome, while her figure was a poem in form. And as I have found it to be a generally received opinion that if there is an American-Indian woman who cannot be described as plain, it is because she is ugly, which indeed is true as regards many tribes; and thinking it but fair to my readers to show the erroneousness of that belief, I will, with the kind indulgence of such ladies as may do me the honour to peruse these recollections, draw a picture of this child of nature, exactly as I have seen her on more than one occasion; premising that, should this book fall into the hands of any person (if such there be) who thinks the Greek statues should be covered with draperies, and that the Creator made the human figure unfit to be seen, the remainder of this chapter is not intended for his reading. Chá-cha was about twenty-two years of age, five feet six inches high, and possibly eleven stone in weight. But it was difficult to estimate what she did weigh; since, though light in the waist, and quite small in the joints, her limbs were very full and well rounded. She had elegantly-sloped shoulders, and a wide, full, deep well-muscled chest—a chest like an athlete's—from which sprung, with a slight upward and outward tendency, the "two young roes that are twins, which feed amongst the lilies." As she stood on the edge of the river's bank some fifteen feet above the water, taking a deep breath preparatory to a header, with her long black hair hanging down her back nearly to the ground, with a look of free fearlessness on her face, with the bright sun shining on her skin and making it look like copper-coloured satin—bringing a warm roseate underglow through its clear texture, and revealing its soft shadow-tints of bronze—she seemed an impersonation of combined strength, grace, and beauty. She embodied a full, complete, and most convincing discourse on the divinity of the human form. Surely, if there are "sermons in stones," *she* was one in flesh and blood. She was at once a realisation of grace in form and beauty in colour, beyond anything I have seen in marble or on canvas, or, before then, was able to have imagined.

CHAPTER XXVII.

A Fight—Irrataba—A Case of Possession—The Body Guard—The Harvest Full-Moon Dance—Mescal—Wild Orgies.

THE Mojaves are a brave people, and a reliable. They made a fair square stand-up fight for their country, when they thought it was invaded; and when thrashed, not only came to terms like men, but have ever since faithfully kept the treaty they then entered into, neither murdering, thieving, nor molesting person or thing.

I have had an account given me of what they call "The Great Battle," by Irrataba, the chief who commanded the Indians at the time, and also by an officer who served with the troops; and the relations being substantially the same and both my informants credible men, I do not hesitate to repeat it here.

The troops—infantry with a few cavalry scouts—were not sent into the upper bottoms of the Colorado with any hostile intent, but to locate and construct a post on the river, at which supplies for the use of the military force in the interior could be landed; in fact, to establish a depôt and distributing point for the military district. This the

Mojaves did not or could not understand, but supposed the soldiers had come to take their country from them ; and therefore gave notice that unless the troops were immediately withdrawn, they would be attacked. And attacked they were in the most plucky manner. It was bow and flint-tipped arrow against gunpowder and bullet; undisciplined valour against trained courage. But the Indians had greatly the advantage in numbers, and though totally unused to contend against firearms, pressed the soldiers steadily back to the edge of the "Mesquite" they had taken position in. The situation becoming critical, the officer commanding determined to risk a charge, preparatory to which the men were ordered to fix bayonets. Irrataba, then but little past middle age, was giving his orders from a tree-top, where, reckless of the danger of being picked off, he had stationed himself to overlook the engagement, and be the better able to direct the movements, of his braves. Seeing the bayonets fixed, he called out to his men, "They have stopped up their guns ; give them the knife ; " and his warriors, casting away their bows and arrows, charged.

Wild yells, flourishes, and savage gestures, intended to strike terror into their foe, are, as a rule, the accompaniment of all Indian attacks, except surprises. The conduct of the Mojaves on this occasion is an instance of their dissimilarity in many things to other tribes.

The assault was delivered in silence. Heads down, shoulder to shoulder, the Mojave warriors came on with a quick, determined rush. It was gallant but fatal. Received with a full volley, fired low, they were piled in heaps, then charged through the smoke, and completely routed.

Soon afterwards the Mojaves made a treaty of peace with the whites, which, as I said before, has been ever since faithfully observed.

During the construction of Fort Mojave, the officer commanding the troops, seeing Irrataba's intelligence and good sense, and the influence he possessed with his people, was inspired with the bright idea that if that chief could only be induced to go to Washington, ostensibly to have an interview with the great white chief to ratify the treaty, he would bring thence a report, which would so impress the Indians, that thereafter they would consider it useless to contend against whites; and such report, getting spread to neighbouring tribes, would induce them also to keep the peace. So the Indian bureau being communicated with, and signifying their approval of the idea, the proper arrangements were made, and Irrataba taken to Washington, presented, and in due time brought back to his country. He returned brimful and running over with tales of wonder. The effect, however, was not exactly what had been expected and hoped. Irrataba called his sachems together and narrated his late experiences. He told them what strange sights and what multitudes of people he had seen. His speech was received with a dead silence, and his wise men dispersed. Then they held a secret council together. After long deliberation they came unanimously to the conclusion it was all lies! The difficulty then presented itself: How was it that their well-beloved and respected chief, whose word hitherto had been truth and law, should have attempted to deceive them so grossly? There was only one possible solution. The whites, the better to secure the destruction of the Mojaves, had cunningly conjured the soul out of the chief's body and replaced it by a lying devil; and to knock him on the head, burn him to ashes, and throw these into the river, was the only safe course to pursue. Fortunately, before this decision was acted upon a notice of his danger came to the ears of Irrataba, and he took refuge with his friends in the Fort. It was only after a lapse of considerable time, and as a result of no little diplomatic ability on his part, that Irrataba was able to go amongst his people again in safety; and it was still longer before he recovered his lost influence over them.

Irrataba was getting to be an old man when I last saw him, but was still straight and hearty. Having been for a long time in daily intercourse with the garrison, he could make himself quite understood in English, and comprehended everything said to him in that language; and being very communicative where he gave his confidence, I often enjoyed long conversations with him. He habitually wore the dress, or rather undress, of his nation; and neither carried insignia, ornament, nor weapon, but was distinguished by being always accompanied by his body-guard. Irrataba's body-guard consisted of an imposing force of one, and such an one! I will describe him. The body-guard was a powerful, well-built, six-foot Indian. His uniform—I enumerate *all* the articles of apparel—a breech-clout, which as a mark of distinction had long overlapping ends dangling down, both before and behind, to below the knees; a dragoon's shell-jacket, dark blue, faced and braided with yellow, much too tight for him, and with sleeves that only reached a little below the body-guard's elbows; and lastly, a sword-belt round the naked waist, from which depended a steel scabbard and a sabretache. In his hand, this extraordinarily-accoutred state official carried his drawn sabre, and upon his head—oh horrors!—an old, battered box-hat—dress-hat if you prefer it so—of the kind which, courteous reader, you and I are obliged to wear to go to church or make our morning calls with. How *such* a hat got into *such* a country, passeth my understanding. It was the one instance that proved the rule, that there they were unknown. It was its quality of uniqueness that was supposed to give the wearer of it such a *distingué* appearance; and no doubt his hat contributed greatly to render the chief's body-guard an efficient equivalent, for purposes of state, to the gentlemen-at-arms, the life-guards, and the sticks in waiting, all "kjummuxed" into one. Such is regal pomp and circumstance among the Mojaves.

It was old Irrataba who told me of the existence, amongst his people, of a very curious rite or semi-religious performance; one that I had never before heard of, nor indeed of any similar to it, amongst other American-Indian tribes. It is therefore well worth describing, and especially so because in many respects it has striking analogies with some of the pagan rites of antiquity, and further because very few white men have seen or know anything about it. The chief informed me it was one of the most ancient and important of the ceremonies practised by his people, for it had always ben observed since the time when the maize

T

had been divinely given to them, having then been enjoined as an annual sacrifice and acknowledgment. And it was believed by all, that its omission would entail bad succeeding crops and other unknown disasters. He added that his people did not like to have strange spectators; but that I, being his friend, would be welcome, and should find the "harvest full-moon dance," for so he called the performance, a sight well worth my witnessing; but that I must not take any weapon with me, as the presence of one would be certain to "spoil the medicine," that is to say, break the charm. In this prohibition, I afterwards recognised the spice of practical sense usually seen to be mixed up with all Indian superstitions; since, on beholding the ceremony, I realised the great desirableness of there being no arms among such a set of wild performers going through such extraordinary rites. Irrataba said he should like me to go with him, but that he would have to attend the chief dance at the main settlement, a long way off, while the one near at hand would be just like it, only on a smaller scale; that the rite would be properly performed there, so I could suit my own convenience. I therefore obtained from him full instructions as to time, place, and route, and determined to attend the dance in the vicinity.

On the appointed night I started off, at about half-past nine, to find my way to the indicated place. My road was by foot trails, through cultivated patches of ground, timber groves, mesquite thickets, and cane-brakes, for a distance of about four miles; and having been told that between ten and eleven o'clock the performance would be in full swing, I confidently expected to be there in good time. But I was much longer on my way than I had anticipated, for, although the moon rendered it almost as light as day in the open, a great portion of the route was under dense foliage, where it was very dark; and there were so many diverging and cross trails from garden to garden, and "wickee-up" to wickee-up, that it was quite bewildering. Several times I went to different wickee-ups to inquire my direction, but invariably found them deserted, except by an occasional old woman and children; the latter always running away and hiding, while from the former I generally failed to get any comprehensible signs. At last, coming within sound of the music, I found my way to the place.

The ceremony was in course of progress in a large grassy natural glade—a sort of savanna—which was surrounded by a wide border of immense cottonwood-trees, and a dense undergrowth of mesquites, canes, and vines. The dancers were in motion, and near to them, under a large tree standing out a little way in the opening, sat, in a semicircle, the musicians; while, close to the trunk of the tree, stood a group of old braves, apparently in charge of, and mounting guard over, what seemed to be a barrel covered with a robe. One of this group, immediately upon its being recognised who and what I was, motioned to me to join them. On doing so, I found my surmise as to the covered object being a barrel was correct. The old savage who had beckoned to me, partially uncovering it, took a gourd drinking-cup, dipped it in, and presented it to me to drink from. A whiff told me what was in the cup; but a refusal being impossible under the circumstances, I accepted it from his hand. Fortunately, although a temperate man, I had, from long sojourning in fever countries, acquired, through taking it for prophylactic purposes, the ability to swallow a fair dose of raw spirts, and so, taking a long breath, and opening my shoulders, "I threw myself outside" of the unavoidable draught.

It was mescal, an intoxicating drink of unknown antiquity, made by the American aborigines from the plant of that name, a species of centaury. This spirit, when old and mellowed, is a pleasant enough drink, being then but little more fiery than new Scotch whisky; but when freshly made, as this was, giving a sensation to the drinker like what one might suppose would be caused by swallowing hot lightning. After drinking, I quietly lit my pipe, and turned my attention to the scene. The band was composed of numerous performers, consisting of old men and old women. They sat in a large semicircle, and their instruments were various, rude, and primitive— stringed ones, constructed of large split gourds and deer-sinews; rattles made of whole gourds, with pebbles in them ; and still less complicated ones—their hands; the majority of the musicians marking time and increasing the noise by clapping their palms together. The band was, however, but an accompaniment, for all the Indians, dancers included, were singing one continuous chant. The tune though full of minor variations, was, in the main, very monotonous. At first the words sounded like "Hié-e-e-hi— ah!—àhe," repeated *ad infinitum;* but upon giving a more critical attention, I discovered that they were singing a set of words or a composition having a regular rhythm. The figures and steps of the dance were simple, and are easy to describe. As I had been led to expect, the gathering was only a small one; there were not many more than a hundred couples dancing, the males being all men capable of bearing arms, and the females marriageable girls and young matrons. For the occasion the ladies had each laid aside her ornaments and fringe, and only retained the hardly-worth-mentioning garment. Full dress—very—*décolleté* to the heels!

The dancers were disposed in four parallel rows, the two inner ones being close together, back to back, and consisting exclusively of women; and the two outer ones which were composed of men, being each about twenty feet from the row of women that it faced. The individuals composing these four parallel rows stood a yard apart from each other in their respective rows, having hold of one another's hands.

The set had only just commenced when I arrived. As yet, the dancers were going it very deliberately. The step was uniformly alike, and executed in admirable time and unison. Throwing their weight on their left legs, the dancers advanced their right ones about a foot, and threw their weight on them, bending the knee and inclining the body slightly forward; then the right foot was retired a much behind the left, and the whole body swayed back. Accompanying these movements, their hands, still clasped each in their neighbours', were simultaneously raised slightly up, and then as slightly depressed.

The chant, though monotonous, sounded strangely plaintive and wild, and its regular rise and fall of cadence was in excellent keeping with the motions of the dancers. There was no attempt at part-singing, but the natural difference between the male and female voice had a good effect.

The whole scene was bathed in a flood of tropical moonlight; and the plaintive wail of the chant as it rose and fell, the four lines of dusky figures swaying and undulating to and fro, the dark solemn forest-trees framing in the scene, and—excepting the chant—the complete stillness, sensibly affected the mind of the beholder. As the dance continued, both it and the music increased in speed; the step forward and backward became longer and longer, and the accompanying swayings of the body more decided. By-and-by, the speed still increasing, two steps to the front and as many back were taken; then more, and still more, ultimately becoming a short run forward until the two lines of women nearly met the two of men, with a backward run of the same distance. The slight inclinations forward and backward became almost prostrations, and the still joined hands of the dancers were raised as high as possible into the air, and then depressed almost to the ground.

The dance had slowly, gradually, and steadily increased in rapidity and energy, from being a slight, quiet, dignified motion to a wild bewildering rush—a glancing kaleidescope of moving arms, legs, and swaying bodies. The effect of the scene, even on a quiet spectator only there from motives of curiosity, was like that of being under a spell. One felt as if enchanted, under the influence of a narcotic, or in a nightmare. The sure, steady, inevitable—as it seemed—way in which accompaniment, chant, and moving figures had imperceptibly progressed from placid slowness to maddening speed, was absolutely fascinating. Continually I had caught myself accompanying the performance with an involuntary Saint Vitus' dance in every limb; and though on each occasion I had stopped it with a determination to control myself and do so no more, I soon became recaptured by the influence of the scene, "the spirit of the revel" seized upon me, my attention, absorbed by chant and dance, was distracted from myself, and the saint resumed his possession of me.

At last increase of speed became impossible; when, on the women falling back until their two lines came together, the men, instead of also retiring as before, followed them up, and the four end men of the lines catching hold of one another, the female dancers were enclosed in a long oval. Instantly the women, leaving go of each other's hands, threw their arms wildly upwards, and a universal yell split the night air. Then, ducking their heads, the Hiloes rushed in every direction against the cordon of men surrounding them, trying to break through it. There was a momentary wild struggling *mêlée*, and then the women broke through in twenty places. Closely pursued by the braves, they scudded away, each on her own line, for the surrounding cover. For a few seconds there was a loud, confused crackling, snapping noise as the two hundred and more Indians crashed headlong into the cane and underbrush. Then a deathlike stillness succeeded. So still was it that the occasional low hum of some straggling mosquito seemed a loud audacious disturbance. Soon all came trooping back and rallied round the cluster of old warriors standing by the barrel. The covering robe was thrown aside. Each guardian angel (?) took his gourd cup, dipped it full of mescal, and *everyone* had a drink.

The band reseated themselves. The dancers reformed. It was, "As you were," and "*En avant.*"

I stopped to see the second dance out, and the third set form—my object being to discover if there was any partnership arrangement, whether the same couples danced opposite each other; but this did not appear to be the case. It all seemed to be an entire matter of chance. The whole performance was gone through, too, without any levity, frolicking, or joking; and I have no doubt it was to the Indians a serious religious rite and sacrifice, upon the due and thorough performance of which they believed the increase and fruitfulness of the ensuing crop depended.

One of the ancients of the barrel assured me that the celebration would continue until all were so drunk that none were able to sing or dance; but that there would be plenty of time to get sober in, since no more mescal could be made until the next season.

The harvest full-moon dance of the Mojave Indians I shall never see again. I am very glad I have seen it. I would not take "a right smart chance of money" not to have seen it. For, the lovely savanna, brilliant with such a moonlight as is only seen in tropical climates—the encircling wall of foliage, of densest black where in the shade, but with edges that glowed like burnished silver, and through whose every crevasse gleamed and glinted arrows of light—the Rembrandt-looking group beneath the spreading branches of the isolated tree—the dancers and the dance—formed, taken all in all, a vision apart from every other experience, as utterly separated from the rest of my life as though I had had a peep into another world.

CHAPTER XXVIII.

Acapulco—The Bay—The Women—The Fandango—Beauty and Ugliness—
La Maripósa — Lozada — My little Speech — The Appointment—Good
Advice—How I keep the Assignation—Throwing Light on a dark Scene
—The Confessor.

THE Mojaves and their country always suggest to me recollections of Acapulco and a Peruvian I met there. I suppose it is a matter of association of ideas; Acapulco being in the matter of heat the comparative to the Colorado bottoms; the place which is the superlative I need not mention, and hope to avoid arriving at; and I suppose Chà-cha brings the Acapulco belle to my remembrance.

Acapulco—*El caliénte*—and well called the hot, where eighty-six degrees Fahrenheit is as low as the thermometer ever goes, and where it mounts to just anywhere. It is so hot; it is so unhealthy; but—it is so beautiful. As a harbour it looks perhaps the loveliest in the world. As you stand on the deck of the ship, riding at anchor, that has brought you in, it seems as though you had come there by magic. An ampitheatre of lofty granite mountains surrounds you, showing no gap through which the vessel could have entered, and how beautifully are those mountains clothed with tropic vegetation.

Acapulco's bay—for the harbour really is a bay—is in its way unique. It is supposed by geologists to be the crater of an extinct volcano that has suffered subsidence, is quite oval, its shores go down almost perpendicularly, and it contains the bluest, clearest sea-water that ever lay in bay. Often into it have I thrown small silver coins for the little native children to dive after, and watched the *reals* glistening down for many a fathom, followed fast by the dusky divers.

Looking east, you see at the edge of the water a crescent sweep of white shell-sand, and just beyond it the town—such a picturesque one. The majority of the buildings are low, having only ground-floors; their whitewashed walls are upright rows of bamboo-canes; their tall steep roofs of reed-cane thatch, two feet thick, with wide overhanging eaves. There they stand, dotted about in all directions with the most charming irregularity, surrounded and overhung with tree-ferns, shady orange-trees, towering palms, and bread-fruits. To your right is the crumbling old Spanish fort, many a time assailed in the olden days by bold buccaneers. Kidd and Drake have both the credit of its capture. The banners of the old Spanish viceroys have waved over it, the Union Jack, and the Tricolour; but patriotism and the climate have always put the flag of the country back again. Long may it wave there! On your left, standing in groups almost to the water's edge, appears a magnificent grove of palms—the city of the dead. The underbrush that once grew beneath the trees is replaced with a carpet of short grass, thickly dotted with the white headstones that preach a sermon as eloquent as it is mute—the milestones of eternity! Behind, a precipitous mountain-side, green and gold, crimson and purple, blazing with the georgeous brightness of the tropics. And the whole scene reflected with wondrous fidelity in the glassy mirror it encircles. No rude wind ever roughens that sheet of burnished, bluest steel—that gem of purest aquamarine set in gold and malachite.

And as Acapulco is beautiful, so are many of her *gentle* inhabitants. *Los hombres* are *muy diabolos*. The most beautiful woman I ever saw was there. She was the cause of my having an adventure—no, of my thinking I was going to have one: it did not amount to an adventure *then*, though for a time it looked likely enough to be a very disagreeable one. I met her first at a fandango, to which I had gone with a friend, a practically speaking naturalized citizen, one of Acapulco's many American resident merchants. It was a pretty little fête— why given I do not recollect, do not think I ever knew. The first thing that rivetted my gaze when, on going into *cása* from the pitchy darkness without, my eyes recovered the shock of the glare from a multitude of hanging lamps, was *she*. Now some people maintain that beauty and ugliness are purely matters of taste, of education, of association; that there is no such thing as absolute beauty, absolute ugliness. I say there is. I have seen both. I then saw an example of the first.

Undoubtedly to a wide range of objects the application of the several terms of the degrees of beauty, and its reverse, would be solely a matter of taste, or want of it. Take for example a pug-dog. I think nothing uglier goes on four legs, but I have seen a fair young creature take one of them in her arms, hug it, and calling it a "perfect beauty," kiss the little monster. I would sooner have kissed a lizard; it would not have been so olfactorally objectionable, and to me much less ugly. Now take a pearl; certainly there are prettier things than pearls, yet where is there a difference of opinion as to a pearl having some beauty? The savage of the lowest grade wears it as an ornament, thinking therefrom to receive reflected beauty; so does the proudest lady in Christendom. The beauty of a pearl, such as it is, is absolute, beyond doubt. I should like to describe this belle of Acapulco, but find the task a difficult one. It is indeed quite out of my line to descant on female loveliness. I have had no practice, for I do not care about describing beauties to my male acquaintances, but prefer to let them find out handsome women for themselves; and as to doing so to other females—no. I may not know much, but I do know too much for that. However, as there are exceptions to every rule, I will "try a stagger" at depicting her. She stood at the upper end of the room, the top lady in a cotillion set just formed; in height five feet three, and rather fully developed in figure. Her complexion, for a mestizo's—and mestizo she certainly was— extremely fair; while her skin had a creamy softness of texture, a warmth of delicate colouring, a rich shading of neutral tints that were most charming; the complexion, of the "blue blood of Castile," and the high arch to the instep of her dainty little feet, the small taper tips of her plump and pretty baby hands, proclaimed that it was there. Her Inca blood only showed in her hair, in her eyes, in her graceful *nonchalant* step, in the look of quiet, set determination that stole over her countenance whenever it was in repose. Her hair, blue-black, and without a wave, was turned back from her face, gathered all together, without a parting, high up on the back of her head, and hung down in one massive fall to within a foot of the ground. Her eyes! They were a revelation—such wonderful eyes. Large brown ones—*dark* eyes, having that expression of dreamy, loving, appealing helplessness, that is the distinguishing characteristic of the loveliest of *blue* eyes, and yet which sometimes flashed and blazed like black diamonds. And their setting—their lids—their lashes—their brows! And her little pearly teeth—her mouth! But hold— this will never do; if I describe all her features I shall run out of adjectives before I get to her figure. That will be where I shall want them most. But first comes, of course, her dress. She was attired in a white muslin gown cut after the fashion of the country; that is to say, with hardly any body to it, *very* low in the neck, and exceedingly short in the waist. Sleeves—call them pieces of tape round the arms—but pray recollect the climate. Dancing in a room heated with many lamps when the thermometer is at ninety-five degrees Fahrenheit out of doors "in the cool," necessitates *and excuses* scanty clothing. The skirt long and flowing, no crinoline, no hidden construction of mechanical invention for *improving*—heaven save the mark—the figure. No! the natural form revealed its charming outlines in every graceful movement. How was her dressed trimmed?

How was her head dressed? With flowers: she was literally covered with natural flowers—flowers that would be priceless exotics here—flowers of every radiant hue, their colours blended and mingled with the innate taste that showed she was a descendant from the ancient race who wrought the marvellous feather-work of old Peru. She stood there, an intoxicating dream of beauty.

To the man who is familiar only with European figures, I can give no adequate idea of her grace of carriage, her elegance of movement, the perfect proportions of her limbs, the matchless beauty of the curves of her muscles: there is no such living perfection of form to be seen in Europe *now.*

The use for generations of stays, of ligatures, of high heels, stomachers, ruffs, steel and whalebone, horse-hair and wire, has settled that question as far as the well-off are concerned; and *pour les autres,* toil, hardship, and privation, disease and vice, have set their marring mark on every line of beauty about them. The woman I am describing was a descendant of the *Conquistadórs*—as fine a body of men as ever left old Spain—and the Incas. Her ancestors, on one side certainly, had been kings when the mammoth trees of California were but seeds. For ages back, the race from which she chiefly sprang had been born rulers; their men had worked not, their women had not toiled; she, until grown up, had run about untrammelled—the children's dress of the country is but a chemise; as a girl she had climbed the tall cocoa-nut for its food, dived in the deep blue bay for shells—a fearless swimmer, a daring horsewoman, an accomplished dancer; no corset had spoiled her waist; no shoe was small enough to pinch her little feet; her tiny gloves alone were aggravations to a man.

I was younger then than now by many a year's hard service. I turned to my friend with—" Who is she? Do you know her?"

"She! Oh, the beauty! know her! I should just think I do. Best-known woman in the state. But go slow, old fellow; that's La Maripósa. If you have any personal objection to attending a funeral in the character of the corpse, you'll steer clear of her."

"Why? Tell me all about her."

"Well, she lives quietly enough with her old mother in very comfortable style at a pretty little place just out of town, known as El Ojo; goes to mass regularly on Sundays and saint-days; is good to the poor, and for Acapulco very discreet in her conduct; but she is under the protection of Lozada." Now Lozada was a robber.

I knew Lozada by reputation very well; he was "no slouch of a road agent." He was "Géfe." He was a "Patriota." There was a price—a good price—upon his head, for he was "King of the Mountains." The country was full of his friends, and they served the brigand well; his enemies feared him, and "lay low;" every *cárga* of bullion paid him tribute or risked capture; every *hacienda* contributed its quota to his revenue, or was harried. Troops had been sent against him, and lo! he was not to be found; but, in the expedition's rear, supplies were captured, mails stopped and robbed, treasure trains pounced upon and carried off; and when it tried back, again he had disappeared. Clearly Lozada was an institution of the country not to be despised, a most irrepressible "Cosa de Mejico."

But what did I care for Lozada? In a few days I was going to leave the country, and he was in the mountains. In reply, therefore, to my friend, I asked him to introduce me. He flatly refused, so, seizing a favourable opportunity, mustering my best Hispaño-Mexicaño, and to the extent of my ability, assuming the true lounging swagger of the Méxican *caballéro* I approached the señorita, laid my hand on my left breast, bowed profoundly, waved by *sombréro* gently, and announced myself. Then I said, "I kissed her feet; that I had too good taste to ask any other lady in the room to dance until I had requested that favour from her; and having observed she was as gracious as beautiful, I had felt emboldened to pray her to accord to me that great honour and happiness." A proceeding and speech which, though they would in an English ball-room have been as improper as ridiculous, and have astonished even the most advanced girl of the period, were, under the circumstances, quite the correct thing to do and say. I had behaved with distinguished politeness. The little speech sounded *there* quite pretty, and my petition was rewarded with a smiling consent.

When the entertainment ended, I requested to be allowed to escort the señorita home (custom of the country). She answered, "Impossible;" but I might come and see her, to-morrow, if I liked. Was I fond of music? She would play the guitar and sing to me. She loved singing, and she had heard I had recently come from

Sinaloa; she had friends there, perhaps I knew some of them; she should so much like to hear about those I knew there ; and I could teach her some more English, and we could smoke and drink chocolate ; and I must come when the night was getting cool and pleasant. I should find her alone, sitting in the verandah, or perhaps in her *salon*. I could come in through the window ; it would be wide open to let the air in, but there would be no light burning because of the mosquitoes. If the house looked dark I was not to think she was away or gone to bed. She would be sure to be there, waiting for me.

As I strolled home with my friend I told him I was going, by appointment, to see the Mariposa the next night. He looked very grave. He made a remark—a personal one. I think personalities very bad form. I do *not* like personal remarks. He said I was an idiot. He went on to say, if I thought because the senorita had permitted me to carry on outrageously with her—he maintained I had done so, the whole company had remarked us—that therefore she was sweet upon me, I was an infatuated fool. How many men did I suppose had gone to—(the Palm Grove)—on account of *that* woman ? Lozada's spies were everywhere. Lozada was everywhere ; was sure to hear of my follies. If I went to El Ojo I should be murdered. "Four aces to a pair of deuces."

I inelegantly answered : "I shall keep my appointment. Lozada be blowed."

My friend turned sharply, almost fiercely, on me. He made another personal remark—a very personal one. I shall not repeat it—it is not necessary. But if I would go,

U

he would go with me; not into the lion's den, but to the mouth of it. He did not want to go inside. He would take post in the shrubbery and wait for me. I need not hurry myself, he had plenty of patience; and if it came to a row, why if one man could pull me through, he would be there doing his level best. But before starting, I should do well to sling myself between a brace of revolvers; on second thoughts, I had better take a bowie instead. A pistol-shot might bring those infernal Mexican police on us. I told him compromise was the chief of wisdom. I would take one six-shooter and my knife. But indeed I was sure there would be no danger. *She* would never let me run into an ambush.

"Oh!" said he. "And so, because she made eyes at you, and at parting permitted——no, there is no use in protestations; I was watching——you think she cares more for your life than his frown. Well! you are a fool," and then with a grip of the hand we parted.

Next evening saw us on our way to El Ojo, the "lion's den," according to my friend; to me, "Beauty's bower." It was late enough to be what in Acapulco is called cool, and the night was as dark as ink. There was no one in the verandah; the window was open, I peeped in. In one of the far corners a small, bright spark was visible —the glow from a *cigáritta;* and a sweet, low voice said, "Quién alli?" I gave my name. "Entrár, senór," was the reply. I was lifting my foot over the low sill of the window, when I heard a movement in the other corner of the room. I dodged to one side as quickly as a lightning-flash. "Will you go back now?" whispered my friend. "No."

"Then this is what I propose. I will stand in front of the window; but far enough from it to be beyond where a burning match can throw a light upon me, with my pistol pointing to *that* corner. You crawl under the window-sill, stretch your hand over the middle of it, strike a match on the inner side, and hold it up—its light will reveal everything in the room; you will be under cover, I in darkness. If that confounded scoundrel, Lozada, or any other infernal 'greaser,' is in there with a drawn weapon, I'll blow the top of his head off, by G——, and we'll cut and run for it." This performance, as far as to the lighting of the match, was carried out without further parley, and greeted with a merry peal of laughter from within the *salon*—the laughter of a woman and of a *man*—familiar laughs both of them. Who was *he*; who *could* he be? I joined my friend, finding him leaning against a tree, quietly chuckling. "What do you suppose," said he, "I was pointing my revolver at? Why, the ample paunch of our jolly old friend, the Pádre José, La Maripósa's confessor; the old gentleman who passes his daily little joke with us in the Plaza. I guess you'll be safe enough while with him. Give me your word of honour you will leave when he does, and I will now go home; otherwise I'll stop here until you rejoin me, or are killed, if I remain till daylight."

As he spoke, a happy suspicion crossed my mind. If the thought that occurred to me had been the senorita's reason for old José's presence, she was as full of finesse as of loveliness, as deep as fascinating. With alacrity I consented to my friend's request. I gave him the required promise. He left. I joined La Maripósa and her confessor.

The Pádre José proved a regular trump of a pádre, full of anecdote, humour, discretion. The senorita was perfectly charming, and I had a most delightful time, though we did have to sit in darkness, " because of the mosquitoes ; " and it was very late when Father José accompanied me to my quarters in town.

It was many a long day before I again saw " Beauty," and far from Acapulco and Lozada. Everything was different; but she, the Maripósa, was as handsome, as charming, as dangerous as ever.

CHAPTER XXIX.

Mojave M.D.'s—Three Mistakes—Polyandry—A Westernised Yankee—The Tin Pot—"A Gentleman and a Scholard."

I MUST give two more peculiar institutions of the Mojaves, and will then change the subject and leave them.

Regal state (?), war, a superstitious observance, have been already glanced at. Medicine now claims our attention.

A strange regulation affects the prospects in life of the Mojave M.D. The "medicine-man" of that tribe has, of course, a certain amount of skill. He is a rough surgeon, and is possessed of some remedial knowledge as a herbalist; but is more of a sorcerer and impostor than anything else. When one of these professors is called in, his first duty is to go through a divination ceremony, and he has then, prior to prescribing, to state whether the patient will recover or die. Should the latter alternative be announced, he receives no fee. Manifestly in such a case, a doctor's aid is unnecessary; and it is not supposed that a feeling of gratitude on the part of the doomed man, his friends, or widow expectant, for the announcement of his approaching dissolution can be sufficiently strong to justify the doctor in demanding a fee for making it. There is, therefore, always a strong incentive to declare the patient's recovery a preordained certainty. Such a declaration must of itself contribute to the sick person's convalescence by sustaining his courage and filling him with confidence; for unbounded faith in their medical practitioners' prognostications is a prevailing feeling amongst savages. But to make this favourable prophecy is a very serious thing for the medicine-man to do. The Mojave M.D. cannot come to a wrong conclusion from the diagnostics of a case with the same impunity that M.D.'s of other *tribes* can. Whatever be the result announced after completing the incantation, should the event be different, the mistake is recorded against him; and if he prove so unreliable as to make *three* mistakes, he is considered a convicted impostor whose ignorance or folly has tended to cause the decease of his patients; and that, having so made himself an active accomplice of Old Death, he deserves to die and be made a warning to all future aspirants for his high office. So, he is stripped of his insignia and ignominiously executed. Much may be said on both sides as to the advantages or otherwise of this system. Certainly it has one effect, it renders the calling of a quack amongst a lot of naked savages as perilous to himself, and as little likely to prove remunerative, as our system makes the career of a medical impostor dangerous to his patients and one of the easiest paths to wealth.

The domestic question shall be touched upon very lightly. One of the strangest customs of this singular people is that polyandry is an honourable state amongst them. This is the more remarkable from the fact that, though in many of the American-Indian tribes there is, on this subject, much looseness of practice, even where polygamy is the rule, yet the Mojaves' immediate neighbours—the Pah-Utes, the Hualapais, and the Yumayas—are distinguished for the constancy of their matrons. Whether this is entirely attributable to an ususual—in the savage state—development of innate female virtue, or to the fact that in those tribes a case of deviation incurs the penalty of divorce and the loss of the nose, or death, at the option of the plaintiff, is a matter quite beyond my skill in casuistry.

Once when at Fort Mojave I met a very queer specimen of a westernised Yankee. He certainly was, as he described himself, "Of a slightually impatient natral disposish," and he gave me such an amusing practical proof of the truth of the assertion, that I think an account of him and his eccentricities will prove interesting to the reader; more especially because he was one of that class of originals only met with on the frontier. I was on the eve of starting for the interior of Arizona to a post in whose neighbourhood gold-seeking was going on, when a tall, wiry stranger, whose speech "bewrayed" him, stalked up to me. He saluted, and requested permission to accompany my party to its destination, and to be allowed to put a small bundle and his blankets in one of the waggons. He would walk and be no trouble, for he would provide himself with provisions and do his own cooking. All he wanted was protection, and some means of transporting his "plunder."

As then there were no public conveyances in those countries, and private "outfits" were very scarce and few, the request was reasonable; and, in reply, I told him he was heartily welcome to put his plunder and himself too in any of the waggons; but to give himself no concern about his supplies *en route*, for that I had a superabundance of such and a good cook, and he would be very welcome to mess with me.

The man was not a gentleman, as that term is conventionally understood, but neither was I in a civilised country, and so could indulge in a simple act of hospitality which in a polished community "would not do, you know," but which in savagedom was a mere matter of course. This in apology for my conduct, as I do not wish the reader to suppose it arose from forgetfulness of the limitations to kindness and goodfellowship which is imposed by the superior (?) claims of conventionality. My offer was, however, declined with thanks on account of the "slightually," &c., of my new acquaintance, and of course I did not press the matter.

The T. W. stranger started with us during the afternoon of the following day, and at the first camp we had a taste of his quality. On arriving, he established himself as far from the camp-fires of myself and men as he could safely do, just at the edge of the light from them. After spreading his blanket for the night, he collected materials for and lit his fire, put his little camp-pot on to boil, set out his frugal fare, and, sitting down on his small bundle of clothes, cut a huge "chaw" off a plug of "navy;" and placing his elbows on his knees, and resting his chin upon his hands, sat staring at the fire, waiting for the water in his pot to boil, and "chawing" steadily. And a strange figure he presented, sitting in the uncertain flickering light, that played over his gaunt, ungainly form and quaint, lantern-jawed visage. His pot was a tin one, brand-new, one that had never known fire; and, freely reflecting the heat from its polished surface, the water in it heated very slowly. I had finished my first cup of coffee, and poured out my second, when the object of my contemplation, who up to that time had maintained his position of expectancy, sprang suddenly to his feet. Striking an attidude, he clenched his fist, and, shaking it menacingly at his pot, apostrophised it thus: "Yeou gol-derned, dod-rotted, dog-gonned son-uv-a-gun uv er shining bilk uv er pot, I'll tetch yer not never to boil ez soon ez eny other blaimed pot—dern yer!" Then he seized upon it, swung it over his head, and uttered a loud cry—a sort of mingled yell and howl. Then he dashed the pot to the ground, leaped high into the air, came down on it heels first, and smashed it flat; then he kicked it furiously all over the place until he lost it in the brush. This extraordinary outbreak was greeted with a prolonged roar of laughter from all hands, upon hearing which the cause of our merriment stopped his antics, and stood glaring upon us in apparently speechless fury. I called out to him: " Never mind your pot or the boys laughing; they don't intend to hurt your feelings. Come and sit down and sup with me; there is plenty cooked and to spare." When he heard these words a change came over the expression of his countenance, the anger faded out of his eyes, and he walked up to me and said: "Strangar! I perceive thet you air a gentleman end a scholard, end doubtless air a fine jedge uv good whisky; tharfore, I thenk yeou keindly, end will partake, if so be es yeou thenk I em fit to eat with Christings; but yeou see I warned yeou truly wen I sed I war naturally uv an impatient disposish." I assured him it did not matter in the least, and that I greatly admired sincerity of conduct; that if a man really was as mad as a hatter about anything, and made no display of his feelings, he was guilty of duplicity. This view of the subject seemed to afford him great satisfaction; he also took great credit to himself for not allowing his "natural disposish" to lead him to use bad expressions; for, said he, "I war raised stric Methodee, end nary a man hev ever hern me say a profane werd nohow nevar."

From that evening, "Old Potsmasher"—as the boys irreverently nicknamed him—remained a guest at my mess, affording much quiet entertainment by his quaint remarks and original views of things in general; and, out of respect, I suppose, to the attributes he had invested me with—those of being a gentleman, a scholar, and a fine judge of good whisky, the three graces of frontierdom—he behaved, on the whole, tolerably reasonably during the time we were together. Sometimes he became very communicative about his personal affairs, but I could never make out why he had come to the frontier. I suppose he had, like many more of his class, simply gravitated there. The reason he gave for wanting to go to Central Arizona was because he had never been there and knew nothing about it, and therefore "jedged" it would suit him, because every place he had been to or knew anything about did not. But he was not going to mine : no, he had tried that. He believed it was sinful, and that there was a curse upon it, all the same as opium-growing and "raising" niggers. "Becase gold is the reout uv all evil end hedent oughter be dug up; it war pison to the soul same like opium's to the body. It oughter be left whar it were; that's why it's hid so pesky keerful."

But *q. s.* of the queer Yank who was "raised Methodee." I was sorry to part with him. I have parted with more polished men with less regret.

CHAPTER XXX.

Indian Campaigning—Apache-Yumayas—The General gives his Views—
"Eminently practical but desperately dangerous"—We make a Start—
Tunas—The Lava Beds—The Programme—Indian Trick.

A NARRATION of active military operations against savages would hardly be interesting to the reader, neither would it recall sufficiently pleasing memories to the writer to induce him to say much on the subject. It would be but a monotonous recital of long fatiguing marches and hard fare; of nights passed in the saddle, and days in concealment; often in pouring rain, without tent and without fire, and living on cold water, hard biscuit, and raw bacon; for operations against the American *indigène*, to be successful, must be surprises, and the smoke of a camp-fire would in the pure clear mountain or desert air be visible for twenty miles, while to travel by day would be to ensure being observed by the Indian scouts. And all for what? If successful, to surprise an unsuspecting camp of semi-nude savages, kill as many as possible, and destroy their stores. If otherwise, and a slight carelessness, folly, or bad luck, has informed your watchful and subtle foe, that you are "out," then, either you will discover your toil and hardship end with the disappointment of failure, with finding but the cold embers of the fires, and old sticks of the wickee-ups of an abandoned camp, or your mistake or misfortune will entail a more unfortunate result, perhaps a disaster. While entangled in some narrow, tortuous, and rugged defile, where formations are impracticable, and mutual support impossible, you may suddenly find yourself surrounded by an unseen foe; the air thick with their flying arrows, and ringing with their yells, mingled with the scream and "ping" of rifle-balls, and the sharp crack of rifles; your men falling fast; your enemy invisible and inaccessible; and yourself in total ignorance whether it is safer to push on or to fall back. Nevertheless, I will give an account of one expedition, and the incidents thereof, as it was so thoroughly out of the common run of such things, that, if at all properly told, it ought to prove interesting.

A large party of well-armed frontiersmen, out "prospecting" for gold, were searching for that "root" in what was known as the Black Cañon country—a chaotic tract of granite mountains, igneous rocks, and lava beds. One day an Indian appeared on a rocky point overlooking their camp, and made signs that he wished to communicate with them. One of the prospectors went out to meet the Indian, and it was ascertained that a chief of the Apache-Yumayas and some of his braves wished to pay a visit to the prospecting camp—under truce—and have a talk with a view to proposing a treaty of peace. It was arranged such visit should take place the following day, but that only a few warriors should attend. When the visit did take place, it was unfortunately discovered no one in the prospecting camp was able to make himself well understood by the Indians, or to do more than hazard wild guesses at what they meant; so, after a short time the Indians left without any definite conclusion being come to. Shortly after the visit of the Indians, some of the prospectors' horses "came up missing," and the late visitors were of course suspected of having stolen them. Their peace talk was considered only a dodge to get into the camp to take observations preparatory to making an attack; and so the prospectors becoming alarmed, "raised camp and dusted," returning to the neighbourhood of the nearest military station, the district headquarters. Their story soon reached the ears of the general in command, and he sent for the author and his old comrade and companion to talk the matter over. Assisted by the weed of wisdom and the drink of deliberation, and paying us the compliment of saying he considered we knew more about savages and their ways and turn of mind than any men whose opinions he could get, the general laid his plans before us.

The general's idea was to send us two out with a strong force of cavalry; if possible, find the camp of the chief of the Apache-Yumayas, obtain a parley with and persuade him to come himself, or send a deputation to him (the general), to open negotiations, or, failing that, to capture any of the tribe we could lay hands on, and bring our temporary prisoner back to the fort, there to have the general's views and wishes thoroughly explained to him; a place for and mode of further communications arranged, and then to liberate and send him back to his tribe with some small presents as earnests of sincerity. We found but one objection to this plan—it would not work.

To move a body of troops in the Indian country with such precautions as would enable it to elude the observations of spies, and for the Indians' first knowledge of soldiers being out to be the finding their camp surprised, would be so exactly following the usual programme of a hostile expedition, that a flight or fight would be inevitable; while should the troops travel openly, the Indians, on getting the first intimation of their being in the field, would in all probability temporarily retreat into Mexico, whither they could not be followed.

We therefore suggested that if it met with our chief's approval, and he would give us authority to exercise our own discretion as to our proceedings in the affair, we two would pick out two or three men on whom we could thoroughly rely, and with them as our entire force undertake the expedition without escort. We would start out in hunters' costume, and steal our way through the country, trusting to our Indian craft to get speech with some of the Apache-Yumayas, if possible with their chief, Pah-Squal, to whom we were known, he having parleyed with us on a prior expedition; and would trust to our caution and luck to avoid being attacked when travelling or surprised in camp. We would take ten days' rations with us, orders on the rancheros in the district for further supplies, and keep the mountains until we succeeded or turned our toes up.

This proposition struck the general as being "eminently

practical but desperately dangerous;" however, as we incurred all the danger, and he would receive much credit should one of the hostile Indian bands be got on to a reservation, he was persuaded, though with evident reluctance and with many recommendations as to the observance of caution, to accept our offer as a volunteer service, for he declared he would not have it on his conscience to order any men on such a hazardous expedition.

The following night we set out—a party of five, in buckskin trousers and hunting-shirts, moccasins on our feet, well-mounted on unshod Californian nags, heavily armed, lightly provisioned, and prepared at all points to run or fight; every man of us as well able to take care of himself, if it came to a case of scatter and *sauve qui peut*, as any one in the country, while at the same time each knew he could count on the rest standing by him if necessary, at the cost of their lives. To such a party, an expedition of the kind was one whose hazard, and the feeling of calm excitement (if such an expression be permissible) engendered by its risks, made it a pleasure-trip.

After stealing our way along the mountain ridges for a few nights, and watching from good look-outs in the day-time, we found the Indian band we sought where, considering the time of the year, we had expected they would be, in the lava beds of the Black Cañon district.

We could see them far away below us, looking like animated dots; bucks, squaws, and papooses, all engaged in gathering their tuna harvest.

Tunas are the fruit of the prickly pear or Indian fig, a

plant that in hot climates grows in great profusion on soil formed of decomposed lava, attaining, when so situated, great size and then bearing " pears " as large as common figs, which fruit the so-called pears indeed greatly resemble not only in general appearance and shape, but by being, like them, full of seeds.

The tuna is covered with barbed prickles, hence it cannot with impunity be rashly handled; varies in colour when ripe according to the variety of the plant, being purple, bright yellow, crimson, and other shades; and is then not only juicy and sweet, but has a most agreeable and refreshing sub-acid flavour.

The Indians, to preserve the tunas for winter use, first roll them backwards and forwards in buckskins to deprive them of their barbed prickles; then beat them into a pulp with stones, flatten the pulp into cakes about half-an-inch thick, and dry them on the rocks in the sun. In a few days the cakes become quite hard, and are covered with a coating of natural fruit sugar, candied all over them, and are a good, nourishing, portable preserve, which will keep in eatable condition for a twelvemonth.

Having ascertained the whereabouts of the objects of our search, the next thing was to determine how an interview with the chief could be best attained.

Every party, to have a fair chance of success, must have a leader or head. In nothing is this truth more apparent than in mountaineering and Indian fighting; accordingly our party had one, whom I will distinguish as X., and after a council of war he determined upon the next move.

The ground before us we knew thoroughly, every foot

of it; on that point, the Indians had no advantage over us. As, on their appearance and disappearance, the Indians came out of or went into the fissures in the lava plain, and were never seen going to or coming from the mountains, it was evident their camps were in the lava beds. Undoubtedly, however, they had watch parties posted on the surrounding eminences, for not only would such a precaution be according to their usual custom, but the confident way the tuna harvesters straggled about showed that they felt thoroughly secure; well they knew their spies could, by making the alarm-smoke, easily give notice of approaching danger, and that the friendly labyrinths of the lava fissures would enable all in the valley to evade and escape pursuit. These outposts had been one source of apprehension to us, but our discovery by one of the numerous small parties of bucks who, to furnish food for the daily consumption of the harvesters, were doubtless hunting game in the mountains adjacent to the Indian camps, had been our greatest danger. To avoid any such we had travelled only by night, taken circuitous routes, and excepting where obliged to traverse passes, kept off the regular trails. We had also refrained from making any fires, worn moccasins, toed in when walking, and had our animals unshod, that should our sign be seen, the smallness of our numbers forbidding the idea of our being a hostile war-party, we should, in all probability, be taken for a band of friendly Indian hunters, and consequently not followed; while, as a further precaution, we had made our trail as blind as possible, and broke it by travelling in streams whenever we could do so.

BLACK CAÑON, IN THE LAVA BEDS.

The lava beds, where the Indians were encamped, are a very extraordinary formation. The valley on which we looked down was about two miles across, opposite to us, with a bounding ridge of rugged mountains on each side of it; and was, from side to side and for its entire length, a solid sea of lava billows. The lava covered the entire valley. This lava deposit was of inconsiderable depth at its edge, close to the foot of the mountains; but as it had filled up all hollows and depressions in the ground to a general level, was of very varying thickness. In the centre of the valley it was from one to two hundred feet thick, occasionally much thicker, as shown by that being the depth of the main fissures in it. These fissures were clefts from the surface of the lava down to the bed-rock of granite, which formed the structural floor of the valley, and they varied in width from a stone's-throw to hundreds of feet; and the inequalities of their almost perpendicular opposite sides had such complete correspondence to one another, that the fissures looked as if they had only just opened. These main fissures were joined by numbers of large and small lateral ones, for all the clefts in the lava converged and united one into the other, until ultimately there was but one — the Black Cañon. The immense depth and volume of lava in the valley inferred the fact that it was the accumulation of a flood, during a geological period, from now long since extinct volcanoes. Whether the fissures were the result of contraction on cooling, of earthquakes, or of a gradual expansion, caused by slow upheaval of the granite floor on which the lava rested, or of all these causes or some unsuggested one, I am not capable of deciding. The major portion of the surface of the lava beds was quite bare, with a glazed vitrified gloss upon it, and was in great, roundish boils. Every hollow and depression in it had from a few inches to some feet of decomposed lava mould, and in this mould flourished luxuriantly the tuna plants, whose fruit was the object of the Indians' search, varieties of the cereus candelaris, other kinds of opuntas, and magueys. In the fissures were several "tanks"—natural water-holes — supplied by the accumulated filtration of the rainfall through the porous lava. In the largest fissure—the main artery of the system, if I may so describe it—there was quite a strong spring, which formed a large pool, bordered by cottonwood trees, sycamores, and willows. From the lower end of this pool ran a small stream, which in the dry season soon lost itself in the cracks of the bed-rock and accumulated sand; but in the wet one, became almost a torrent, and was one of the wet weather upper feeders of the river, known as the Salinas.

At these several water-holes, the Apache-Yumayas were undoubtedly encamped, and there was an exceeding probability that, close to the pool formed by the spring, the chief had his headquarters; for it was only there that water was abundant, and the place had besides wood for fuel, and was the natural rallying-point from all camps in the fissures converging to it; and, excepting through them, was only accessible by a very steep and narrow path down that side of the fissure it was in, which was next to us.

To ride out into the plain in daylight was not to be thought of. Doing so would at once reveal our strength, or rather our weakness; and though these Indians had professed a desire for peace, they were in a state of hostility, and being Indians, their professions counted for little. Neither would such a step on our part be conducive to obtaining a conference; for the Indians not knowing the object of our being there, would in all probability either run off before we could get within hailing distance of any of them, or, seeing we were so few in number, would suddenly conceal themselves, surround and kill us.

This, therefore, was the programme: to remain where we were until within a few hours of daybreak of the following morning; then make such repast as the circumstances admitted, namely, a meal of army biscuit, raw bacon, and cold water; give our horses a feed of corn, and start for the main water-hole, situated some five miles off and about a thousand feet below us; approach noiselessly the edge of the cleft in the lava close to the head of the path down to the pool, dismount, and, every man holding his horse, wait for daylight; then make our way down the narrow path as quickly as possible and get among the women and children before the Indians could do anything. This bold move would, if successful, achieve for us an interview under circumstances which would deter the Indians from making an immediate attack upon us, since they always seek to avoid a fight in which there would be danger to their squaws or papooses. Should we succeed in getting amongst them and commence a parley we should be comparatively safe, so long as they— the women and children—were present; that is to say, so long as we kept together, faced out, and did not give the Indians a chance to practise a favourite trick of theirs on such occasions. This trick is to enter into general talk, mingle with their visitors, and—apparently so accidentally as not to attract attention—contrive to get each individual visitor separated from the others with two Indians close to him. At a preconcerted signal every man is pinioned by one of the Indians near him, and knifed by the other. It was chiefly enjoined by X. that all the time the party were amongst the Indians every one was to continually keep an eye upon him, and should he at any time "go for" his revolver with his right hand, then each man was instantly, and without hesitation, to draw and shoot down Indians until further orders.

CHAPTER XXXI.

Face to Face—Pah-Squal—A joint Breakfast—Wood-rats—On the *Qui Vive*—An Ancient—The Terms—An unwelcome Invitation—Winchester's Henry's—A good Shot—A Chat with Pah-Squal.

OUR early march was made without accident; and, as the morning star commenced to pale, we cautiously descended the path down into the Black Cañon on our surefooted Californian "cayuses," dashed at a gallop to the front of a large wickee-up, and sprang to the ground in the midst of a startled group of bucks, squaws, and papooses, who had leaped to their feet at the sound of our rush. The children howled, the women wailed, the men yelled; and all scattered in every direction; the women and children to hide like so many partridges and their broods, and the men to get their arms. Quickly as his feet struck the ground, every man of us threw his right arm in the air and made the peace sign. Our conjecture as to the probable whereabouts of the chief we sought proved correct. The one Indian who had stood his ground and was face to face with us, answering our sign of peace with a like gesture, was Pah-Squal! Calling out to his men to come back, and to the women and children not to be afraid, he advanced to us with "the smile that was childlike and bland," shook hands all round, and said, "You are welcome."

X. addressed the Apache-Yumayas chief in a *patois* that was fearfully and wonderfully made up of Mexican-Spanish, English, and Indian dialect, with a running accompaniment or translation thereof in first-class sign-language, and stated the object of the visit. Pah-Squal listened with attention, and replied in a like manner. He said, in effect, that he was very glad to see us, as he much wished for peace, but that to talk when hungry was no good, and so, being his friends, we must eat breakfast with him; his women would soon have it ready. He was answered we had our provisions with us; but that, as friends could not do better than eat together, we would take a joint meal with him, and furnish towards it coffee, sugar, bacon, and biscuit; and the provisions were produced. The Indians grinned the grin of satisfaction. They are inordinately fond of both sugar and coffee, and greatly relish bacon and biscuit. It was a step towards their hearts by the proverbial down-the-throat road; and having fasted from coffee or a hot meal since we had started on our expedition, we also were nothing loath to sit down to a "good square meal," even if it had to be eaten with the sauce of personal danger. By this time all the women in camp were busy, building fires, fetching water, and otherwise engaged in culinary affairs. Ever and anon they cast timid glances of curiosity towards us. It was probably the first time any of them had ever seen a white man, except shooting at them from afar, a prisoner, or dead. The little children, however, did not seem able to get over their fear, and persisted in hiding themselves, but, with sharp black eyes, stared through bush or over rock, regarding us with wondering inquisitiveness. The men, having nothing to do but wait for their breakfast, stood round at a respectful distance, eyeing us closely, and talking together in low tones. Suddenly two stalwart bucks, naked excepting breech-clout and moccasins, and with their bows and arrows slung at their backs, dashed through the circle. They were quite out of breath, and covered with perspiration and dust, and seeing us in peaceable conversation with their chief, struck an attitude of amazement. Their appearance was so comical that none of us could resist a laugh. They were two scouts who had that morning seen our sign in the mountains, and, without losing time to follow it, had rushed off to warn their chief there were strangers on the range.

Ere long we sat down to an appetising meal, and did ample justice to it. The Indians appeared to have plenty of game. There was one dish that was a novelty to us— wood-rats! These were pouched, roasted in their skins in hot ashes, skinned, and served on a large leaf. They were fat, their flesh looked as white and fine as a frog's, was piping hot, and smelt very savoury. I took one, seasoned it well with pepper and salt, eat him, and hereby testify, by these presents, that wood-rat, properly cooked, is most excellent eating. After breakfast Pah-Squal told us he was only the war or fighting chief, his father, who was yet alive, being the head of the tribe, and that it would be necessary for us to see and explain all things to him. He was very old and very wise; what he said was right, and ought to be done, all the tribe would consent to do; that the old man was not there, but not far off; and that he (Pah-Squal) would send some of his young men to fetch him, for he was sure we were talking straight talk about making peace. He knew we would wait for his father. In the meantime our horses would want grass; some of his boys would take them to where there was plenty until we should require them again. This statement and proposition we did not quite relish; it looked very much like a plausible tale got up to quietly deprive us of our mounts. X. replied that the horses had had plenty of grass, as they had been eating it all night; that corn was better for them, as it was what they were most accustomed to; that we had some with us, and would feed them presently; that we would wait for his father, and hoped he would not be long, as we were in a hurry to get back to the mountains where the soldiers were; for if we did not do so soon, they would think we had been killed, and then all start out and shoot every Indian they saw, since, as he well knew, soldiers could not tell one Indian from another; and we should be very sorry for any of his people to be killed on our account, as he wished for peace, and had been so friendly.

Of course there was nothing for it but to wait; so we passed the time talking with the Indians to the best of our inability, about game, horses, their tribal customs, and mutually examining arms and equipments; but all the time on the *qui vive* for any intimation of treachery, and ready at any and every moment for a fight. I can vouch for it as a fact, there is nothing more trying than to spend a few hours in apparently total carelessness and *abandon*, but really in partial expectation of being made the objects of a sudden murderous attack at close quarters by a numerically overwhelming force standing round you, and that, too, in a place from which, under such circumstances, escape would be miraculous, and where succour and reinforcement are out of the question.

It was late in the afternoon when the old chief made his appearance—for at last he came—and his doing so was quite a relief to us, as it was an earnest of good faith. He was a wonderful old man. I have no doubt he was the oldest man I have ever seen, and appeared to be shrivelled and wrinkled up to a mummy. He arrived in the arms of two young fellows, to whom he seemed a feather weight, who set him down on a folded blanket before his son's wickee-up. The old man was so bent and doubled up with age that he could not straighten himself, neither could he stand up without support. He had still a luxuriant head of hair—I have yet to see a bald Indian—but it was snowy white, his teeth were all in his head, but worn down level with his gums, his eyes still keen and piercing, and he appeared to notice everything. We conversed with him through his son as interpreter. Whether the ancient savage could not understand anything but his native dialect, or would not as a matter of dignity, I do not know, but suspect the latter to have been the true reason. He seemed to be a very reasonable old man, and really anxious to make a treaty and go on a reservation. He spoke to this effect: His enemies the Pinal-Apaches had been harassing his people cruelly. No longer ago than the last moon they had killed fourteen of his braves, and carried off their women and children prisoners. On the other hand were the whites, who were getting stronger and more numerous every day. Between the two, though his warriors were brave and wise, the tribe, his children, would be crushed into nothing. He remembered the time when all the world feared the great Yumayas nation ; now, they were only a little handful; but if he could see his people settled on a reserve at peace with and protected by the whites, as the Mojaves were, he would die glad. He himself had always wished for peace between his nation and the whites, but his young men were ambitious and would steal horses and kill people, because the women admired them for so doing: that had made all the trouble. He feared it would be difficult to persuade the young warriors to make and keep a peace. This is what should be done. In one moon's time, his son Pah-Sqaul would go to the rancho of the red-headed man on the Agua Taména with all the chief men and warriors of the tribe, and we should meet them there, and settle all things. In the meantime he would be able to talk to all his children and persuade them to make peace and go on a reserve. We must bring a present of meat and flour, and such other things as they would get when on a reserve, so as to make their stomachs our friends and induce them to go on one ; and plenty too, for their wives and children would be with them, and be much hungry, but we must not bring any soldiers with us, as they would be frightened of them—and a lot more, unnecessary to repeat.

When Pah-Squal *père* had done "spreading himself, enlarging, and slopping over," X., in reply, promised to give the proposed meeting, and bring with him, as a present, two fat steers, and two army waggons loaded with flour, and a little coffee, sugar, and salt; some of it for him to keep for himself, and the rest for him to divide amongst his head men.

Then the old pirate of the wilderness was hoisted up in the arms of his bearers, and—escorted for a short distance by his son—carried, whence he came, or somewhere else.

Twilight's shades were falling when Pah-Squal returned, and be was informed we were about to leave. But that chief insisted on our remaining all night, said the dark was no time for travelling in the mountains, and plainly intimated that a refusal to stop would be construed with an indication of want of confidence on our part in his good faith, and a rejection of proffered hospitality and friendship. It was of the first importance to gain the confidence of the savages with whom the making of a treaty was desired, and as the readiest way of doing so was to show it towards them, X. determined to remain, influenced also by the consideration that if treachery was intended we should be in danger, if we travelled in the dark, of being followed up and set upon during the night while *en route* or in camp; so after watering our horses and giving them the remainder of our corn, we sat down to supper with our new friends, and afterwards smoked and talked with them for some hours.

During the day we had seen a great many of the Indians, for they had been coming and going all the time from and to the other camps, no doubt to satisfy their curiosity about us; each fresh batch having questions to ask, and wanting to examine our "rig." Our rifles especially interested them, being of a pattern they had never seen before, for they were a then lately invented arm —Winchester's improved Henry's; to my notion the most perfect rifle in existence—the very prince of weapons! Ours were carbine size, having, when loaded, fourteen shots in them, capable of being reloaded after the first or any succeeding discharge; and of being reloaded as quickly per shot as an ordinary muzzle loader can be capped. To show what could be done with our rifles, and thereby impress the Indians with a sense of our formidableness, one of our party notched a cross in a sycamore tree, and at a distance of a hundred yards threw his fourteen shots at it; firing with the utmost rapidity, and without once taking his gun from his shoulder. When the lead was chopped out of the tree by the Indians, six of the balls were found welded together, while the remaining eight were clustered quite close round the mass. The performance created—as the French would put it—a profound sensation! A hawk, which soon afterwards sailed over camp, being killed in mid air by X., the prestige of our party was still further increased.

I had observed, during the day, that the Indians possessed many articles of civilized manufacture; and those amongst them who had fire-arms (got no doubt from murdered whites) had plenty of ammunition. All of them had knives, principally of cheap Sheffield make. These knives were certainly not captured from frontiersmen. No frontiersmen would carry such ill-designed, badly-tempered things. They had evidently been "made for exportation." I was anxious to ascertain whence they obtained such goods, as, apart from a feeling of curiosity about the matter, it would be very desirable to be able to stop any channel through which ammunition was obtained by hostile Indians. Therefore, while we smoked our pipes after supper, I led the conversation so as to find this out, if possible. Pah-Squal made no bones about telling me. He said they were bought at San Bernardino, in Southern California, and to that place a party of his tribe went annually on a trading trip. To the question, were they not afraid, being at war with the whites, to venture into one of their towns? he replied, not at all, they always passed themselves off as Mission Indians; adding, with a smile (I give his own words this time), "Los blancos no heap sabe Indiános."

Now, San Bernardino is about four hundred miles from where we sat talking, and it seemed impossible that they should wander so far to trade. To test the statement, I asked if he knew the names of the men they traded with. To my astonishment, he, without hesitation, pronounced those of some Jewish firms that I was well acquainted with. Then, to try his topographical knowledge, I told him that by-and-by I was going to San Bernardino; could he tell me the best route to take? He took an arrow, smoothed the sandy ground, marked out the cardinal points, and drew a map of the country between where we sat and there, showing the number of "sleeps," where there was water, where grass, and where wood; and all this as accurately as I could have done it myself, who knew the route, not only by personal experience, but from being familiar with the military surveys and itineraries of it.

Then I asked what they had to give to the traders for the goods, and was answered : " Buckskins, gold-dust, and horses." But you have no horses, and you do not mine." "True," was the reply, "but we get the gold-dust from those who do, and the horses from those who have them. We are obliged to. We must have powder, lead, and caps, knives, blankets, and salt."

At last the time came, beyond which we could not in courtesy prolong the sitting; we had to turn in, and so rolling ourselves up in our blankets, all lay down in a row. Of course it would not have done to set a watch openly, but secretly we did, each man taking his two hours. Guard was relieved by a quiet kick from the one coming off to the one going on. The sentinel's chief duty was to notice if the horses were molested, or if the women and children should commence to withdraw themselves ; if he observed either of these things happening, he was immediately to arouse all hands. Such proceedings would have been conclusive that an attack on us was contemplated, and without waiting for it, we should at once have "opened the ball."

At daybreak we excused ourselves from stopping for breakfast, alleging that, on account of the extreme heat during the middle of the day we were anxious to make a good march before taking that meal, and thus utilise the cool of the morning for travelling. Shaking hands with Pah-Squal, and all who came forward to bid us *á dios*, we sprung into our saddles and rode away.

A WELCOME PARTING.

We left the "Hôtel de Pah-Squal" with very great pleasure. Not because the board was objectionable—on the contrary, it had been very good; not on account of the lodging—the lodging accommodation had been excessively ample; not because it was expensive. Oh no, we did not object to it on any of these grounds; but we did not like the *attendance.* We may have been fastidious, perhaps we were, but we did *not* want to stay there any longer. We had had enough of that little game.

CHAPTER XXXII.

The three Rancheros—The two W.'s—Our Arrangements—A military Picnic —Preparations to receive the Apaches—The Indians arrive—A Warparty—X.'s Speech—Pah-Squal's Reply—A Feast.

WHEN, after leaving the encampment of the Apache-Yumayas' chief, we found ourselves on the level lava plain, we directed our course immediately across it, so as to strike into the cover at a place where we should not be expected to do so; and, when out of sight of the plain, swung half round and started for the rancho of "The red-headed man" —that nickname stuck. The rancho was about twenty miles from us, and situated in a wide, deep, "box" cañon— a cañon with perpendicular walls—through which flowed the Rio Taména. The red-headed man was an old acquaintance of ours, a bold Kentuckian who had come out to Arizona to seek for gold; and who, finding none, or next to none, had turned farmer. Associated with him in the enterprise of establishing a rancho under difficulties were two gentlemen, old friends of the author's; in fact, one of them had been a mining partner of his, and was a son of a distinguished ex-governor of Missouri. The other, old

Major von B., was an ex-officer of the once celebrated Texan Rangers, a gallant old gentleman of sixty, whom love of adventure, the charms of semi-civilised life—in short, the "mustang fever," had kept on the frontier. Poor old fellow! Soon after the time I am writing about, jungle fever carried him off. The old campaigner died delirious, cheering on his Rangers.

Our friends the rancheros were delighted and surprised to see us and to hear our news. They expressed themselves strongly about the prospective treaty, and were very wishful for our success in the matter; since they had been much troubled by the Indians, who had been, and were, the chief obstacle to their success, and from whom their lives were never quite safe. They gave us a stunning breakfast, and we eat off crockery, seated upon chairs! They were, indeed, bloated aristocrats. We lounged about all day; shot at a mark; smoked; took an occasional "snifter," a semi-occasional "go down;" and we dined sumptuously. We had, indeed, *Arizona strawberries* for dinner, fried in bacon grease. Then we took a "settler" and inspected the improvements and the stock. "A refresher" and an "eye-opener" made us feel equal to despatching supper; and, with the assistance of the two W.'s, or wants of the frontier, "weed and whisky," we sat up until late, "swapping lies." Oh! happy day. And we slept soundly and long. Oh! happy night. Were we not in a good block-house, with a garrison of desperado frontiersmen; trusty rifles stacked in every corner; and watchful hounds lying outside? We liked the attendance this time.

Before leaving in the morning, it was arranged that ere

the time came for the Apache-Yumayas to meet us at their rancho, our friends would strengthen its garrison by smuggling as many good men as they could into the place, keeping them as dark as possible, so that the Indians should not know they were there.

We arrived at head quarters without further adventure, found our chief glad to see us again, and were congratulated and complimented by him. Indeed, he was pleased to say many handsome things about the conduct of the expedition. He was, however, far from sanguine as to the ultimate result of negotiations; thinking, as his experience well warranted him in doing, that the Indians had been "talking good" with the sole idea of getting presents and lulling vigilance; and offered to place under our orders, when we gave them the proposed meeting, whatever escort we liked to take with us.

Lounging about, killing time, soon became monotonous, and we were beginning to *ennui* terribly; when, to our great relief, the general sent us out again. This time on a scout through the countries of the Tontos, Yavapais, and Hualapais, with *carte blanche* as to its direction. Interpreting this order into leave of absence to go shooting and fishing with an escort for protection, we took our shot-guns and tackle, and went away rejoicing. Than we, none knew better where game was plenty, and good camps to be found. We had besides with us all creature comforts and camp appliances. "A good time," was a foregone conclusion. We saw no fresh Indian sign while out, and were not, therefore, obliged to abandon pleasure for duty. Indirectly our scout did good. It kept so many soldiers from getting lazy and dissatisfied, lying around the fort doing nothing but guard-mounting, &c., was an encouragement to the settlers and miners whose ranchos and camps we visited and undoubtedly acted as a check on the hostile Indians; for, while we were in the mountains, no raid of consequence was made by them—the capture of a small búrro train and the killing of its arréaros, an attack on the Californian mail, and the murdering of two adventurous mining prospectors, being, if I recollect rightly, the extent of their operations. We returned to district head-quarters in time to make preparations for the trip to the Rio Taména rancho, and the pow-wow there with the Apache-Yumayas, bringing with us a welcome contribution to the garrison mess—fat venison, wild turkeys, quails, and sun-dried Gila trout.

We remembered the injunction of Pah-Squal *père* not to bring any soldiers with us, but, as it might prove a most fatal policy to allow the Apache-Yumayas to find themselves preponderately strong when we held our conference with them, to avoid any display of force, and still have some additional strength, we had recourse to the following arrangements: Four dragoons, in stable dress and only carrying their Colt's holster-pistols, and each with a stockwhip in his hand, drove the two bullocks. The two six-mule covered army-waggons had each its postilion on the near wheeler, and a man on the box, all dragoons, looking as unlike soldiers as they could. In each waggon, sitting on the flour sacks and concealed by the waggon covers, were more dragoons, packed like sardines in a box, a dozen in each waggon. So, in addition to our select embassy of five, we had with us a non-commissioned officer, a bugler, and thirty troopers, picked men, selected for the special service they were on, and armed with Spencer-magazine carbines (seven-shooters) and their holster-pistols (six-shooters). Sabres were very carefully left behind—no use for them.

It had been suggested to run a force into the rancho at night, but as the place was undoubtedly watched all the time, such a move would most probably have been detected; and then the suspicious Indians, coming at once to the conclusion a trap was being set for them, would have bolted.

Though we made a very early start, and travelled as rapidly as we could, it was late at night when we arrived at the rancho, but that suited well enough; for as it was quite dark it enabled the men to get from the waggons to their quarters unseen by any distant watcher. The troopers were placed in an "adobe" stable at the end of the corral, with their arms, accoutrements, camp equipage, and provisions; ordered to keep their weapons loaded, and themselves out of sight, and, to prevent accidents, the sergeant locked the door and pocketed the key.

We found the ranch-house full, for our friends the rancheros, especially the old ranger, had no confidence in the professions of the Indians. Their opinion was, that either the whole arrangement was a sell, the Indians having no serious intention to keep any appointment, or, more probably, that it was a plant; first, to humbug us out of so much beef and flour; and secondly, to get an excuse, without molestation, to concentrate a force at the rancho which would enable them to take it. So they had mustered all the assistance they could get; twenty-two was, I think, their number. They were all more or less well-known mountaineers and desperadoes; men who valued their own lives very lightly, and other people's not at all. With such auxiliaries we felt we had the game in our own hands.

Next morning the appearance of the Apache-Yumayas was anxiously looked for. As hour succeeded hour without any signs of them, those who had backed the opinion that it was a sell began to give odds; but about eleven o'clock a faint far-off shout was heard, and on looking in the direction whence it came a group of Indians were seen, standing on the ridge of the cañon's bluff, and waving their blankets to attract attention. Signs were made to them to come down. Then one of the Indians advanced a few paces and stopped still. He stood on a rock, and also on his dignity. He was evidently waiting to be met in regular Indian style. Immediately X. concealed his belt-pistols under his hunting-shirt, put his holster-pistols in his belt, picked up a rifle, and started out towards him. When the Indian perceived X. approaching, he also commenced to advance. The Indian was armed with a carbine (Sharp's) and his bow and arrows. When the two were about a hundred yards apart, they halted and made the sign of peace. X. raised his rifle in the air, and laid it down on the ground, and the Indian did the same with his carbine. They advanced on each other to almost half that distance, and halted again. X. drew the pistols out of his belt, displayed them, and laid them down. So did the Indian his bow and arrows. Then they walked up to each other and shook hands. The Indian was Pah-Squal. X. produced his pipe; it was filled, lit, the mystic whiffs were blown by each of them, and then the two walked into the rancho together, followed by a string of warriors, one of whom picked up his chief's weapons, X. recovering his as he came to them.

For some time the Indians continued to arrive, and at last the corral was full of them. When they had ceased coming Pah-Squal stepped up, announced that all were assembled, and demanded to have the oxen and flour turned over to him. I had tried to count the Indians as they poured into the corral; there were between a hundred and thirty-five and a hundred and forty of them. They were as fine a body of men, physically speaking, as I had ever seen, evidently the pick of the tribe: tall, stout, broad-shouldered fellows, heavily-muscled, straight-limbed, and light in the flank; having a depth of chest, from front to back, not seen among civilised men; active, able-bodied warriors. With the exception of the chief and a very few others, breech-clout, leggings, and moccasins constituted their attire. Every man of them had his knife and tomahawk in his belt, his full quiver at his back, and held his bow *and three arrows* in his left hand. I glanced at the arrows; they all had war-tips to them, not hunting ones, and there was not a man of the party younger than twenty-five, or older than forty-five.

If ever there was a well-chosen, well-armed war-party, ready for instant action, it was that party standing before us.

Word was passed to the frontiersmen in the ranch-house and the troopers in the stable to slip quietly out, a few at a time, but prepared for action, and to quickly and noiselessly surround the corral. X. then began a speech, to gain time and by way of reply. Put into understandable English, he said : " I see none here but braves. Where are the old men, the wise men who are to counsel about the treaty? Where are the young men ? the women and children, who are so hungry ? When they come you shall have the oxen and flour, not before." While he had been speaking, the troopers and frontiersmen had obeyed their orders. As the Indians caught sight of them they showed evident surprise, got together in little knots, and commenced talking earnestly to each other. Pah-Squal never moved a muscle or appeared to see them. When X. had ceased talking, Pah-Squal replied to this effect : " The old men are not yet here, for they cannot walk fast like we can. The women and children are not come, for they are not brave ; they are afraid of white men. The young men are with them, because of the Pinalás. Perhaps, when they hear you will not give us what you promised unless they come they will get braver, for they are very hungry." Then he sent off a couple of runners, the Indians put their arrows into the quivers and their bows into their cases, the troopers slung their carbines, the frontiersmen stacked their rifles in the house, and whites and Indians became quite friendly.

In less than half an hour, old men, boys, women, and children, all came swarming into and around the corral. There was quite a crowd of them, and they had been doubtlessly hidden in the rocks not far off, awaiting eventualities. The oxen were slaughtered and cut up, the flour distributed, fuel collected, fires lit, and our wild visitors were grinning, chattering, laughing, and singing, elated with the anticipation of the coming revel. There was no immediate danger to be apprehended; and we, as spectators, were as much amused at the scene as the Indians were pleased at being performers; Indians in a state of hilarity and friendliness, their women singing and quarrelling, and the little ones playing about, being a most novel sight to the soldiers, and an entertaining one to us all.

Pah-Squal stated there could be no council that day, for that as soon as his people commenced to eat they would think of nothing else, and never stop until they could hold no more, which would not be before night. The event more than proved the truth of this statement; for, indeed, they were eating all night; those who had "choked off" first sleeping awhile, and then, recovering a second appetite towards the small hours, going to work again, and trying to eat some more. But daylight found all the Apache-Yumayas lying around, sleeping soundly, like so many gorged boa-constrictors.

CHAPTER XXXIII.

A Council—The big White War-Chief—A Challenge—Muncho Bravo, Muncho Sabé — Departure — Precaution — The three Chiefs — An Indian Wag.

ABOUT noon the council was opened in due form. It was, like all such scenes, a succession of speeches, most of them amounting to little. But Indians are naturally fond of oratorical display, and greatly enjoy hearing themselves speak in public. The pow-wow was commenced by X., who informed the assembled Apache-Yumayas of the locality of their intended reservation, told them a resident white agent would be appointed to it, and enumerated his duties. He (the agent) would distribute, from time to time, such rations as might be necessary for their subsistence; give them seeds, implements, and instructions in their use; prevent them being in any way molested by other Indians or whites, and give passes to go beyond the reservation's limits for hunting purposes to such of the braves as should be recommended to him for that favour by their chiefs. On their part they were to undertake not to leave the reserve without such passes, and to behave themselves peaceably and honestly.

These were very liberal terms, but not more so than are always offered to Indians by the United States Government, for it has been found much cheaper to feed than to fight savages. The difficulty is to prevail upon such to forego the pleasures of thieving and killing at any price.

The talkee-talkee continued until late in the day; but at length the council was closed, and Pah-Squal, stepping up to X. and party, who were standing clustered together, chatting and looking on, announced the result. It was to the effect that he, and many more, were willing to accept the terms of the treaty at once, and go on the reserve, but that many of the wise men said no—they ought first to see the big white war-chief, who lived at the fort, and hear him speak, so that there might be no back talk or mistakes; therefore, there must be another meeting. In another moon the big white war chief must meet them all; and if he would speak to their face like what they had heard that day, then would they know it was all true, and everybody would be satisfied. That the big white war-chief must then give them some more beef and flour. As he was a great brave, he would no doubt give greatly.

This answer was discouraging, and thoroughly Indian. It looked more as if they were trying to humbug us out of presents than seriously wishing for peace.

In reply, Pah-Squal was told that the great chief at the fort had more important things to attend to than to come to see them; that he would *not* give them any more presents except through the agent when they were on the reserve ; that he was tired of *talk* about peace. This should be done : Pah-Squal and two warriors, as witnesses, should go with us to the fort, and speak face to face with the big war-chief there, and in four sleeps be brought back in safety to where they then stood. That they need have no fear. Had we not trusted them? Did not we—only five—ride into their camp amongst their whole tribe? Did we not eat with them? did we not lie down and sleep among them in perfect confidence, setting no guard? How could we have done such things if our hearts had not been straight? Where *they* less brave than we were? or were their hearts crooked, and did that make them fear to trust us?

This answer Pah-Squal took back to his councillors, and they had a short confab together.

He returned and said : "It is *not* good. The big white war-chief must come and talk to us all, and bring beef and flour, in one moon's time."

Upon this X. feigned to get very angry. He said : " Now I know you have been lying to me all the time ! You only wanted beef and flour. Now I am sure you do not want peace, but prefer war. *I am glad of it.* I am 'on the fight.' if it is to be war, and not peace, let us begin—NOW ! You have your warriors here : I have mine. Decide instantly : either for peace, and go with me to see my great war-chief ; or for war, and we are ready."

Then the bugler sounded the assembly. X. and party drew their revolvers. The troopers fell in, carbine in hand, and the frontiersmen, snatching up their rifles, took up such positions as seemed to them most advantageous.

The Indian warriors rushed together, fitted arrows to their bow-strings, half drew them, and stood waiting their chief's commands. The women threw themselves flat on the ground, with their arms round their children.

The situation was becoming interesting.

Pah-Squal stood like a statue, but he spoke a few words in Yumaya. Then two Indian swells stepped up and placed themselves one on each side of him, and all three came close to X. Pah-Squal laid the palm of his open right hand on X.'s breast, and said, "Muncho bravo! Muncho sabé! We will go with you—I and these two. We are ready."

X. replied, "It is well," and replaced his pistols; the Indians sheathed their bows and returned their arrows to the quivers; the troops fell out, and the frontiersmen "derned the luck," and said it was "a cussed shame ter threow away . setch a bully chance uv wiping eout the hull caboodle uv the pesky varmunts."

While our horses were being saddled, Pah-Squal stated that though he and the other two wished to go with us to the fort, we must leave all the soldiers behind, because they did not want any soldiers with them; they would *not* go if there were to be any soldiers. So the non-commissioned officer was put in charge of the troopers, with orders to remain on the rancho until the Indians had all gone; and then, should he not in the interval have received further commands, to return to the fort without longer delay; and a report in duplicate was drawn up of what had transpired, one copy given to the sergeant, and the other to old Major von B., to hand to the officer in command of a cavalry scout, whose arrival we told him might be expected in a day or two.

Then mounting our steeds, and accompanied by the three chiefs on foot, our little expeditionary party of five struck out into the wilderness.

As my companion and I rode quietly along, we tried to come to some conclusion why Pah-Squal had objected to our taking an escort with us, to, in fact, figure out his little game. In the first place, was such a request consistent with good faith on his part? There was only one light in which we could consider it so. His objection might arise from a feeling of Indian pride. Had there been soldiers with us it would have looked as if he was going on compulsion, was more or less a prisoner; whereas, as it was, his party was so nearly of equal strength to ours that their continuing with us had the appearance of being voluntary. On the other hand, his compliance with the request to go with us to the fort, and his objection to an escort, was quite a masterstroke of Indian policy; it had extricated him and his people from danger, from a position in which we had completely the advantage, and had placed us in peril. How could we know what orders he had given to the hundred and thirty odd picked warriors we had just left behind us? We were only five, separated from our supports, with no assistance within striking distance. The Indians knew our destination; even as we spoke, a party of them might be pushing along parallel with us, could easily pass us, and we might go headlong into an ambuscade; or the intention might be to attack us in the night. It would be so easy for the Indians with us to make sign enough on the trail to run it up on; but these dangers were, in a manner, provided for. Before leaving the fort it had been arranged that the general would send out, the day after we left, a detachment of cavalry to camp on Ash Creek, which was about ten miles from the rancho, with orders that if the officer in command did not hear from us within two days' time after his arrival, he was to push on to the rancho and put his force at X.'s disposal; or should he not require assistance, or have left, then to act as the circumstances of the case might require. Our intention was, therefore, so soon as it became dark, to alter our course and make for Ash Creek and camp there for the night, travelling in the mean time as much as possible in the open ground.

There was another danger to be guarded against. The three Indians being on foot, could, if they thought fit, and without appearing to do so purposely, contrive to drop behind all of us, then three noiseless arrows would make the odds in their favour—three to two—and the remaining two might also be easily shot down ere they knew their comrades had fallen. To prevent any such game as that, it was arranged that one of us should be always behind the last Indian; but the three chiefs showed no inclination to lag; they took a steady dog-trot of about six miles an hour, and went along with such an appearance of ease that it gave the impression they could go on *ad infinitum*. I suspect they were showing-off. We had made about three miles when it became necessary to cross a strip of broken ground masked with juniper trees and dwarf-cedars. On the edge of this covered way the Indians halted. Pah-Squal unslung his carbine and cocked it, and each of the other

Indians took his bow and three arrows in his left hand, and fitted a fourth arrow to the string. We asked their reason for what they had done, and were told we were about to traverse a line of direction the Pinal-Apaches frequently took in going from and returning to their country when on a raid; there was a strong war-party of them in the neighbourhood somewhere, and we might run across them at any time. So we also prepared for action, and proceeded on our way with increased circumspection and caution. A couple of miles more brought us once again into open country, and we took our old gait. It had become dark enough for our movements to be no longer visible from a distance, and we commenced swerving, from the course in which the fort was situated, towards Ash Creek. The change of direction was instantly detected by Pah-Squal, who exclaimed that we were going wrong. He was informed we had friends camped not very far off, and were going to spend the night with them, as then we should be quite safe from the Pinalás, and would besides have a good supper and breakfast given to us. The idea seemed to please him, and he answered, "Buena!"

I may as well here give some account of these Apache-Yumayas chiefs, for such they were, Pah-Squal being fighting chief of the tribe, the two others being chiefs of bands.

Of Pah-Squal I need not say much, for he sat for the portrait of him which is given in this book, and it is an excellent likeness; therefore, it will be sufficient to state he was over six feet high, apparently about thirty years of age, had a handsome, well-proportioned figure, and a quiet, dignified manner. To eyes unaccustomed, however, to Indian physiognomy, Pah-Squal's portrait will seem to have something incongruous about it, looking womanish and yet showing a man's determination and somewhat of savage ferocity. This is partly caused by the tribal style the hair is dressed in, but principally from lack of evidence of a beard. American Indians have naturally hardly any hair upon lips, cheek, or chin. Some tribes, I believe have none, and all the uncivilized aborigines of that continent pluck out by the roots the hairs that do grow upon their faces below their eyes.

Pi-Nolé shall receive our next attention. The name signifies two tracks, and was probably given to the individual who bore it from the fact that his feet were unusually large for an Indian's. He was a shortish, thick-set man of about forty years of age, and unusually dark-skinned for a man of his tribe; the Apache-Yumayas being, comparatively speaking, a light-complexioned race, little if any darker than gipsies. His face beamed with an amount of drollery and *bonhomie* which is most uncommon for an American *indigène* ; and, indeed, I suspect that Indian was something of a wag in his way, for he was constantly saying with a solemn air things that appeared to greatly amuse those to whom he addressed himself. Unfortunately I understood hardly any words that he used, but Pi-Nolé tried his best to make himself companionable, pointing out to me as he trotted along by the side of my horse different objects, and attempting to tell me something about them.

Mocha-Smar, or Three-sleeps, was a man of very different cast, nearly as tall as Pah-Squal, but without his grace, and with nothing nearly so good an expression of countenance. In age he was probably midway between the other two. He was an openly-pronounced dandy. His large nose-ring and ear-drops of green obsidian (volcanic glass), the elaborate charms hung round his neck, the highly-ornamented bowstring-guard round his left wrist, his stained moccasins, his paint, feathers, strut, and general importance of demeanour, left no room for doubt on that point; and he appeared to think that to dress himself up, and look supercilious, was to discharge "the whole duty of man."

Ere long we reached Ash Creek, and had not penetrated far into the timber of its bottoms when "Halt!" rung out, and we found ourselves before a sentinel. When he saw who we were he permitted us to pass, and we made our way into an encampment of a troop of dragoons. Our Indians were evidently surprised at coming suddenly on a camp of such size, and by seeing upwards of a hundred horses tied in a double line to the picket-rope. Captain S. invited us cordially to his tent, and the three chiefs and our companions were hospitably entertained by the soldiers, to whom three live Indians in full fig were objects of special and peculiar interest. They gathered around and watched them eating, as though they (the Indians) were lions being fed in a menagerie. But the savages seemed to rather like it, and to consider it all as a flattering attention.

CHAPTER XXXIV.

The Lone Oak—A Surprise—We open the Ball—A Panic—The Chase — A dead Chieftain—The Spoils of War—A sad Tale—A big Fire—Al fresco Toilette—We excite Attention.

A BREAKFAST eaten at the first peep of dawn enabled our little party of eight to make a sufficiently early start to have a fair chance of covering the distance to the fort ere nightfall, and our Indians taking up their old dog-trot we pushed along at a good pace. No incident worthy of note befell until the middle of the day, when a very lively interlude, one that had not at all been included in our programme, diversified our proceedings considerably.

The time was approaching when it was advisable to seek some advantageous camping-ground for the noon-halt to be made at: some place where we could water our horses, let them graze awhile, cook and eat our dinner at, and have shade to repose in, for it was blazing hot. X. fixed upon one not far from the direct course : one we had often used for such a purpose before, and to which we had long ago given the name of the "Lone Oak Camp." It was situated on the left bank of the Escarabájo Grande, an auriferous mountain stream, at that place and time of year twenty yards more or less in width and about knee-deep.

Lone Oak Camp had received its name because the spot used as a halting-place was the shaded ground beneath the boughs of a large ilex, that grew at a distance of about thirty yards from the water's edge, and stood there solitary and alone; the country on the side of the stream it was on being an open rolling grass plain, without, excepting it, either tree or bush for many miles.

The nature of the ground on the opposite or right side of the Escarabájo Grande was in every respect the reverse. Immediately across the stream there commenced the " breaks" of the foothills of a lofty mountain range, which rose up at a distance of a couple of miles or so from its banks. These breaks were a jumble of hillocks gradually increasing in size, and of intervening hollows and ravines, all thickly covered with scrub-oaks, bearberry-bushes, and numerous other varieties of dwarf-trees and shrubs, and with occasional matted and impenetrable thickets of grape-vines and wild hop-bines.

In the cool shade of the Lone Oak, we were going to eat and drink, and take our ease; for we were hungry, thirsty, and tired with so many hours' travelling.

We approached the place over the undulating grass plain, but it was concealed from our view by a ridge or roll of the ground.

This roll continued for some miles parallel with the course of the Escarabájo Grande, at an average distance of fifty yards from it, and had in all probability been at some remote geological period its left bank, for it was a boulder and gravel deposit, looking not unlike a moraine, and for its entire length yielded more or less placer gold.

We crossed diagonally this ridge at a distance of about seventy yards from the Lone Oak, and "a surprise" was the immediate consequence.

As we came suddenly in view of the spot, our appearance was the signal for a war-party of about forty or fifty Indians to start to their feet right from under the oak itself.

We opened the ball instantly. Without deliberation, without hesitation, our rifles came to our shoulders, and we delivered our fire, blazing a volley—so simultaneous as to sound like a single shot—right into "the brown of them."

As the rifles flashed, two warriors pitched headlong out of the cluster to the ground. The remainder scattered like the fragments of an exploding shell. Panic-struck, they all rushed across the stream, and fled in every direction through the cover.

X., not wishing to give the flying foe a chance to recover their presence of mind, to rally while his party remained in the open, and so perceive its numerical weakness, and anxious, moreover, to profit by the occasion, cried out, "Sail in, boys." Suiting the action to the word, he sprung to the ground, and without even looking back to see if he was followed, pursued the fugitives across the water, firing his magazine-gun as he ran.

This example was quickly followed by the rest of the white party, except one, who gathered together and held the five horses; and almost as quickly by the three chiefs, who, making ready as they went, followed up close behind. A shout drew X.'s attention to the three Apache-Yumayas, and he imperatively ordered them back, a command they complied with in the most sulky manner possible.

The attacking party, diverging as they ran, took the water about thirty yards apart, and plunging into the cover on the other side, were instantly lost to view. They could only conjecture each other's whereabouts by the firing, but that was so fast as to be almost continuous. The pursuit was pushed on with the utmost rapidity that the nature of the ground admitted; the assailants firing whenever they obtained the slightest glimpse of an Indian, or, from the crashing and swaying of the brush, knew where one of them was plunging through it. Though there were only four guns at work they were magazine ones, in the hands of old bush-fighters and expert shots, men well acquainted with their weapons, and the brush appeared to be actually alive with sharpshooters.

The holder of the horses had a good view of what was going on. He was in an elevated position, that looked over and on the broken ground where the fight was progressing. He could see the flying Indians and their pursuers, as they darted across or ran up the different glades and openings in the cover. And he stood an interested spectator, with his cocked revolver in his hand, ready to fire the recall signal as a warning sign, should any of the Indians sufficiently recover their confidence to get together and make a stand in force, or halt in ambush to shoot his comrades. But the savages seemed too scattered and demoralised to make any such attempt—occasionally to turn half round as they ran, and discharge arrows in the direction of their pursuers, being about the extent of their offensive attempts; until, nearly a dozen of them, coming simultaneously in view of each other on emerging into an open glade that lay across their line of flight, not seeing their foes and possibly thinking themselves unseen, took courage from numbers, and came together to consult or make a stand. As they did so three quick puffs of smoke, from as many different directions, showed they had been observed; and before the sound of the sharp crack of the rifles reached the ear of the watcher, he saw two more Indians fall to the ground, and another reel a few paces, drop to his hands and knees, and crawl into a thicket of vines. Soon the shooting ceased. The rifles were emptied. Fifty-seven shots had been fired in the most rapid succession; for not only had X. and "the boys" been anxious to lose no chance of "saving" an Indian, but well knew their safety depended on keeping the enemy on the run, not allowing their flying foes to recover from surprise, until they were thoroughly dispersed and stampeded. On the firing ceasing, X. gave the recall signal, and he and the rest returned, refilling the magazines of their rifles as they walked back. They arrived at the Lone Oak quite out of breath from their sharp running, and were there joined by the rest of the party.

Beneath the spreading branches of the tree lay the dead bodies of the two Indians who had fallen at the first fire, and occasional blood drops on the tracks of the fugitives thence announced that some of them were wounded.

One of the dead had received a ball through his chest, which had broken his spine; the other had been hit by two balls, one passing through his shoulder, the other striking him in his forehead. This double attention he had most likely owed to his conspicuousness. Judging from the size of the corpse, the Indian had probably been the tallest man in the group. Certainly he was the biggest Apache I had ever seen; doubtless also a distinguished warrior, for all his trappings were unusually handsome. His leggings and bowstring-guard were hung with Mexican silver buttons. A gorget of thin silver plate, shaped like a half-moon, hung at his throat; and two large buckskin plaques depending from a string round his neck—one in front over his chest, the other behind over his shoulders—were covered with figure writing, hieroglyphically setting forth his great exploits. On his head he carried the plume that denoted chieftainship, and he was the most hideously-painted object possible. A line down the middle of his face divided it into two, one half was coal-black, the other as red as vermilion could make it; and his ribs were all painted white, giving his body a skeleton-like appearance. He was evidently a most distinguished personage, and may have been the leader of the party; if so, his sudden fall at the first fire had without doubt added greatly to their panic and demoralisation.

Pah-Squal stepped up to the body, and turning it over contemptuously with his foot, shook his clenched hand at it; and, speaking for our benefit in what he considered plain white man's talk, exclaimed: "Muncho C——jo. Pinalá no mas you kilee Apache-Yumayas." Then he explained that the party of Indians we had attacked were his enemies, and indignantly demanded why he and his companions had not been allowed to take a share in the combat? and could hardly be appeased by having it explained to him that, as he and the other chiefs were accompanying us as delegates from his tribe to our chief, we were responsible to them and him for their safety, and that therefore, glad as we should have been for the assistance of three such allies, we had not dared to risk their being killed or wounded.

We took stock of the plunder which had become our spoil, and from the sign in sight, tried to determine what the party we had recently surprised had been about when we came so unexpectedly upon them, where they came from, and what they had been doing. Alas! the story was only too plain. They were a return war-party, on their way back from a successful foray upon a mining camp. As we gathered together the plunder, the different articles clearly told the tale. The fresh skins of two horses bore on their flanks brands which we well knew. A lot of tobacco was wrapped up in a piece of paper, covered with memoranda in the handwriting of an old associate of the author's. A pair of buckskin trousers—no doubt brought away to be cut into Indian leggings—were instantly recognised by their peculiar cut and fringes. They had belonged to another member of the same mining camp. Packages of fresh horse-meat (the horses had no doubt been killed in the attack on the miners), of bacon, sugar, coffee, salt, flour, beans, and other stores, and about thirty pounds of blasting-powder, tied up in an empty flour sack, were incontestable evidences of a captured and plundered mining *hacienda*, and of murdered miners. This party of Indians was unquestionably the band of Pinalás, of whose presence in the neighbourhood we had been informed by Pah-Squal, and we had come upon them while busily engaged either in dividing their plunder, preparatory to scattering, or making it up into more portable shape than it had been hitherto in; for there were strips of freshly-peeled bark twisted into strings lying about, several newly made-up and tied bundles, and many articles scattered around loose or partly packed. Not only had these things been abandoned by the Pinalás, but many had left their bows and quivers lying on the ground where they had placed them, while employed making up their packs; a most convincing proof of the completeness of the panic which had seized them, and an excellent reason for *their* not rallying. We gathered up the weapons as trophies and articles of curiosity. For a like reason we despoiled the big Indian of his plaques, of his gorget, of his silver Mexican buttons, and his other braveries.

It went against our principles, being men who had often suffered from hunger, to destroy good food; but, considering the distance still before us, X. decided the remainder of the captured articles could not be taken along, and so a bonfire was made of them, which we finished off with a grand explosion of the thirty pounds of blasting-powder. Our dinner was then cooked and eaten with the good appetite engendered by our long tramp and lively skirmish.

There was much speculation amongst us all as to the numbers of the Pinal-Apaches who had been killed and wounded. Each participant in the pursuit was confident of having made several successful shots, which, indeed, was quite possible. All were too experienced to become excited, and being in full practice in shooting deer on the run with the rifle, it was not reasonable to suppose a large majority of shots had been misses. The proposition, rashly made, that there should be a search for dead Indians, though backed up by the assertion of more than one that he knew where he could find some, was instantly negatived as being altogether too dangerous an undertaking, for if any of the wounded Indians lying in the brush were armed and not quite *hors de combat*, we might easily have one of our party killed by them should we venture into the jungle. Pah-Squal remarked that if the place was watched it could be learned how many had been killed; for, according to their invariable custom on all such occasions, the Pinalás would return when the coast was clear, find the slain, and, piling brush and wood on the bodies where they lay, consume the corpses and everything belonging to them. And he quaintly added, " I think there will be many smokes this night."

When refreshed and rested we resumed our journey, and, keeping an extra sharp look-out as we travelled on, pushed forward at the best pace the Indians could accomplish.

A little before sunset we arrived at a stream near the fort, and the three chiefs asked us to stop awhile, to enable them to prepare themselves for their coming public appearance. We halted accordingly, and they proceeded at once and in full view to make their toilets. We sat down to take a rest, smoke a comfortable pipe, and see how it was all done.

First, they took a good wallow and souse in the stream, then they dressed their hair while the sun and air dried them. I must confess to my thorough astonishment when Pah-Squal drew the ornamented skewer out of the coil at the back of his head, and his hair fell down in a thick, heavy switch to below his calves. When dry, our three chiefs resumed their few articles of Indian apparel, and, producing from unsuspected places of concealment little packages of paints and bunches of feathers, made each other as nearly hideous for ever as the perishable nature of their cosmetics would permit.

Having thus succeeded in rendering themselves "fit to be seen," the three Adoni announced they were ready to proceed, and we all took up our line of march again.

As we passed through the settlement which had sprung up under the protection of the fort, a sort of trading centre and general rendezvous for the mining camps and ranchos in the country, we became objects of absorbing interest and curiosity. Our horses were hung all over with Indian weapons and trophies, and the three Apache-Yumayas swells, who swaggered along with us, their full quivers at their backs, their weapons in their hands, and arrayed principally in paint, feathers, and nakedness, were clearly not prisoners. Certainly the sight was *the* novelty of the season. We felt, indeed, as if we were a circus.

As our party rode along we were assailed with innumerable questions, and with many a hearty "Hold on a minute—let's all take a drink;" but we cared not to lose time talking and drinking; so, showering promises right and left that we would give our interrogators full information next day and then take the proffered drinks, we went on steadily to the fort.

On arrival, a sufficiently commodious tent was pitched in the cavalry square and turned over to our friends, Pah-Squal, Pi-Nolé, and Mocha-Smar, for their accommodation, a liberal number of rations furnished them from the commissary stores, and a sufficiency of fuel and camp equipage from the quartermaster's supplies, and they proceeded to make themselves quite at home. We reported, and then returned to our old quarters.

The following day a conference was held, terminating to the satisfaction of all parties concerned, especially to that of our brave and gallant chief and kind friend, the general commanding the district; all the articles of a treaty being determined and agreed to; which treaty, I am happy to be able to state, was subsequently kept—a most unusual *finale* to peace negotiations with American-Indian savages.

CHAPTER XXXV.

Apachedom—Is Truth stranger than Fiction ?—What Trappers say of the Apaches—What the Philanthropists—Apache Notions of Generosity— The mental Differences between Races—Impossibility of Civilising the Apaches—Their consequent natural Extinction—The Mexican of To-day.

SOME years spent in the heart of Apachedom between Mexico and Arizona have given me perhaps as fair a chance as any other man to know something about the wildest and most untamable of American savages, and stored my memory with many an incident and adventure of frontier life. But which of them would interest, which be but inflictions and bores, is hard to determine. To the man to whom it would be "a most strange and extraordinary adventure, you know," to spend a night sleeping in the open air, only his clothes between him and the ground, only clouds between him and the sky, incidents and details that would appear trivial and unworthy of mention to the old campaigner may from their novelty be interesting ; while to him, stirring actions and startling adventures, from their resemblance to what he has read in works of imagination, and from lacking the dramatic completeness and *dénouement* that all well-constructed fictitious adventures possess, but which is so unusual in fact, may appear flat, unnatural, or disappointing. That truth is stranger than fiction is, if true, most strange. Hume's History of England is popularly supposed to be a true story. It contains the strange events of centuries. What part of it, however, is as strange as the "Arabian Nights' Entertainments," or "Alice in Wonderland"? But perhaps I mistake the adage. To be strange is to be uncommon, unusual, not often met with. Verily, truth *is* stranger than fiction. About some things truth is very hard to tell, because there is no getting at it. As the bear said of the mosquito in his ear, "there are not adequate means for the purpose." In everything relating to the Apache Indian this is most applicable. When he is making a treaty with you he is probably lying; if not, you cannot tell. Anyway he will break the compact before you find out. You rarely see him except to fight him; he has no literature that you can decipher, no home that you can find, no industries worth mentioning; you cannot collect statistics about him —how can you count what you cannot see? He will not trade with you, nor tell you his religious beliefs, nor let you behold his ceremonies, except his torture ones, and then only on condition that you personally furnish the victim; no reports have been published; no, you *cannot* find out much about him. How many are there of them to the square mile? How many square miles are there to the Indian? Is there a confederated nation of them, or is every family a nation to itself? Have they a head chief? Have they a supreme council? Have they anything? What is it they have not got or its Indian equivalent for?

I have heard "all about them" from learned lecturers—I went as escort to some ancient ladies; I have read official reports—I have had to read them—that told "all about them"; I have been informed that several tourists have written "all about them" in their books; I have talked with old mountaineers, old pioneersmen who had traded and travelled with them, fought with and killed them, married them and had children by them, or most of these things—Kit Carson, Paul Weaver, Joe Walker, Jim Bent, the two Roubedeaux, Cherokee Bill, old Maxwell—but their names are legion: *they* did not profess to tell me "all about them."

Thus sayeth ye ancient trapper: Apaches are cruel, cowardly, skulking, murdering thieves; the only good ones are dead ones. Government should give five dollars a scalp reward money, and the pesky varmints would be wiped off the face of the earth. Government is a parcel of soft-headed, maundering old women, with their Indian agents, their missionaries, their Quaker peace commissioners. Should just like to see old Government making tracks through a prickly-pear plain with a hundred of the howling devils after him for his scalp.

Ye withdrawing-room theorist propoundeth: The Apaches are unjustly and shamefully used; they are full of noble traits; they are the rightful owners of the country, defending their homes, their altars, and the sacred ashes of their sires against unprincipled miscreants, whose thirst for gold, whose greed for gain, whose contempt for order, right, and religion has led them to violate the principles of Christianity and the laws of God and man.

There! What does the reader think of those two specimens of "the evidence in the case"? There is just enough truth in each to make them mischievous, enough falsehood to make them worthless; and they very fairly represent the respective sincere opinion of thousands.

The chief source of error in judging what, considering the circumstances of the case, an Apache will do or has done is a natural tendency in us to attribute to him, as the reason for his intentions or acts, a like impulse, motive, and train of thought to what we should experience if similarly placed. He judges the white man on the same principle, and misjudges us as much as we do him.

The times when black-mailing was an every-day event, when payment of tribute as propitiation to the wielder of superior force was the ordinary rule of life, are long since passed in England, and generosity is a universally known and admired sentiment; every gift made in England is presumably made from that motive, and its looked-for effect and return is gratitude. The reverse is true with the Apache. Generosity is no more an ever-present thought in his mind or common act of his life than is fear of being black-mailed before night, or the providing tribute for a marauding baron, a familiar thought and act of an English country squire. But the giving to another as *tribute* is a most familiar practice of the Apache. He gives his goods as tribute to the spirits of air, water, fire, by tearing them up and scattering the fragments to the winds, by throwing them into the river, by consuming them to ashes. Why? Because they are devils he fears. He gives to his priests. Why? Because they are sorcerers, and can bewitch him.

Does a neighbouring tribe prevail against the Apaches? negotiations for peace is only a bargain about tribute. What is the logical expectation of result from a gift to an Apache? That he can and should do you an injury. To his mind your gift is *tribute*—an indication and *result* of fear. If he can only do you an injury, then you will give him more.

I have inferred that generosity is unknown to the Apaches. Perhaps I have wronged them. Their minds are so differently constituted from ours that it is almost impossible not to do so; probably their idea of generosity is different from ours. One form it takes is hospitality. When an Apache feasts—and all his meals are feasts if he has plenty of food—each and every one are welcome. You may bring all your own relations, all your *wives'* relations (I am supposing you to be a savage); they will all be heartily welcome, though the result of numbers be insufficiency for each; but you may sit down with him to the greatest superabundance, and though he knows your family are hungry at home, he will not give you a morsel to take to them. A gift, except as a tribute of fear, never once suggests itself to his mind.

That there is a radical mental difference between the races is as certain as that there are physical ones. The dog and wolf—as we are told mankind had—may have had one pair of ancestors, but the dog is naturally a domestic animal; so is the white man, and so are some of the American tribes. The wolf still is—he always will be —a savage; so has been—so always will be—the Apache.

The philanthropist sees no apparent reason why, with

proper culture, the Apache should not become a useful member of society. I see no apparent reason the wolf should not become as domestic as the dog. But he won't. The reason is a *mental* difference. Therein is the root of endless misunderstandings, of mutual injustice, between the races. But if the earth was made for man to increase and multiply thereon, and have possession, as it requires a greater number of square miles to support one Apache than a square mile will support civilised families, his extinction is justified by the inevitable logic of the fitness of things. He cannot be developed into a civilised man; he must give place to him. Circumstances and early training will sometimes make a white boy into a first-rate savage, but that is no argument to prove the converse, only a case of reversion. Our remote ancestors were painted savages. The cleverest collie is a descendant of dogs that lived like wolves and foxes. Every country has, perhaps, had its true wild men—tribes incapable of civilisation; some countries have them yet. Every country, sooner or later, has its civilised races, sometimes historically known to be immigrant ones; sometimes, presumably, of an equal antiquity of location to the wild ones near them. Mexico is a case in point. The *Conquistadóres* found in that country an ancient, highly-developed, apparently indigenous civilisation, with a most complete system of government and *taxation;* an established state religion, a thorough organisation of classes, an elaborate school of manners and etiquette; a civilisation, in some respects, superior to their own; and in the same country wild, nearly naked savage tribes, equally indigenous—the Apaches of then and to-day. Time, soil, climate, natural resources, had been equal to them all, and behold the difference of result! It was a case of *indigènes* capable of self-development, and not capable. Now look at Mexico of to-day. The old civilisation was utterly destroyed. The immigration of civilised people has been too small to materially affect so vast a country and such a scattered population; but the Mexican of to-day is not a savage. The mass of the people, though showing no trace of European blood, are more industrious, more reliable, more honest, more law-abiding, than the mixed bloods. They are steadily developing their civilisation again, because it is in them to do so. The descendant of the wild savage of the time of Cortez is not one whit better now than he was the day his ancestors, the old Apaches, murdered, robbed, and harassed the ancient house-dwellers of America. Doubtlessly, too, old England had her wild men, who, like her wolves, have been extirpated.

To-day a mixed breed of so-called British-Flemish, Gallic-Irish and Scottish-Celts, Norman and Picard-French, Hispaño-Irish, Saxons and Romans, form her population. All these races are known to have been immigrant, and, when they arrived, partly civilised ones— certainly people capable of self-development. None are supposed to have amalgamated with the savage found in possession; he is not alluded to but as a foe to be killed or enslaved; indeed, probably the aboriginal ancient Briton had, long before the advent of the Romans on the scene, gone where the Australian nearly is—where the Apache soon will be.

CHAPTER XXXVI.

Caution of the Apaches—Their Bands—The Rancho—A Government Contract—An Attack—The Storm—A solitary Apache—The Stampede—A fruitless Chase.

AMONGST the many reproaches brought against the Apache, a charge of cowardice is the most frequent and the least true. His excessive caution is continually mistaken for fear. Caution is perhaps his most strongly-developed trait. From the beginning it has been an essential of his existence. The law of heredity has developed it to the fullest extent; it has become in him an innate instinct. Apache is now an inclusive name, by which is called a large group of small bands—they can hardly be called tribes—all physically and mentally one people, however, though speaking different dialects, with diverse minor customs, and distinguishable from each other by dissimilarities of costume and make of weapons. Some of these bands number but a few dozen individuals; some can muster five hundred fighting men. The larger bands are continually breaking up amongst themselves. Secession appears to have been always prevalent. The small bands often join to form large ones; sometimes only temporarily, sometimes amalgamating. Immemorially at war with each other, but collectively in hostility to civilisation, ancient or modern, their hand has been against every man, every man's hand against them; and Indian warfare being a succession of treacheries and surprises, the Apache necessarily carries his life in his hand. Hence his excessive caution; but the very circumstances that have made him careful have also rendered him constitutionally brave. Always in a state of warfare, unprotected by walls, by armour, by political combinations, the victory has been to the daring and the brave. With these Indians defeat is synonymous with extinction. The Israelite of old did not more utterly destroy his vanquished foe than does the Apache. The most courageous bands increased and multiplied, the least so were exterminated. The increased bands inevitably broke up into small ones; these quarrelled with a like result. And besides the bravery that is constitutional, the ever-present thought from childhood that their life is in continual danger, that its preservation depends entirely upon themselves, is to the Apache an education in courage. It is as much to the high development of those qualities, caution and courage, as to the inaccessibility of, and difficulty to campaign in, the country ranged over by the Apaches, that has enabled them not only to have defied and held their own against one of the most powerful military nations of the world, but to have besides utterly destroyed the modern Mexican civilisation of a strip of country six hundred miles long and two hundred wide.

An instance of an Apache's cool calculating daring, of

his deliberately incurring personal risk for what was considered an adequate object, comes to my recollection. Its recital, however, necessitates a long preamble; fortunately, one not totally devoid of interest. Two years prior to the occurrence, a friend of mine, having some capital, engaged a number of *employés*, principally Mexicans, and went into the country now known as the territory of Arizona, intending—for he was of an enterprising and adventurous turn of mind—to establish a rancho near to the probable site of a then-talked-of military post, with the view of supplying it, at great prices, with grain, forage, and cattle, and so to become quickly enriched. It was a good idea, and was well carried out. The place chosen for the rancho had great natural advantages, and my friend's information must have been good, for the district head-quarters was established only thirty miles by mountain trail, and forty-five by practicable waggon-way, from his rancho soon after its being "taken up"—near enough to give a practical monopoly. My friend's settlement was on the site of an ancient, a prehistoric city. Wide low mounds scattered over the valley it was in, looking like undulations in its surface, where the partly standing walls of large stone buildings, buried by the accumulated dust of ages, and fragments of broken pottery were found everywhere. The stonework used about his house and outbuildings were excavated from these mounds, already squared and finished to his hand; he got paving-tiles from their floorings, curious crockery out of their rubbish.

The valley was about six miles in length, two at its widest, and in form resembled the longitudinal section of a

١

pear. Excepting a pass at each end, it was surrounded with lofty mountains of a most broken and rugged character, covered from their bases to their summits with thick chaparrals and heavy timber, which, beginning with ilexes, ended with large pines and balsams. This valley's surface was naturally nearly level, the greater part covered with "grama" grass—admirable feed for stock all the year round —and having groups of cedar and juniper trees scattered over it. At its lower end were three hundred acres of "cienaga" land, which though firm and apparently dry above, has water below; holes sunk anywhere for a few feet filling immediately. Such land, lying as it did, subjected to the influence of an almost tropical sun, produced a succession of crops all the year round. At the end of the cienaga numerous springs of intensely cold water burst forth, forming at once a considerable stream, the source of the Agua Frio river. At the head of this stream my friend's *haçienda* (rancho head-quarters) was built. It was constructed after the regular block-house pattern, with a "dirt" roof, so as to be fire-proof. Adjoining was a courtyard round which were sheds, quarters for extra hands, and the stabling, and adjacent thereto stood a corral or stock-yard. The corral was capable of containing about a thousand head, its adobe walls were eight feet high and two feet thick, and its single entrance, a strongly ironed oak gate, commanded by a cross fire from house and courtyard. In this corral the rancho herd was nightly secured.

More than one attack had been made upon the rancho by Apaches, but there had always been in it a garrison of thirty to forty well-armed and experienced frontiersmen, and each assault had been easily beaten off with loss to the assailants and without any to the defending party. At the time of the incident I am about to relate, an unusually large and valuable lot of animals were on the premises, for in the stables stood my friend's and his major-domo's saddle-nags, the mounts for the herders, and the work-mules at that time in use, while the corral was nightly full. First, there was in it the "patron's" herd : twenty horses and mares, as many mules, a dozen yoke of work oxen, and about eighty milch cows with their respective calves. Secondly, a band of about thirty saddle-horses, owned by men who, having ridden into the country, had sent them to be "ranched." There were no stages or other conveyances into Arizona at that time, and few men liked to part with their saddle-horses, knowing it was often impossible to buy a mount when wanted, while no man cared to keep his steed in a stable, which it would cost more in one month to do than the horse would sell for "inside," as these pioneers call the United States. Thirdly and lastly, but far from least, the corral held the Government herd of over four hundred beeves.

This herd of Government cattle was what remained of a drove that had come from Mexico to supply with beef the district head-quarters, and which had been herded close thereto, until, having eaten all the grass, it had to be moved further off, where—though strongly guarded by cavalry—the ground being a succession of rocky ravines, timber groves, chaparral thickets, open glades and mountain spurs, some of the beeves were almost daily "lifted," while the cavalry in charge, who furnished herders, continually lost men, picked off by Indians ambushed behind the rocks and in the thickets. Under these circumstances, our enterprising patron thought he saw a chance to "surround a few dollars," and offered to take the entire charge of the drove at a price per head per month, representing how much better it would be for them to feed on the abundance of first quality grass in his valley, how much safer they would be, and that the arrangement would not only liberate the cavalry from an arduous service, and—considering the object of their being in the country—useless duty, but save valuable lives from being literally thrown away. At the same time he did not neglect to ask the biggest consideration he thought it possible to obtain as an equivalent for so many advantages. An officer had gone down from the district head-quarters to view the rancho, and ascertain how its owner proposed to take care of the cattle, and his report being favourable, there they were.

It had been stipulated my friend should keep sufficient force on his premises to render an attack on the corral hopeless, that the cattle should be corralled every night, and adequate provision made for their safety during daytime. In fulfilment of which last obligation he had arranged that every morning at daybreak two reliable herders should ride out into the valley, take positions on elevated ground and see it was clear of Indians, that the herd should then be turned out and driven to the feeding-ground by six more herders, two of whom would leave it on arrival there, and, joining the two men who had preceded them, take post right and left in couples on commanding eminences as vedettes, and that the herd should not be driven under any circumstances so far up the valley as to give the Indians a chance to cut it out by a rush from cover between the *hacienda* and the cattle ere the herders could drive them in.

Before the beeves had long been on the rancho, an effort to capture them was made. As the Apaches broke cover, the vedettes fired the alarm, and started for the herd; the herdsmen who were with it instantly "bunched" the stock and drove at a gallop for the corral. There was a race, and the Indians lost it.

Again the Apaches undertook a similar attempt. This time the rush was made closer to the *hacienda*, so that the cattle having farther to go, there might be a better chance to cut them out. It very nearly succeeded; in fact the Indians and the herd met at right angles, but in charging distance of the *hacienda*. Nearly two score men, armed with carbines and six-shooters, dashed out to the rescue, and over a dozen Indians were stretched before they knew what struck them; the remainder turned and fled, and the herd was again saved. This affair seemed to settle the question, no signs of intentions to further molest the stock were given; everybody considered them perfectly safe.

Two months elapsed, and there came a storm—a howler! The valley lay in about the same latitude as does the Arabian desert, and at an elevation of about six thousand feet above the level of the sea, nestled in the midst of the immense mountain tract that constitutes the central plateau of Arizona. The storm was such as only a country so situated could produce. All day long the thunder-clouds had been banking up, and at nine o'clock at night they "turned themselves loose."

During the storm a solitary Apache, naked, unarmed, with only a small red blanket to protect him from the cold rain of a mountain storm, climbed unperceived the corral's wall. Crouched quietly in a corner he patiently waited for day.

Morn broke clear and calm, the storm had only lasted five hours, and the light, porous soil was already dry on its surface. Eight well-mounted and armed "vaquéros" have as usual ranged themselves, waiting for the herd to be turned out. The look-outs have reported "No Indians in sight." The ranch-hands are at breakfast. The gate is opened, the stock commences to pour out; the gateway gets full of them, to shut it would be impossible. Up springs the Apache, vaults on the nearest horse, with one hand clutches his mane, with the other waves his red blanket in the air, yells like a demon, and *en masse* every "hoof" stampedes, with the Indian in their midst, the horse beneath him the most terrified animal of all. As they clear the gateway in a frenzied rush, the Indian clasps his arms around the neck of the unbridled, unsaddled steed he has seized upon, throws his head and body under the horse's neck, and disappears from sight, and in clouds of dust, raised by the quick tramp of more than two thousand feet, the herd tear up the valley. Did the vaquéros attempt to stop that rush? Not they. The steadiest square that stood at Waterloo would have gone down before that solid column of six hundred maddened brutes. A scattered volley is fired, on the chance of "fetching" *that* Indian. It only serves to kill and wound some of the animals. Then two bodies of mounted Apaches dart out from cover, on opposite sides of the valley, close up behind the herd, and they are lost—captured by strategy, courage, and dash, without the loss of a man!

Messengers were instantly despatched to the fort, to report the disaster. A dangerous task, as it was likely, in anticipation of such a step, a small party of Indians might have been left behind to watch the rancho, and cut off its communications; but men in that country were accustomed to brave danger, and they started without hesitation, taking different directions, and—not to run into any already-formed ambush—avoiding all trails and dangerous places, and making their way by circuitous and zigzag courses, arrived in safety. But it was ten o'clock ere the first got to the district head-quarters. By noon a detachment of cavalry was in pursuit, in *very* light marching order. Every man carried his entire shelter and subsistence on his horse. One double blanket, ten days' rations of army biscuit, of bacon, coffee, and sugar; and for camp equipage, one tin cup, one tin plate, a sheath knife, and a water canteen per trooper; and every tenth man, one small fryingpan.

The orders were to follow the lost stock with all speed; stay out, if necessary, while rations could be made to last; recapture what it was possible, and inflict some punishment on the depredators. The expedition was well mounted on Californian horses—the very best for such service—led by an old member of the Indian scout and guide corps, who knew the country well. But the Indians had too great a start for success to be possible except through some lucky chance. By the time the cavalry were in motion the cattle-lifters had been able to drive the stock fifty miles, and had, therefore, eighty miles start. The troops were sixteen days in the field—having eked out their rations with game killed on the march—had followed a most difficult trail nearly two hundred miles into the country of the Pinal-Ápaches, through tremendous cañons, across lava beds, rivers, and mountain ranges; but, except an occasional distant spy, had not seen an Indian, or anything of the lifted herd but their tracks, and the wolf and jaguar-mangled remains of such of them as, giving out from fatigue, had been killed *en route*, or been slaughtered for food by the Indians at their nightly camps. They returned, men and horses done up with rapid travelling, short commons, exposure, and disappointment; and so ended this and many another hard scout I have been on in that desperately difficult country to campaign in—the home of the Apache.

CHAPTER XXXVII.

Pi-Nolé turns his Toes up—A sad Scene—A Privilege of Chiefship—Indian
Impulses—" Hold, enough ! "—The End.

ACCOMPANIED by a sufficient cavalry escort to ensure against any danger of possible complications arising from another Indian "affair," we returned the three chiefs of the Apache-Yumayas according to promise, and parted with our old foes—now friends—with many mutual protestations of admiration and regard, and with a small present of tobacco, &c., from us to them on our own private account.

We had seen the last, excepting one sad scene, of any of that tribe of Indians; the "exigences of the service" soon after causing our removal from the district.

The melancholy interview referred to, one especially so for poor Pi-Nolé, took place some little time after the conclusion of the Apache-Yumayas treaty, when it was supposed all the Indians of that tribe had collected on their reservation, and thus came to pass. While engaged on a general scout we struck quite fresh Indian signs—moccasin tracks—and, following them at a gallop, dashed through a broad belt of chaparral down an open glade, right into a small encampment of Indians. To our amazement they all stood their ground, neither making hostile demonstrations nor evincing any fear of us, and we immediately perceived that they were some of the new " Treaty Indians."

A few men were standing listlessly around, apparently doing nothing, looking, it might be sulky, it might be dejected; and a number of women sat in a circle, rocking themselves to and fro, and uttering a continuous low wailing cry.

Dismounting and stepping up to the group, I asked an old Indian what was the matter. He answered by a gesture, and pointed to a wickee-up close by. I looked into it. There lay poor Pi-Nolé! He was evidently in the last stage of an attack of malignant ague, and although not in a state of unconsciousness, was delirious, for he not only failed to recognise me, even as being a white man, but in muttered tones addressed me as though I had been someone else. Perhaps he thought I was a spirit—who can tell? The words he uttered could bear that construction. Turning to the old Indian who was standing by me, a sorrowful expression softening his stern countenance, I shook my head and said, " Poor Pi-Nolé, he will be dead before many days." " He will be dead before morning," was the reply.

In a rude, unartificial, and inelegant jargon of Indo-Mexican, rendered impressive and intelligible by that extraordinary product of savage intellect, the American-Indian sign-language, the old man, pointing to his prostrate leader, addressed me as follows : " He was a great brave, and he was a chief. He must not die like a dog. No ; a chief should die facing his enemies; but if that cannot be, then he must be killed. To-night, when all are asleep, his own tomahawk will send him home. Are not the women singing the death-song of the brave? None will know the hand that held the weapon. His youngest wife will be watching by her chief, but *she* will never say. In the morning all his arms and possessions will be laid by him; food and water for his journey; dry wood be piled around his wickee-up, and set on fire; we shall go hence, and no Indian will camp here again for ever!"

Here was a custom that was quite new to me; so I made further inquiries, thinking I might have happened on an exceptional case, but it was not so. I ascertained the custom in question was one of the oldest and most imperative of all the tribal regulations of the Apache-Yumayas, that it was a privilege that belonged of right to the dignity of chiefship.

The successful termination to the efforts made to bring the Apache-Yumayas on a reservation may incline the reader to suspect that during the course of the preliminary incidents we had needlessly troubled ourselves with fears and precautions; had, in fact, done those Indians injustice in thought, and disquieted ourselves and others in vain, by our doubts of their *bona fides*. But it must be kept in view that the savage mind is not as the civilised; that the American *indigène*, with all his cunning and *finesse*, is as liable as a child to sudden, apparently irresistible impulses; which, however, are very different from a child's in their intensity and force. Savagery is civilisation's childhood. To the wild, unregulated mind of a savage, a temptation to seize a present advantage, to possess himself of some coveted object, *which is immediately in sight*, or to gratify his natural propensity to kill, by availing himself of a presented chance to murder, is almost irresistible. Irrespective of all ulterior consequences, forgetful of all determinations and deliberations, of all or any settled plans, he will often give way to a frenzy of unreasoning savagery. It is this disturbing element in all calculations of what will be the conduct of the American *wild* Indian, under given circumstances—this unknown quantity in the calculation—that is generally the cause of the disappointments and disasters, which are the common results of all dealings with him.

But I must now cry, "Hold, enough!" hoping not to incur the penalty denounced against him who doth so first, though I greatly fear my tediousness has deserved it. It is written, "A visitor should not wear out his welcome," neither should a writer wear out his readers' patience. Perhaps I may have done so long ago. How can I tell? As I have sat writing, many a half-remembered, many a hitherto forgotten scene, has come again vividly before me. The name of a place, a frontier phrase, a sporting term, has brought with each a long train of old remembrances; some told, more left unmentioned. Of those which have been here set down, many are likely enough of insufficient interest; some better deserving, perhaps, to have been told, have been omitted. Many, from personal considerations and out of regard to others—actors in them—could not be related. Others again, perhaps the most interesting of them all, have been passed over, out of respect to the great sense of propriety, and extreme regard for correctness of expression, moderation of conduct, and generally speaking *les convenances*, that is characteristic of the reading public, before whom I have ventured to appear in print.

The manner of life, which the recollections that have been told give imperfect and insufficient glimpses at, has a charm and freedom all its own; but it entails on him who makes of it practical trial, *real* hardships, great deprivation, not a few dangers.

Therefore, though not regretting the past, I am well satisfied to find myself once more in the enjoyment of the comforts and securities of a high state of civilisation. And as I mentally review my wild experiences, a feeling of deep gratitude comes over me. I cannot fail to realise that I am one who, having often tempted Providence, has been by Him mercifully protected through great and many perils.

THE END.

193, PICCADILLY, LONDON, W.
NOVEMBER, 1877.

Chapman and Hall's

CATALOGUE OF BOOKS,

INCLUDING

DRAWING EXAMPLES, DIAGRAMS, MODELS,
INSTRUMENTS, ETC.

ISSUED UNDER THE AUTHORITY OF

THE SCIENCE AND ART DEPARTMENT,
SOUTH KENSINGTON,

FOR THE USE OF SCHOOLS AND ART AND SCIENCE CLASSES.

NEW NOVELS.

NEW NOVEL, BY THE DUKE DE POMAR.

A SECRET MARRIAGE.
By THE DUKE DE POMAR.
Author of "Fashion and Passion," &c. &c. [3 Vols.

NEW NOVEL, BY ANNIE THOMAS.

A LAGGARD IN LOVE.
By ANNIE THOMAS (Mrs. Pender Cudlip).
Author of "Dennis Donne" and "Called to Account," &c. &c.
Will be ready in a few days. [3 Vols.

NEW NOVEL, BY LADY WOOD.

SHEEN'S FOREMAN
A NOVEL.
By LADY WOOD.
Author of "Sabrina," "Wild Weather," "Through Fire and Water," &c. &c. [3 Vols.

NEW NOVEL, BY JOSEPH HATTON.

THE QUEEN OF BOHEMIA.
A NOVEL.
By JOSEPH HATTON. [2 Vols.

GREY ABBEY.
By OLD CALABAR.
Author of "Jack Blake," "Over Turf and Stubble," &c. &c. [2 Vols.

ROTHERY SELFERT, Q.C.
By JOHN OLLIVE.
Author of "A Wooing of Até."

ARTIST AND AMATEUR;
OR, THE SURFACE OF LIFE.
A NOVEL.
By MRS. CADDY. [3 Vols.

BOOKS

PUBLISHED BY

CHAPMAN AND HALL.

ABBOTT (EDWIN)—Formerly Head-Master of the Philological School—]
A CONCORDANCE OF THE ORIGINAL POETICAL WORKS OF ALEXANDER POPE. With an Introduction on the English of Pope, by EDWIN A. ABBOTT, D.D., Author of "A Shakespearian Grammar," &c. &c. Medium 8vo, price £1 1s.

ABBOTT (SAMUEL)—
ARDENMOHR: AMONG THE HILLS. A Record of Scenery and Sport in the Highlands of Scotland. With Sketches and Etchings by the Author. Demy 8vo, 12s. 6d.

ADAMS (FRANCIS)—
THE FREE-SCHOOL SYSTEM OF THE UNITED STATES. Demy 8vo, 9s.

ADON—
LAYS OF MODERN OXFORD. Illustrated by M. E. EDWARDS, F. LOCKWOOD, and THE AUTHOR. Fcap. 4to, cloth, 6s.

AUSTIN (ALFRED)—
LESZKO THE BASTARD. A Tale of Polish Grief. Crown 8vo, 3s. 6d.

BARTLEY (G. C. T.)—
A HANDY BOOK FOR GUARDIANS OF THE POOR: being a Complete Manual of the Duties of the Office, the Treatment of Typical Cases, with Practical Examples, &c. Crown 8vo, cloth, 3s.

THE PARISH NET: HOW IT'S DRAGGED AND WHAT IT CATCHES. Crown 8vo, cloth, 7s. 6d.

THE SEVEN AGES OF A VILLAGE PAUPER. Crown 8vo, cloth, 5s.

BENSON (W.)—
MANUAL OF THE SCIENCE OF COLOUR. Coloured Frontispiece and Illustrations. 12mo, cloth, 2s. 6d.

PRINCIPLES OF THE SCIENCE OF COLOUR. Small 4to, cloth, 15s.

BLAKE (EDITH OSBORNE)—
TWELVE MONTHS IN SOUTHERN EUROPE. With Illustrations. Demy 8vo, 14s.

A 2

BLANC (CHARLES)—
ART IN ORNAMENT AND DRESS. Translated from the French of CHARLES BLANC, Member of the Institute, and formerly Director of Fine Arts. With Illustrations. Demy 8vo, 10s. 6d.

BLYTH (COLONEL)—
THE WHIST-PLAYER. With Coloured Plates of "Hands." Third Edition. Imp. 16mo, cloth, 5s.

BRADLEY (THOMAS)—*of the Royal Military Academy, Woolwich*—
ELEMENTS OF GEOMETRICAL DRAWING. In Two Parts, with Sixty Plates. Oblong-folio, half-bound, each Part 16s.
Selection (from the above) of Twenty Plates for the use of the Royal Military Academy, Woolwich. Oblong folio, half-bound, 16s.

BRYANT (W. C.)—
THE CIVIL SERVICE OF THE CROWN: its Rise and its Constitution. Small 8vo, cloth, 4s.

BUCKLAND (FRANK)—
LOG-BOOK OF A FISHERMAN AND ZOOLOGIST. Second Edition. With numerous Illustrations. Large crown 8vo, 12s.

BUCKMASTER (J. C.)—
THE ELEMENTS OF MECHANICAL PHYSICS. With numerous Illustrations. Fcap. 8vo, cloth. [*Reprinting.*

BURCHETT (R.)—
DEFINITIONS OF GEOMETRY. New Edition. 24mo, cloth, 5d.
LINEAR PERSPECTIVE, for the Use of Schools of Art. Twenty-first Thousand. With Illustrations. Post 8vo, cloth, 7s.
PRACTICAL GEOMETRY: The Course of Construction of Plane Geometrical Figures. With 137 Diagrams. Eighteenth Edition. Post 8vo, cloth, 5s.

CADDY (MRS.)—
HOUSEHOLD ORGANIZATION. Crown 8vo, 4s.

CAITHNESS (COUNTESS)—
OLD TRUTHS IN A NEW LIGHT: or an Earnest Endeavour to Reconcile Material Science with Spiritual Science and Scripture. Demy 8vo, 15s.

CAMPION (J. S.), *late Major, Staff, 1st Br. C.N.G., U.S.A.*—
ON THE FRONTIER. Reminiscences of Wild Sport, Personal Adventures, and Strange Scenes. With Illustrations. Demy 8vo.
[*In November.*

CARLYLE (DR.)—
DANTE'S DIVINE COMEDY.—Literal Prose Translation of THE INFERNO, with Text and Notes. Second Edition. Post 8vo, 14s.

CARLYLE (THOMAS)—*See pages 17 and 18.*

CLINTON (R. H.)—
A COMPENDIUM OF ENGLISH HISTORY, from the Earliest Times to A.D. 1872. With Copious Quotations on the Leading Events and the Constitutional History, together with Appendices. Post 8vo, 7s. 6d.

CRAIK (GEORGE LILLIE)—
ENGLISH OF SHAKESPEARE. Illustrated in a Philological Commentary on his Julius Cæsar. Fifth Edition. Post 8vo, cloth, 5s.
OUTLINES OF THE HISTORY OF THE ENGLISH LANGUAGE. Ninth Edition. Post 8vo, cloth, 2s. 6d.

DASENT (SIR G. W.)—
JEST AND EARNEST. A Collection of Reviews and Essays. 2 vols. Post 8vo, cloth, £1 1s.
TALES FROM THE FJELD. A Second Series of Popular Tales from the Norse of P. Ch. Asbjörnsen. Small 8vo, cloth, 10s. 6d.

DAUBOURG (E.)—
INTERIOR ARCHITECTURE. Doors, Vestibules, Staircases, Anterooms, Drawing, Dining, and Bed rooms, Libraries, Bank and Newspaper Offices, Shop Fronts and Interiors. With detailed Plans, Sections, and Elevations. A purely practical work, intended for Architects, Joiners, Cabinet Makers, Marble Workers, Decorators; as well as for the owners of houses who wish to have them ornamented by artisans of their own choice. Half-imperial, cloth, £2 12s. 6d.

DAVIDSON (ELLIS A.)—
THE AMATEUR HOUSE CARPENTER: a Guide in Building, Making, and Repairing. With numerous Illustrations, drawn on Wood by the Author. Royal 8vo, 10s. 6d.

DAVISON (THE MISSES)—
TRIQUETI MARBLES IN THE ALBERT MEMORIAL CHAPEL, WINDSOR. A Series of Photographs. Dedicated by express permission to Her Majesty the Queen. The Work consists of 117 Photographs, with descriptive Letterpress, mounted on 49 sheets of cardboard, half-imperial. Price £10 10s.

DE COIN (COLONEL ROBERT L.)—
HISTORY AND CULTIVATION OF COTTON AND TOBACCO. Post 8vo, cloth, 9s.

DE KONINCK (L. L.) and DIETZ (E.)—
PRACTICAL MANUAL OF CHEMICAL ASSAYING, as applied to the Manufacture of Iron from its Ores, and to Cast Iron, Wrought Iron, and Steel, as found in Commerce. Edited, with notes, by ROBERT MALLET. Post 8vo, cloth, 6s.

DE LEUVILLE (LE MARQUIS)—
ENTRE-NOUS. With Portrait. Fourth Edition. Demy 8vo, 5s.
A Smaller Edition, with Portrait. Crown 8vo, 3s.

DE POMAR (THE DUKE)—
FASHION AND PASSION; or, Life in Mayfair. New Edition, in 1 vol. Crown 8vo, 6s.
THE HEIR TO THE CROWN. Crown 8vo, 7s. 6d.

DE WORMS (BARON HENRY)—
ENGLAND'S POLICY IN THE EAST. An Account of the Policy and Interest of England in the Eastern Question, as compared with those of the other European Powers. Sixth Edition. To this Edition has been added the Tripartite Treaty of 1856, and the Black Sea Treaty of 1871. Sixth Edition. Demy 8vo, 5s.
THE AUSTRO - HUNGARIAN EMPIRE: A Political Sketch of Men and Events since 1868. Revised and Corrected, with an Additional Chapter on the Present Crisis in the East. With Maps. Second Edition. Demy 8vo, cloth, 9s.

DICKENS (CHARLES)—See pages 19—22.

DYCE'S COLLECTION. A Catalogue of Printed Books and
Manuscripts bequeathed by the REV. ALEXANDER DYCE to the South Kensington
Museum. 2 vols. Royal 8vo, half-morocco, 14s.

A Collection of Paintings, Miniatures, Drawings, Engravings,
Rings, and Miscellaneous Objects, bequeathed by the REV. ALEXANDER DYCE
to the South Kensington Museum. 1 vol. Royal 8vo, half-morocco, 7s.

DICKENS (CHARLES)—Conducted by—
ALL THE YEAR ROUND. First Series. 20 vols.
Royal 8vo, cloth, 5s. 6d. each.
New Series. Vols. 1 to 12. Royal 8vo, cloth, 5s. 6d. each.

DIXON (W. HEPWORTH)—
THE HOLY LAND. Fourth Edition. With 2 Steel and
12 Wood Engravings. Post 8vo, 10s. 6d.

DRAYSON (LIEUT.-COL. A. W.)—
THE CAUSE OF THE SUPPOSED PROPER MOTION
OF THE FIXED STARS, with other Geometrical Problems in Astronomy hitherto
unsolved. Demy 8vo, cloth, 10s.
THE CAUSE, DATE, AND DURATION OF THE
LAST GLACIAL EPOCH OF GEOLOGY, with an Investigation of a New
Movement of the Earth. Demy 8vo, cloth, 10s.
PRACTICAL MILITARY SURVEYING AND
SKETCHING. Fifth Edition. Post 8vo, cloth, 4s. 6d.

DYCE (WILLIAM), R.A.—
DRAWING-BOOK OF THE GOVERNMENT SCHOOL
OF DESIGN; OR, ELEMENTARY OUTLINES OF ORNAMENT. Fifty
selected Plates. Folio, sewed, 5s.; mounted, 18s.
Text to Ditto. Sewed, 6d.

ELLIOT (FRANCES)—
OLD COURT LIFE IN FRANCE. Third Edition.
Demy 8vo, cloth, 10s. 6d.
THE DIARY OF AN IDLE WOMAN IN ITALY.
Second Edition. Post 8vo, cloth, 6s.
PICTURES OF OLD ROME. New Edition. Post 8vo,
cloth, 6s.

ELLIOT (ROBERT H.)—
EXPERIENCES OF A PLANTER IN THE JUNGLES
OF MYSORE. With Illustrations and a Map. 2 vols. 8vo, cloth, £1 4s
CONCERNING JOHN'S INDIAN AFFAIRS. 8vo,
cloth, 9s.

ENGEL (CARL)—
A DESCRIPTIVE AND ILLUSTRATED CATALOGUE
OF THE MUSICAL INSTRUMENTS in the SOUTH KENSINGTON
MUSEUM, preceded by an Essay on the History of Musical Instruments. Second
Edition. Royal 8vo, half-morocco, 12s.

EWALD (ALEXANDER CHARLES), F.S.A.—
THE LIFE AND TIMES OF PRINCE CHARLES
STUART, COUNT OF ALBANY, commonly called The Young Pretender.
From the State Papers and other Sources. Author of "The Life and Times of
Algernon Sydney," "The Crown and its Advisers," &c. 2 vols. Demy 8vo, £1 8s
SIR ROBERT WALPOLE. A Political Biography,
1676—1745. Demy 8vo, 18s.

CHAPMAN & HALL, 193, PICCADILLY. 7

FALLOUX (COUNT DE), of the French Academy—
AUGUSTIN COCHIN. Translated from the French by
AUGUSTUS CRAVEN. Large crown 8vo, 9s.

FANE (VIOLET)—
DENZIL PLACE : a Story in Verse. Crown 8vo, cloth, 8s.
QUEEN OF THE FAIRIES (A Village Story), and other
Poems. By the Author of "Denzil Place." Crown 8vo, 6s.
ANTHONY BABINGTON : a Drama. By the Author of
"Denzil Place," "The Queen of the Fairies," &c. Crown 8vo, 6s.

FINLAISON (ALEXANDER GLEN)—
NEW GOVERNMENT SUCCESSION-DUTY TABLES.
Third Edition. Post 8vo, cloth, 5s.

FLEMING (GEORGE), F.R.C.S.—
ANIMAL PLAGUES : THEIR HISTORY, NATURE,
AND PREVENTION. 8vo, cloth, 15s.
HORSES AND HORSE-SHOEING : their Origin, History,
Uses, and Abuses. 210 Engravings. 8vo, cloth, £1 1s.
PRACTICAL HORSE-SHOEING : With 37 Illustrations.
Second Edition, enlarged. 8vo, sewed, 2s.
RABIES AND HYDROPHOBIA : THEIR HISTORY,
NATURE, CAUSES, SYMPTOMS, AND PREVENTION. With 8 Illustrations. 8vo, cloth, 15s.
A MANUAL OF VETERINARY SANITARY SCIENCE
AND POLICE. With 33 Illustrations. 2 vols. Demy 8vo, 36s.

FORSTER (JOHN)—
THE LIFE OF CHARLES DICKENS. Uniform with
the "C. D." Edition of his Works. With Numerous Illustrations. 2 vols. 7s.
THE LIFE OF CHARLES DICKENS. With Portraits
and other Illustrations. 15th Thousand. 3 vols. 8vo, cloth, £2 2s.
A New Edition in 2 vols. Demy 8vo, uniform with the
Illustrated Edition of Dickens's Works. Price £1 8s.
SIR JOHN ELIOT : a Biography. With Portraits. New
and cheaper Edition. 2 vols. Post 8vo, cloth, 14s.
OLIVER GOLDSMITH : a Biography. Cheap Edition in
one volume. Small 8vo, cloth, 6s.
WALTER SAVAGE LANDOR : a Biography, 1775–1864.
With Portraits and Vignettes. A New and Revised Edition, in 1 vol. Demy 8vo, 14s.

FORTNUM (C. D. E.)—
A DESCRIPTIVE AND ILLUSTRATED CATALOGUE
OF THE BRONZES OF EUROPEAN ORIGIN in the SOUTH KENSINGTON MUSEUM, with an Introductory Notice. Royal 8vo, half-morocco, £1 10s.
A DESCRIPTIVE AND ILLUSTRATED CATALOGUE
OF MAIOLICA, HISPANO-MORESCO, PERSIAN, DAMASCUS, AND RHODIAN WARES in the SOUTH KENSINGTON MUSEUM. Royal 8vo, half-morocco, £2.

FRANCATELLI (C. E.)—
ROYAL CONFECTIONER : English and Foreign. A
Practical Treatise. With Coloured Illustrations. 3rd Edition. Post 8vo, cloth, 7s. 6d.

GALLENGA (A.)—
THE PEARL OF THE ANTILLES. Post 8vo, cloth, 9s.
GILLMORE (PARKER)—
PRAIRIE AND FOREST: a Description of the Game of North America, with personal Adventures in their pursuit. With numerous Illustrations. 8vo, cloth, 12s.
GOULD (W. BARING)—
HOW TO SAVE FUEL. With Illustrations. Post 8vo, 1s.
HOLBEIN—
TWELVE HEADS AFTER HOLBEIN. Selected from Drawings in Her Majesty's Collection at Windsor. Reproduced in Autotype, in portfolio. 36s.
HALL (SIDNEY)—
A TRAVELLING ATLAS OF THE ENGLISH COUNTIES. Fifty Maps, coloured. New Edition, including the Railways, corrected up to the present date. Demy 8vo, in roan tuck, 10s. 6d.
HARDY (CAPT. C.)—
FOREST LIFE IN ACADIE; and Sketches of Sport and Natural History in the Lower Provinces of the Canadian Dominion. With Illustrations. 8vo, cloth, 18s.
HOVELACQUE (ABEL)—
THE SCIENCE OF LANGUAGE: LINGUISTICS, PHILOLOGY, AND ETYMOLOGY. With Maps. Large crown 8vo, cloth, 5s. Being the first volume of "The Library of Contemporary Science."
(*For list of other Works of the same Series, see page 24.*)
HULME (F. E.)—
A Series of 60 Outline Examples of Free-hand Ornament. Royal 8vo, mounted, 10s. 6d.
HUMPHRIS (H. D.)—
PRINCIPLES OF PERSPECTIVE. Illustrated in a Series of Examples. Oblong-folio, half-bound, and Text 8vo, cloth, £1 1s.
JACQUEMART (ALBERT)—
THE HISTORY OF FURNITURE. Researches and Notes on Objects of Art which form Articles of Furniture, or would be interesting to Collectors. Translated from the French and Edited by Mrs. BURY PALLISER. With 200 Illustrations. Imperial 8vo. [*In November.*
JAGOR (F.)—
PHILIPPINE ISLANDS, THE. With numerous Illustrations and a Map. Demy 8vo, 16s.
JARRY (GENERAL)—
NAPIER (MAJ.-GEN. W. C. E.)—OUTPOST DUTY. Translated, with TREATISES ON MILITARY RECONNAISSANCE AND ON ROAD-MAKING. Third Edition. Crown 8vo, 5s.
KEBBEL (T. E.)—
THE AGRICULTURAL LABOURER. A Short Survey of his Position. Crown 8vo, 6s.
KEMPIS (THOMAS À)—
THE IMITATION OF CHRIST. Beautifully Illustrated Edition. Demy 8vo. [*In November.*

KLACZKO (M. JULIAN)—
TWO CHANCELLORS: PRINCE GORTCHAKOF and
PRINCE BISMARCK. Translated by Mrs. Tait. New and cheaper edition, 6s.

LACROIX (P.)—
SCIENCE AND LITERATURE IN THE MIDDLE
AGES AND AT THE PERIOD OF THE RENAISSANCE. With 13
Coloured Illustrations and 400 Wood Engravings. (This Volume completes the
Series.) Imperial 8vo. [In November.

THE ARTS OF THE MIDDLE AGES AND AT THE
PERIOD OF THE RENAISSANCE. With 19 Chromo-lithographs and over
400 Woodcuts. A New Edition, on large paper. Imperial 8vo, half-morocco,
£1 11s. 6d.

THE MANNERS, CUSTOMS, AND DRESS OF THE
MIDDLE AGES. With 15 Chromo-lithographs and over 400 Wood Engravings.
A New Edition, on large paper. Imperial 8vo, half-morocco, £1 11s. 6d.

THE MILITARY AND RELIGIOUS LIFE IN THE
MIDDLE AGES AND OF THE PERIOD OF THE RENAISSANCE.
With 14 Chromo-lithographs and upwards of 400 Engravings on Wood. Imperial
8vo, half-morocco, £1 11s. 6d.

THE EIGHTEENTH CENTURY: its Institutions, Customs, and Costumes. France 1700-1789. Illustrated with 21 Chromo-lithographs
and 351 Wood Engravings. On large paper. Imperial 8vo, half-morocco, £2 2s.

LEE (HENRY, F.L.S., F.G.S., F.Z.S., &c., Naturalist of the Brighton
Aquarium)—
AQUARIUM NOTES. THE OCTOPUS; or, The
"Devil-fish of Fiction and of Fact." With Illustrations. Crown 8vo, 3s.

LEGGE (ALFRED OWEN)—
PIUS IX. The Story of his Life to the Restoration in
1850, with Glimpses of the National Movement in Italy. Author of "The Growth
of the Temporal Power in Italy." 2 vols. Demy 8vo, £1 12s.

LETOURNEAU (DR. CHARLES)—
BIOLOGY. With Illustrations. Forming a new volume
of "The Library of Contemporary Science." [In October.

LYNCH (REV. T. T.)—
MEMORIALS OF THEOPHILUS TRINAL,
STUDENT. New Edition, enlarged. Crown 8vo, cloth extra, 6s.

LYTTON (ROBERT, LORD)—
POETICAL WORKS—COLLECTED EDITION. Now
Issuing in Monthly Volumes.
 FABLES IN SONG. 2 vols. Fcap. 8vo, 12s.
 LUCILE. 1 vol. Fcap. 8vo, 6s.
 THE WANDERER. 1 vol. Fcap. 8vo, 6s.
 Vol. V. in the Press.

MALLET (DR. J. W.)—
COTTON: THE CHEMICAL, &c., CONDITIONS OF
ITS SUCCESSFUL CULTIVATION. Post 8vo, cloth, 7s. 6d.

MALLET (ROBERT)—
GREAT NEAPOLITAN EARTHQUAKE OF 1857.
First Principles of Observational Seismology, as developed in the Report to the
Royal Society of London, of the Expedition made into the Interior of the Kingdom
of Naples, to investigate the circumstances of the great Earthquake of December,
1857. Maps and numerous Illustrations. 2 vols. Royal 8vo, cloth, £3 3s.

MASKELL (WILLIAM)—
A DESCRIPTION OF THE IVORIES, ANCIENT AND
MEDIÆVAL, in the SOUTH KENSINGTON MUSEUM, with a Preface. With numerous Photographs and Woodcuts. Royal 8vo, half-morocco, £1 1s.

MAZADE (CHARLES DE)—
THE LIFE OF COUNT CAVOUR. Translated from the French. Demy 8vo, 16s.

MELVILLE (G. J. WHYTE-)—
ROSINE. With Illustrations. Demy 8vo. Uniform with "Katerfelto," 16s.

SISTER LOUISE; or, The Story of a Woman's Repentance. With Illustrations by MIRIAM KERNS. Demy 8vo, 16s.

KATERFELTO: A Story of Exmoor. With 12 Illustrations by COLONEL H. HOPE CREALOCKE. Fourth Edition. Large crown, 8s.
(*For Cheap Editions of other Works, see page 25.*)

MEREDITH (GEORGE)—
MODERN LOVE, AND POEMS OF THE ENGLISH
ROADSIDE, with Poems and Ballads. Fcap. 8vo, cloth, 6s.

MILLER (JOAQUIN)—
THE SHIP IN THE DESERT. By the Author of "Songs of the Sierras," &c. Fcap. 8vo, 6s.

MOLESWORTH (W. NASSAU)—
HISTORY OF ENGLAND FROM THE YEAR 1830
TO THE RESIGNATION OF THE GLADSTONE MINISTRY.
A Cheap Edition, carefully revised, and carried up to March 1874 crown 8vo, 18s.
A School Edition, in 1 vol. Post 8vo, 7s. 6d.

MONTAGU (THE RIGHT HON. LORD ROBERT, M.P.)—
FOREIGN POLICY: ENGLAND AND THE EASTERN
QUESTION. Second Edition. Demy 8vo, 14s.

MORLEY (HENRY)—
ENGLISH WRITERS. Vol. I. Part I. THE CELTS
AND ANGLO-SAXONS. With an Introductory Sketch of the Four Periods of English Literature. Part II. FROM THE CONQUEST TO CHAUCER. (Making 2 vols.) 8vo, cloth, £1 2s.
*** Each Part is indexed separately. The Two Parts complete the account of English Literature during the Period of the Formation of the Language, or of THE WRITERS BEFORE CHAUCER.

Vol. II. Part I. **FROM CHAUCER TO DUNBAR.**
8vo, cloth, 12s.

TABLES OF ENGLISH LITERATURE. Containing 20 Charts. Second Edition, with Index. Royal 4to, cloth, 12s.
In Three Parts. Parts I. and II., containing Three Charts, each 1s. 6d. Part III., containing 14 Charts, 7s. Part III. also kept in Sections, 1, 2, and 5, 1s. 6d. each; 3 and 4 together, 3s. *** The Charts sold separately.

MORLEY (JOHN)—
CRITICAL MISCELLANIES. Second Series. France in the Eighteenth Century—Robespierre—Turgot—Death of Mr. Mill—Mr. Mill on Religion—On Popular Culture—Macaulay. Demy 8vo, cloth, 14s.

CRITICAL MISCELLANIES. First Series. Demy 8vo, 14s.

MORLEY (JOHN) *Continued—*

ROUSSEAU. 2 vols. 8vo, cloth, £1 6s.

VOLTAIRE. Cheap Edition. Crown 8vo, 6s.

STRUGGLE FOR NATIONAL EDUCATION. Third Edition. 8vo, cloth, 3s.

ON COMPROMISE. New Edition. Crown 8vo, 3s. 6d.

MORRIS (M. O'CONNOR)—

HIBERNICA VENATICA. Large crown 8vo. [*In October.*

TRIVIATA; or, Cross Road Chronicles of Passages in Irish Hunting History during the season of 1875-76. With Illustrations. Large crown 8vo, 16s.

NEWTON (E. TULLEY, F.G.S.)—Assistant-Naturalist H.M. Geological Survey—

THE TYPICAL PARTS IN THE SKELETONS OF A CAT, DUCK, AND CODFISH, being a Catalogue with Comparative Descriptions arranged in a Tabular Form. Demy 8vo, cloth, 3s.

OLIVER (PROFESSOR), F.R.S., &c.—

ILLUSTRATIONS OF THE PRINCIPAL NATURAL ORDERS OF THE VEGETABLE KINGDOM, PREPARED FOR THE SCIENCE AND ART DEPARTMENT, SOUTH KENSINGTON. Oblong 8vo, with 109 Plates. Price, plain, 16s. ; coloured, £1 6s.

PARR (HARRIETT)—Author of "Essays in the Silver Age," &c.—

DE GUÉRIN (MAURICE AND EUGÉNIE). A Monograph. Crown 8vo, cloth, 6s.

PIM (B.) and SEEMAN (B.)—

DOTTINGS ON THE ROADSIDE IN PANAMA, NICARAGUA, AND MOSQUITO. With Plates and Maps. 8vo, cloth, 18s.

POLLEN (J. H.)—

ANCIENT AND MODERN FURNITURE AND WOODWORK IN THE SOUTH KENSINGTON MUSEUM. With an Introduction, and Illustrated with numerous Coloured Photographs and Woodcuts. Royal 8vo, half-morocco, £1 1s.

PUCKETT (R. CAMPBELL)—Head-Master of the Bath School of Art—

SCIOGRAPHY; or, Radial Projection of Shadows. New Edition. Crown 8vo, cloth, 6s.

RANKEN (W. H. L.)—

THE DOMINION OF AUSTRALIA. An Account of its Foundations. Post 8vo, cloth, 12s.

REDGRAVE (RICHARD)—

MANUAL AND CATECHISM ON COLOUR. 24mo, cloth, 9d.

REDGRAVE (SAMUEL)—

A DESCRIPTIVE CATALOGUE OF THE HISTORICAL COLLECTION OF WATER-COLOUR PAINTINGS IN THE SOUTH KENSINGTON MUSEUM. With an Introductory Notice by SAMUEL REDGRAVE. With numerous Chromo-lithographs and other Illustrations. Published for the Science and Art Department of the Committee of Council on Education. Royal 8vo, £1 1s.

RIDGE (DR. BENJAMIN)—
OURSELVES, OUR FOOD, AND OUR PHYSIC.
Twelfth Edition. Fcap 8vo, cloth, 1s. 6d.

ROBINSON (C. E.)—
THE CRUISE OF THE *WIDGEON*: 700 Miles in
a Ten-Ton Yawl, from Swanage to Hamburg, through the Dutch Canals and the Zuyder Zee, German Ocean, and the River Elbe. With 4 Illustrations, drawn on Wood, by the Author. Second Edition. Large crown 8vo, 9s.

ROBINSON (J. C.)—
ITALIAN SCULPTURE OF THE MIDDLE AGES
AND PERIOD OF THE REVIVAL OF ART. A descriptive Catalogue of that Section of the South Kensington Museum comprising an Account of the Acquisitions from the Gigli and Campana Collections. With 20 Engravings. Royal 8vo, cloth, 7s. 6d.

ROBSON (GEORGE)—
ELEMENTARY BUILDING CONSTRUCTION. Illus-
trated by a Design for an Entrance, Lodge, and Gate. 15 Plates. Oblong folio, sewed, 8s.

ROBSON (REV. J. H., M.A., LL.M.)—late Foundation Scholar of Downing College, Cambridge—
AN ELEMENTARY TREATISE ON ALGEBRA.
Post 8vo, 6s.

ROCK (THE VERY REV. CANON, D.D.)—
ON TEXTILE FABRICS. A Descriptive and Illustrated
Catalogue of the Collection of Church Vestments, Dresses, Silk Stuffs, Needlework, and Tapestries in the South Kensington Museum. Royal 8vo, half-morocco, £1 11s. 6d.

SALUSBURY (PHILIP H. B.)—Lieut. 1st Royal Cheshire Light Infantry—
TWO MONTHS WITH TCHERNAIEFF IN SERVIA.
Large crown 8vo, 9s.

SCHMID (HERMAN) and STIELER (KARL)—
BAVARIAN HIGHLANDS (THE) AND THE SALZ-
KAMMERGUT. Profusely illustrated by G. Closs, W. Diez, A. von Ramberg, K. Raup, J. G. Steffan, F. Volty, J. Watter, and others. With an Account of the Habits and Manners of the Hunters, Poachers, and Peasantry of these Districts. Super-royal 4to, cloth, £1 5s.

SCOTT (SIR SIBBALD D.)—
TO JAMAICA AND BACK. With Frontispiece. Crown
8vo, 10s. 6d.

SHIRREFF (EMILY)—
A SKETCH OF THE LIFE OF FRIEDRICH
FRÖBEL, together with a Notice of MADAME VON MARENHOLTZ BULOW'S Personal Recollections of F. FROBEL. Crown 8vo, sewn, 1s.

SHUTE (ANNA CLARA)—
POSTHUMOUS POEMS. Crown 8vo, cloth, 8s.

SKERTCHLY (J. A.)—
DAHOMEY AS IT IS: being a Narrative of Eight
Months' Residence in that Country, with a Full Account of the Notorious Annual Customs, and the Social and Religious Institutions of the Ffons. With Illustrations. 8vo, cloth, £1 1s.

SPALDING (CAPTAIN)—
    KHIVA AND TURKESTAN, translated from the Russian,
    with Map. Large crown 8vo, 9s.

SPICER (HENRY)—
    ACTED DRAMAS. Crown 8vo, 8s.

ST. CLAIR (S. G. B., Captain late 21st Fusiliers) and CHARLES A. BROPHY—
    TWELVE YEARS' RESIDENCE IN BULGARIA.
    Revised Edition. Demy 8vo, 9s.

STORY (W. W.)—
    ROBA DI ROMA. Seventh Edition, with Additions and
    Portrait. Post 8vo, cloth, 10s. 6d.
    THE PROPORTIONS OF THE HUMAN FRAME,
    ACCORDING TO A NEW CANON. With Plates. Royal 8vo, cloth, 10s.
    CASTLE ST. ANGELO. Uniform with "Roba di Roma."
    With Illustrations. Large crown 8vo, 10s. 6d.

STREETER (E. W.)—
    PRECIOUS STONES AND GEMS. An exhaustive and
    practical Work for the Merchant, Connoisseur, or the Private Buyer. Treats
    upon all descriptions of Precious Stones, giving their History, Habitat, Value, and
    Uses for Ornament, together with much Information regarding their Matrices or
    Rough State. With Coloured Illustrations, Photographs, &c. Demy 8vo, 18s.
    GOLD; OR, LEGAL REGULATIONS FOR THIS
    METAL N DIFFERENT COUNTRIES OF THE WORLD. [In the Press.

TOPINARD (DR. PAUL)—
    ANTHROPOLOGY. With a Preface by Professor PAUL
    BROCA, Secretary of the Société d'Anthropologie. With numerous Illustrations
    Forming a new volume of "The Library of Contemporary Science." [In November.

TROLLOPE (ANTHONY)—
    THE PRIME MINISTER. 4 vols. Crown 8vo, cloth,
    £2 2s.
    AUSTRALIA AND NEW ZEALAND. A Cheap Edition
    in Four Parts, with the Maps. Small 8vo, cloth, 3s. each.
        NEW ZEALAND.
        VICTORIA AND TASMANIA.
        NEW SOUTH WALES AND QUEENSLAND.
        SOUTH AUSTRALIA AND WESTERN AUSTRALIA.
    HUNTING SKETCHES. Cloth, 3s. 6d.
    TRAVELLING SKETCHES. Cloth, 3s. 6d.
    CLERGYMEN OF THE CHURCH OF ENGLAND.
    3s. 6d.
    THE BELTON ESTATE. 5s.
    THE WAY WE LIVE NOW. With 40 Illustrations.
    2 vols. Demy 8vo, £1 1s.
        (For Cheap Editions of other Works, see page 25.)

TROLLOPE (T. A.)—
HISTORY OF THE PAPAL CONCLAVES. Demy 8vo, 16s.

TWINING (T.)—
SCIENCE MADE EASY. By the Author of "Technical Training." Being a Progressive Course of Elementary Lectures for delivery by amateurs, for use in schools, and for home study. To be completed in Six Parts, at 1s. each. The first Four Parts are now ready. Special Sets of Apparatus and Diagrams. Explanatory Prospectuses supplied post free.

VON GUNTHER (LA COMTESSE)—
TALES AND LEGENDS OF THE TYROL. Collected and Arranged. Crown 8vo, cloth, 5s.

WAHL (O. H.)—
THE LAND OF THE CZAR. Demy 8vo, 16s.

WESTWOOD (J. O.), M.A., F.L.S., &c. &c.—
A DESCRIPTIVE AND ILLUSTRATED CATALOGUE OF THE FICTILE IVORIES IN THE SOUTH KENSINGTON MUSEUM. With an Account of the Continental Collections of Classical and Mediæval Ivories. Royal 8vo, half-morocco, £1 4s.

WHEELER (G. P.)—
VISIT OF THE PRINCE OF WALES. A Chronicle of H.R.H.'s Journeyings in India, Ceylon, Spain, and Portugal. Large crown 8vo, 12s.

WHITE (WALTER)—
HOLIDAYS IN TYROL: Kufstein, Klobenstein, and Paneveggio. Large crown 8vo, 14s.

EASTERN ENGLAND. From the Thames to the Humber. 2 vols. Post 8vo, cloth, 18s.

MONTH IN YORKSHIRE. Fourth Edition. With a Map. Post 8vo, cloth, 4s.

LONDONER'S WALK TO THE LAND'S END, AND A TRIP TO THE SCILLY ISLES. With 4 Maps. Second Edition. Post 8vo, 4s.

WORNUM (R. N.)—
HOLBEIN (HANS)—LIFE. With Portrait and Illustrations. Imperial 8vo, cloth, £1 11s. 6d.

THE EPOCHS OF PAINTING. A Biographical and Critical Essay on Painting and Painters of all Times and many Places. With numerous Illustrations. Demy 8vo, cloth, £1.

ANALYSIS OF ORNAMENT: THE CHARACTERISTICS OF STYLES. An Introduction to the Study of the History of Ornamental Art. With many Illustrations. Sixth Edition. Royal 8vo, cloth, 8s.

WYNTER (DR.)—
FRUIT BETWEEN THE LEAVES. By the Author of "Curiosities of Civilisation," "Our Social Bees," "Peeps into the Human Hive," &c. &c. 2 vols. Crown 8vo, 18s.

WYON (F. W.)—
HISTORY OF GREAT BRITAIN DURING THE
REIGN OF QUEEN ANNE. 2 vols. Demy·8vo, £1 12s.

YOUNGE (C. D.)—
PARALLEL LIVES OF ANCIENT AND MODERN
HEROES. New Edition. 12mo, cloth, 4s. 6d.

AUSTRALIAN MEAT: RECIPES FOR COOKING AUS-
TRALIAN MEAT, with Directions for Preparing Sauces suitable for the same.
By a Cook. 12mo, sewed, 9d.

CEYLON : being a General Description of the Island, Historical,
Physical, Statistical. Containing the most Recent Information. With Map. By
an Officer, late of the Ceylon Rifles. 2 vols. Demy 8vo, £1 8s.

COLONIAL EXPERIENCES ; or, Incidents and Reminiscences
of Thirty-four Years in New Zealand. By an Old Colonist. With a Map.
Crown 8vo. [In October.

ELEMENTARY DRAWING-BOOK. Directions for Intro-
ducing the First Steps of Elementary Drawing in Schools and among Workmen.
Small 4to, cloth, 4s. 6d.

FORTNIGHTLY REVIEW.—First Series, May, 1865, to Dec.
1866. 6 vols. Cloth, 13s. each.

New Series, 1867 to 1872. In Half-yearly Volumes. Cloth,
13s. each.

From January, 1873, to December, 1876, in Half-yearly
Volumes. Cloth, 16s. each.

GERMAN NATIONAL COOKERY FOR ENGLISH
KITCHENS. With Practical Descriptions of the Art of Cookery as performed in
Germany, including small Pastry and Confectionery, Preserving, Pickling, and
making of Vinegars, Liqueurs, and Beverages, warm and cold, also the Manufacture
of the various German Sausages. Post 8vo, cloth, 7s.

OUR CREED : Being an Appeal to the Church of England
regarding some Doubts about the Truth of Ecclesiastical Christianity. By a
BARRISTER. Demy 8vo, 6s.

OUR OWN MISANTHROPE. Reprinted from " Vanity Fair."
By ISHMAEL. Crown 8vo, 7s.

PAST DAYS IN INDIA ; or, Sporting Reminiscences of the
Valley of the Saone and the Basin of Singrowlee. By a late CUSTOMS OFFICER,
N.W. Provinces, India. Post 8vo, 10s. 6d.

PRO NIHILO: THE PRELUDE TO THE ARNIM
TRIAL. An English Edition. Demy 8vo, 7s. 6d.

SHOOTING, YACHTING, AND SEA-FISHING TRIPS,
at Home and on the Continent. Second Series. By "WILDFOWLER," "SNAP-
SHOT." 2 vols., crown 8vo, £1 1s.

SHOOTING AND FISHING TRIPS IN ENGLAND,
FRANCE, ALSACE, BELGIUM, HOLLAND, AND BAVARIA. By "WILD-
FOWLER," "SNAPSHOT." 2 vols. Large crown 8vo, £1 1s.

SPORT IN MANY LANDS. By " The Old Shekarry." With
164 Illustrations. 2 vols. Demy 8vo, £1 10s.

UNIVERSAL CATALOGUE OF BOOKS ON ART. Compiled for the use of the National Art Library, and the Schools of Art in the United Kingdom. In 2 vols. Crown 4to, half-morocco, £2 2s.

WOLF HUNTING AND WILD SPORT IN BRITTANY. By the Author of "Dartmoor Days," &c. With Illustrations by COLONEL CREALOCKE, C.B. Large crown 8vo, 12s.

SOUTH KENSINGTON MUSEUM SCIENCE AND ART HANDBOOKS.

Published for the Committee of Council on Education.

BRONZES. By C. DRURY E. FORTNUM, F.S.A. With numerous Woodcuts. Forming a new volume of "The South Kensington Museum Art Handbooks." [*In October.*

PLAIN WORDS ABOUT WATER. By A. H. CHURCH, M.A., Oxon., Professor of Chemistry in the Agricultural College, Cirencester. Published for the Committee of Council on Education. In the Press.

ANIMAL PRODUCTS: their Preparation, Commercial Uses, and Value. By T. L. SIMMONDS, Editor of the *Journal of Applied Science*. Large crown 8vo, 7s. 6d.

FOOD: A Short Account of the Sources, Constituents, and Uses of Food; intended chiefly as a Guide to the Food Collection in the Bethnal Green Museum. By A. H. CHURCH, M.A., Oxon., Professor of Chemistry in the Agricultural College, Cirencester. Large crown 8vo, 3s.

SCIENCE CONFERENCES. Delivered at the South Kensington Museum. Crown 8vo, 6s.

ECONOMIC ENTOMOLOGY. By ANDREW MURRAY, F.L.S., APTERA. With numerous Illustrations. Large crown 8vo, 7s. 6d.

HANDBOOK TO THE SPECIAL LOAN COLLECTION of Scientific Apparatus. Large crown 8vo, 3s.

THE INDUSTRIAL ARTS: Historical Sketches. With 242 Illustrations. Demy 8vo, 7s. 6d.

TEXTILE FABRICS. By the Very Rev. DANIEL ROCK, D.D. With numerous Woodcuts. Large crown 8vo, 2s. 6d.

IVORIES: ANCIENT AND MEDIÆVAL. By WILLIAM MASKELL. With numerous Woodcuts. Large crown 8vo, 2s. 6d.

ANCIENT & MODERN FURNITURE & WOODWORK. By JOHN HUNGERFORD POLLEN. With numerous Woodcuts. Large crown 8vo, 2s. 6d.

MAIOLICA. By C. DRURY E. FORTNUM, F.S.A. With numerous Woodcuts. Large crown 8vo, 2s. 6d.

MUSICAL INSTRUMENTS. By CARL ENGEL. With numerous Woodcuts. Large crown 8vo, 2s. 6d.

MANUAL OF DESIGN, compiled from the Writings and Addresses of RICHARD REDGRAVE, R.A., Surveyor of Her Majesty's Pictures, late Inspector-General for Art, Science and Art Department. By GILBERT R. REDGRAVE. With Woodcuts. Large crown 8vo, 2s. 6d.

PERSIAN ART. By MAJOR R. MURDOCK SMITH, R.E. With Additional Illustrations. [*In November.*

CARLYLE'S (THOMAS) WORKS.

LIBRARY EDITION COMPLETE.

Handsomely printed in 34 vols. Demy 8vo, cloth,£15.

SARTOR RESARTUS. The Life and Opinions of Herr
Teufelsdrockh. With a Portrait, 7s. 6d.

THE FRENCH REVOLUTION. A History. 3 vols., each 9s.

LIFE OF FREDERICK SCHILLER AND EXAMINATION
OF HIS WORKS. With Supplement of 1872. Portrait and Plates, 9s. The Supplement *separately*, 2s.

CRITICAL AND MISCELLANEOUS ESSAYS. With Portrait.
6 vols., each 9s.

ON HEROES, HERO WORSHIP, AND THE HEROIC
IN HISTORY. 7s. 6d.

PAST AND PRESENT. 9s.

OLIVER CROMWELL'S LETTERS AND SPEECHES. With
Portraits. 5 vols., each 9s.

LATTER-DAY PAMPHLETS. 9s.

LIFE OF JOHN STERLING. With Portrait, 9s.

HISTORY OF FREDERICK THE SECOND. 10 vols.,
each 9s.

TRANSLATIONS FROM THE GERMAN. 3 vols., each 9s.

GENERAL INDEX TO THE LIBRARY EDITION. 8vo,
cloth, 6s.

EARLY KINGS OF NORWAY: also AN ESSAY ON THE
PORTRAITS OF JOHN KNOX. Crown 8vo, with Portrait Illustrations, 7s. 6d.

CARLYLE'S (THOMAS) WORKS—*Continued*—

CHEAP AND UNIFORM EDITION.

In 23 vols., Crown 8vo, cloth, £7 5s.

THE FRENCH REVOLUTION:
A History. 2 vols., 12s.

OLIVER CROMWELL'S LETTERS AND SPEECHES, with Elucidations, &c. 3 vols., 18s.

LIVES OF SCHILLER AND JOHN STERLING. 1 vol., 6s.

CRITICAL AND MISCELLANEOUS ESSAYS. 4 vols., £1 4s.

SARTOR RESARTUS AND LECTURES ON HEROES. 1 vol., 6s.

LATTER-DAY PAMPHLETS. 1 vol., 6s.

CHARTISM AND PAST AND PRESENT. 1 vol., 6s.

TRANSLATIONS FROM THE GERMAN OF MUSÆUS, TIECK, AND RICHTER. 1 vol., 6s.

WILHELM MEISTER, by Göthe. A Translation. 2 vols., 12s.

HISTORY OF FRIEDRICH THE SECOND, called Frederick the Great. Vols. I. and II., containing Part I.—" Friedrich till his Accession." 14s. Vols. III. and IV., containing Part II.—" The First Two Silesian Wars." 14s. Vols. V., VI., VII., completing the Work, £1 1s.

PEOPLE'S EDITION.

In 37 vols., small Crown 8vo. Price 2s. each vol., bound in cloth; or in sets of 37 vols. in 18, cloth gilt, for £3 14s.

SARTOR RESARTUS.

FRENCH REVOLUTION. 3 vols.

LIFE OF JOHN STERLING.

OLIVER CROMWELL'S LETTERS AND SPEECHES. 5 vols.

ON HEROES AND HERO WORSHIP.

PAST AND PRESENT.

CRITICAL AND MISCELLANEOUS ESSAYS. 7 vols.

LATTER-DAY PAMPHLETS.

LIFE OF SCHILLER.

FREDERICK THE GREAT. 10 vols.

WILHELM MEISTER. 3 vols.

TRANSLATIONS FROM MUSÆUS, TIECK, AND RICHTER. 2 vols.

GENERAL INDEX.

DICKENS'S (CHARLES) WORKS.
ORIGINAL EDITIONS.
In Demy 8vo.

THE MYSTERY OF EDWIN DROOD. With Illustrations by S. L. Fildes, and a Portrait engraved by Baker. Cloth, 7s. 6d.

OUR MUTUAL FRIEND. With Forty Illustrations by Marcus Stone. Cloth, £1 1s.

THE PICKWICK PAPERS. With Forty-three Illustrations by Seymour and Phiz. Cloth, £1 1s.

NICHOLAS NICKLEBY. With Forty Illustrations by Phiz. Cloth, £1 1s.

SKETCHES BY "BOZ." With Forty Illustrations by George Cruikshank. Cloth, £1 1s.

MARTIN CHUZZLEWIT. With Forty Illustrations by Phiz. Cloth, £1 1s.

DOMBEY AND SON. With Forty Illustrations by Phiz. Cloth, £1 1s.

DAVID COPPERFIELD. With Forty Illustrations by Phiz. Cloth, £1 1s.

BLEAK HOUSE. With Forty Illustrations by Phiz. Cloth, £1 1s.

LITTLE DORRIT. With Forty Illustrations by Phiz. Cloth, £1 1s.

THE OLD CURIOSITY SHOP. With Seventy-five Illustrations by George Cattermole and H. K. Browne. A New Edition. Uniform with the other volumes, £1 1s.

BARNABY RUDGE: a Tale of the Riots of 'Eighty. With Seventy-eight Illustrations by G. Cattermole and H. K. Browne. Uniform with the other volumes, £1 1s.

CHRISTMAS BOOKS: Containing—The Christmas Carol; The Cricket on the Hearth; The Chimes; The Battle of Life; The Haunted House. With all the original Illustrations. Cloth, 12s.

OLIVER TWIST and TALE OF TWO CITIES. In one volume. Cloth, £1 1s.

OLIVER TWIST. Separately. With Twenty-four Illustrations by George Cruikshank.

A TALE OF TWO CITIES. Separately. With Sixteen Illustrations by Phiz. Cloth, 9s.

*** *The remainder of Dickens's Works were not originally printed in Demy 8vo.*

DICKENS'S (CHARLES) WORKS—*Continued*—

LIBRARY EDITION.

In Post 8vo. With the Original Illustrations, 30 vols., cloth, £12.

				s.	d.
PICKWICK PAPERS	43 Illustrns.,	2 vols.	..	16	0
NICHOLAS NICKLEBY	39 "	2 vols.	..	16	0
MARTIN CHUZZLEWIT	40 "	2 vols.	..	16	0
OLD CURIOSITY SHOP and REPRINTED PIECES	36 "	2 vols.	..	16	0
BARNABY RUDGE and HARD TIMES..	36 "	2 vols.	..	16	0
BLEAK HOUSE	40 "	2 vols.	..	16	0
LITTLE DORRIT	40 "	2 vols.	..	16	0
DOMBEY AND SON	38 "	2 vols.	..	16	0
DAVID COPPERFIELD	38 "	2 vols.	..	16	0
OUR MUTUAL FRIEND	40 "	2 vols.	..	16	0
SKETCHES BY "BOZ"	39 "	1 vol.	..	8	0
OLIVER TWIST	24 "	1 vol.	..	8	0
CHRISTMAS BOOKS	17 "	1 vol.	..	8	0
A TALE OF TWO CITIES	16 "	1 vol.	..	8	0
GREAT EXPECTATIONS	8 "	1 vol.	..	8	0
PICTURES FROM ITALY and AMERICAN NOTES	8 "	1 vol.	..	8	0
UNCOMMERCIAL TRAVELLER	8 "	1 vol.	..	8	0
CHILD'S HISTORY OF ENGLAND	8 "	1 vol.	..	8	0
EDWIN DROOD and MISCELLANIES	12 "	1 vol.	..	8	0
CHRISTMAS STORIES from "Household Words," &c..	16 "	1 vol.	..	8	0

THE "CHARLES DICKENS" EDITION.

In Crown 8vo. In 21 vols., cloth, with Illustrations, £3 9s. 6d.

			s.	d.
PICKWICK PAPERS	8 Illustrations	..	3	6
MARTIN CHUZZLEWIT	8 "	..	3	6
DOMBEY AND SON	8 "	..	3	6
NICHOLAS NICKLEBY	8 "	..	3	6
DAVID COPPERFIELD	8 "	..	3	6
BLEAK HOUSE	8 "	..	3	6
LITTLE DORRIT	8 "	..	3	6
OUR MUTUAL FRIEND	8 "	..	3	6
BARNABY RUDGE	8 "	..	3	6
OLD CURIOSITY SHOP	8 "	..	3	6
A CHILD'S HISTORY OF ENGLAND	4 "	..	3	6
EDWIN DROOD and OTHER STORIES	8 "	..	3	6
CHRISTMAS STORIES, from "Household Words"	8 "	..	3	0
TALE OF TWO CITIES	8 "	..	3	0
SKETCHES BY "BOZ"	8 "	..	3	0
AMERICAN NOTES and REPRINTED PIECES	8 "	..	3	0
CHRISTMAS BOOKS	8 "	..	3	0
OLIVER TWIST	8 "	..	3	0
GREAT EXPECTATIONS	8 "	..	3	0
HARD TIMES and PICTURES FROM ITALY	8 "	..	3	0
UNCOMMERCIAL TRAVELLER	4 "	..	3	0

THE LIFE OF CHARLES DICKENS. Uniform with this Edition, with Numerous Illustrations. 2 vols. 3s. 6d. each.

DICKENS'S (CHARLES) WORKS—*Continued—*

THE ILLUSTRATED LIBRARY EDITION.

Complete in 30 Volumes. Demy 8vo, 10s. each; or set, £15.

This Edition is printed on a finer paper and in a larger type than has been employed in any previous edition. The type has been cast especially for it, and the page is of a size to admit of the introduction of all the original illustrations.

No such attractive issue has been made of the writings of Mr. Dickens, which, various as have been the forms of publication adapted to the demands of an ever widely-increasing popularity, have never yet been worthily presented in a really handsome library form.

The collection comprises all the minor writings it was Mr. Dickens's wish to preserve.

SKETCHES BY "BOZ." With 40 Illustrations by George Cruikshank.

PICKWICK PAPERS. 2 vols. With 42 Illustrations by Phiz.

OLIVER TWIST. With 24 Illustrations by Cruikshank.

NICHOLAS NICKLEBY. 2 vols. With 40 Illustrations by Phiz.

OLD CURIOSITY SHOP and REPRINTED PIECES. 2 vols. With Illustrations by Cattermole, &c.

BARNABY RUDGE and HARD TIMES. 2 vols. With Illustrations by Cattermole, &c.

MARTIN CHUZZLEWIT. 2 vols. With 40 Illustrations by Phiz.

AMERICAN NOTES and PICTURES FROM ITALY. 1 vol. With 8 Illustrations.

DOMBEY AND SON. 2 vols. With 40 Illustrations by Phiz.

DAVID COPPERFIELD. 2 vols. With 40 Illustrations by Phiz.

BLEAK HOUSE. 2 vols. With 40 Illustrations by Phiz.

LITTLE DORRIT. 2 vols. With 40 Illustrations by Phiz.

A TALE OF TWO CITIES. With 16 Illustrations by Phiz.

THE UNCOMMERCIAL TRAVELLER. With 8 Illustrations by Marcus Stone.

GREAT EXPECTATIONS. With 8 Illustrations by Marcus Stone.

OUR MUTUAL FRIEND. 2 vols. With 40 Illustrations by Marcus Stone.

CHRISTMAS BOOKS. With 17 Illustrations by Sir Edwin Landseer, R.A., Maclise, R.A., &c. &c.

HISTORY OF ENGLAND. With 8 Illustrations by Marcus Stone.

CHRISTMAS STORIES. (From "Household Words" and "All the Year Round.") With 14 Illustrations.

EDWIN DROOD AND OTHER STORIES. With 12 Illustrations by S. L. Fildes.

DICKENS'S (CHARLES) WORKS—*Continued—*

HOUSEHOLD EDITION.

In Crown 4to vols. Now Publishing in Weekly Penny Numbers and Sixpenny Monthly Parts. Each Penny Number will contain Two Illustrations.

15 Volumes completed.

OLIVER TWIST, with 28 Illustrations, cloth, 2s. 6d.; paper, 1s. 6d.
MARTIN CHUZZLEWIT, with 59 Illustrations, cloth, 4s.; paper, 3s.
DAVID COPPERFIELD, with 60 Illustrations and a Portrait, cloth, 4s.; paper, 3s.
BLEAK HOUSE, with 61 Illustrations, cloth, 4s.; paper, 3s.
LITTLE DORRIT, with 58 Illustrations, cloth, 4s.; paper, 3s.
PICKWICK PAPERS, with 56 Illustrations, cloth, 4s.; paper, 3s.
BARNABY RUDGE, with 46 Illustrations, cloth, 4s.; paper, 3s.
A TALE OF TWO CITIES, with 25 Illustrations, cloth, 2s. 6d.; paper, 1s. 6d.
OUR MUTUAL FRIEND, with 58 Illustrations, cloth, 4s.; paper, 3s.
NICHOLAS NICKLEBY, with 59 Illustrations by F. Barnard, cloth, 4s.; paper, 3s.
GREAT EXPECTATIONS, with 26 Illustrations by F. A. Frazer, cloth, 2s. 6d.; paper, 1s. 9d.
OLD CURIOSITY SHOP, with 39 Illustrations by Charles Green, cloth, 4s.; paper, 3s.
SKETCHES BY "BOZ," with 36 Illustrations by F. Barnard, cloth, 2s. 6d.; paper, 1s. 9d.
HARD TIMES, with 20 Illustrations by H. French, cloth, 2s.; paper, 1s. 6d.
DOMBEY AND SON, with 61 Illustrations by F. Barnard, cloth, 4s.; paper, 3s.
UNCOMMERCIAL TRAVELLER, with 26 Illustrations by E. G. Dalziel, cloth, 2s. 6d.; paper, 1s. 9d.

Messrs. CHAPMAN & HALL trust that by this Edition they will be enabled to place the works of the most popular British Author of the present day in the hands of all English readers.

The next Volume will be CHRISTMAS BOOKS.

PEOPLE'S EDITION.

PICKWICK PAPERS. In Boards. Illustrated. 2s.
SKETCHES BY BOZ. In Boards. Illustrated. 2s.
OLIVER TWIST. In Boards. Illustrated. 2s.
NICHOLAS NICKLEBY. In Boards. Illustrated. 2s.

MR. DICKENS'S READINGS.

Fcap. 8vo, sewed.

CHRISTMAS CAROL IN PROSE. 1s.
CRICKET ON THE HEARTH. 1s.
CHIMES: A GOBLIN STORY. 1s.
STORY OF LITTLE DOMBEY. 1s.
POOR TRAVELLER, BOOTS AT THE HOLLY-TREE INN, and MRS. GAMP. 1s.

A CHRISTMAS CAROL, with the Original Coloured Plates; being a reprint of the Original Edition. Small 8vo, red cloth, gilt edges, 5s.

# THE LIBRARY
OF
CONTEMPORARY SCIENCE.

Some degree of truth has been admitted in the charge not unfrequently brought against the English, that they are assiduous rather than solid readers. They give themselves too much to the lighter forms of literature. Technical Science is almost exclusively restricted to its professed votaries, and, but for some of the Quarterlies and Monthlies, very little solid matter would come within the reach of the general public.

But the circulation enjoyed by many of these very periodicals, and the increase of the scientific journals, may be taken for sufficient proof that a taste for more serious subjects of study is now growing. Indeed there is good reason to believe that if strictly scientific subjects are not more universally cultivated, it is mainly because they are not rendered more accessible to the people. Such themes are treated either too elaborately, or in too forbidding a style, or else brought out in too costly a form to be easily available to all classes.

With the view of remedying this manifold and increasing inconvenience, we are glad to be able to take advantage of a comprehensive project recently set on foot in France, emphatically the land of Popular Science. The well-known publishers MM. Reinwald and Co., have made satisfactory arrangements with some of the leading *savants* of that country to supply an exhaustive series of works on each and all of the sciences of the day, treated in a style at once lucid, popular, and strictly methodic.

The names of MM. P. Broca, Secretary of the Société d'Anthropologie; Ch. Martins, Montpellier University; C. Vogt, University of Geneva; G. de Mortillet, Museum of Saint Germain; A. Guillemin, author of "Ciel" and "Phénomènes de la Physique;" A. Hovelacque, editor of the "Revue de Linguistique;" Dr. Dally, Dr. Letourneau, and many others, whose co-operation has already been secured, are a guarantee that their respective subjects will receive thorough treatment, and will in all cases be written up to the very latest discoveries, and kept in every respect fully abreast of the times.

We have, on our part, been fortunate in making such further arrangements with some of the best writers and recognised authorities here, as will enable us to present the series in a thoroughly English dress to the reading public of this country. In so doing we feel convinced that we are taking the best means of supplying a want that has long been deeply felt.

[OVER.

BOOKS PUBLISHED BY

LIBRARY OF CONTEMPORARY SCIENCE—*Continued*—

The volumes in actual course of execution, or contemplated, will embrace such subjects as:

SCIENCE OF LANGUAGE. [*Ready.*	PHILOSOPHY.
BIOLOGY. [*In November.*	ARCHITECTURE.
ANTHROPOLOGY. [*In December.*	CHEMISTRY.
COMPARATIVE MYTHOLOGY.	EDUCATION.
ASTRONOMY.	GENERAL ANATOMY.
PREHISTORIC ARCHÆOLOGY.	ZOOLOGY.
ETHNOGRAPHY.	BOTANY.
GEOLOGY.	METEOROLOGY.
HYGIENE.	HISTORY.
POLITICAL ECONOMY.	FINANCE.
PHYSICAL AND COMMERCIAL GEOGRAPHY.	MECHANICS. STATISTICS, &c. &c.

All the volumes, while complete and so far independent in themselves, will be of uniform appearance, slightly varying, according to the nature of the subject, in bulk and in price.

When finished they will form a Complete Collection of Standard Works of Reference on all the physical and mental sciences, thus fully justifying the general title chosen for the series—"LIBRARY OF CONTEMPORARY SCIENCE."

"This is a translation of the first work of a new French series of Popular Scientific Works. The high character of the series, and also its bias, may be inferred from the names of some of its writers, *e.g.* P. Broca, Ch. Martins, C. Vogt, &c. The English publishers announce that the present volume will be followed immediately by others on Anthropology and Biology. If they are like their precursor, they will be clear and well written, somewhat polemical, and nobly contemptuous of opponents. . . . The translator has done his work throughout with care and success."—*Athenæum*, Sept. 22, 1877.

LEVER'S (CHARLES) WORKS.

THE ORIGINAL EDITION with THE ILLUSTRATIONS.
In 17 vols. Demy 8vo. Cloth, 6s. each.

CHEAP EDITION.
Fancy boards, 2s. 6d.

CHARLES O'MALLEY.	DAVENPORT DUNN.
TOM BURKE.	DODD FAMILY.
THE KNIGHT OF GWYNNE.	SIR BROOKE FOSBROOKE.
MARTINS OF CROMARTIN.	BRAMLEIGHS OF BISHOP'S FOLLY.
THE DALTONS.	LORD KILGOBBIN.
ROLAND CASHEL.	

Fancy boards, 2s.

THE O'DONOGHUE.	LUTTRELL OF ARRAN.
FORTUNES OF GLENCORE.	RENT IN THE CLOUD and ST. PATRICK'S EVE.
HARRY LORREQUER.	
ONE OF THEM.	CON CREGAN.
A DAY'S RIDE.	ARTHUR O'LEARY.
JACK HINTON.	THAT BOY OF NORCOTT'S.
BARRINGTON.	CORNELIUS O'DOWD.
TONY BUTLER.	SIR JASPER CAREW.
MAURICE TIERNAY.	

Also in sets, 27 vols. Cloth, for £4 4s.

TROLLOPE'S (ANTHONY) WORKS.
CHEAP EDITION.
Boards, 2s. 6d., cloth, 3s. 6d.

PHINEAS FINN.
ORLEY FARM.
CAN YOU FORGIVE HER?
PHINEAS REDUX.
HE KNEW HE WAS RIGHT

RALPH THE HEIR.
THE BERTRAMS.
EUSTACE DIAMONDS.
VICAR OF BULLHAMPTON.

Boards, 2s., cloth, 3s.

KELLYS AND O'KELLYS.
McDERMOT OF BALLYCLORAN.
CASTLE RICHMOND.
BELTON ESTATE.
MISS MACKENSIE.
LADY ANNA.

RACHEL RAY.
TALES OF ALL COUNTRIES.
MARY GRESLEY.
LOTTA SCHMIDT.
LA VENDÉE.
DOCTOR THORNE.

WHYTE-MELVILLE'S WORKS.
CHEAP EDITION.
Crown 8vo, fancy boards, 2s. each, or 2s. 6d. in cloth.

UNCLE JOHN. A Novel.
THE WHITE ROSE.
CERISE. A Tale of the Last Century.
BROOKES OF BRIDLEMERÈ.
"BONES AND I;" or, The Skeleton at Home.
"M., OR N." Similia Similibus Curantur.
CONTRABAND; or, A Losing Hazard.
MARKET HARBOROUGH; or, How Mr. Sawyer went to the Shires.
SARCHEDON. A Legend of the Great Queen.
SONGS AND VERSES.
SATANELLA. A Story of Punchestown.
THE TRUE CROSS. A Legend of the Church.
KATERFELTO. A Story of Exmoor.
SISTER LOUISE; or, A Story of a Woman's Repentance.

CHAPMAN & HALL'S
List of Books, Drawing Examples, Diagrams, Models, Instruments, &c.

INCLUDING

THOSE ISSUED UNDER THE AUTHORITY OF THE SCIENCE AND ART DEPARTMENT, SOUTH KENSINGTON, FOR THE USE OF SCHOOLS AND ART AND SCIENCE CLASSES.

BARTLEY (G. C. T.)—
CATALOGUE OF MODERN WORKS ON SCIENCE AND TECHNOLOGY. Post 8vo, sewed, 1s.

BENSON (W.)—
PRINCIPLES OF THE SCIENCE OF COLOUR. Small 4to, cloth, 15s.

MANUAL OF THE SCIENCE OF COLOUR. Coloured Frontispiece and Illustrations. 12mo, cloth, 2s. 6d.

BRADLEY (THOMAS)—of the Royal Military Academy, Woolwich—
ELEMENTS OF GEOMETRICAL DRAWING. In Two Parts, with 60 Plates. Oblong-folio, half-bound, each part 16s.
Selections (from the above) of 20 Plates, for the use of the Royal Military Academy, Woolwich. Oblong-folio, half-bound, 16s.

BURCHETT—
LINEAR PERSPECTIVE. With Illustrations. Post 8vo, cloth, 7s.

PRACTICAL GEOMETRY. Post 8vo, cloth, 5s.

DEFINITIONS OF GEOMETRY. Third Edition. 24mo, sewed, 5d.

CUBLEY (W. H.)—
A SYSTEM OF ELEMENTARY DRAWING. With Illustrations and Examples. Imperial 4to, sewed, 8s.

DAVISON (ELLIS A.)—
DRAWING FOR ELEMENTARY SCHOOLS. Post 8vo, cloth, 3s.

MODEL DRAWING. 12mo, cloth, 3s.

THE AMATEUR HOUSE CARPENTER: A Guide in Building, Making, and Repairing. With numerous Illustrations, drawn on Wood by the Author. Demy 8vo, 10s. 6d.

DELAMOTTE (P. H.)—
PROGRESSIVE DRAWING-BOOK FOR BEGINNERS. 12mo, 3s. 6d.

DICKSEE (J. R.)—
SCHOOL PERSPECTIVE. 8vo, cloth, 5s.

DYCE—
DRAWING-BOOK OF THE GOVERNMENT SCHOOL OF DESIGN: ELEMENTARY OUTLINES OF ORNAMENT. 50 Plates. Small folio, sewed, 5s.; mounted, 18s.

INTRODUCTION TO DITTO. Fcap. 8vo, 6d.

FOSTER (VERE)—
DRAWING-BOOKS:
(*a*) Forty Numbers, at 1d. each.
(*b*) Fifty-two Numbers, at 3d. each. The set *b* includes the subjects in *a*.

HENSLOW (PROFESSOR)—
ILLUSTRATIONS TO BE EMPLOYED IN THE PRACTICAL LESSONS ON BOTANY. Prepared for South Kensington Museum. Post 8vo, sewed, 6d.

HULME (F. E.)—
SIXTY OUTLINE EXAMPLES OF FREEHAND ORNAMENT. Royal 8vo, mounted, 10s. 6d.

JEWITT—
HANDBOOK OF PRACTICAL PERSPECTIVE. 18mo, cloth, 1s. 6d.

KENNEDY (JOHN)—
FIRST GRADE PRACTICAL GEOMETRY. 12mo, 6d.
FREEHAND DRAWING-BOOK. 16mo, cloth, 1s. 6d.

LINDLEY (JOHN)—
SYMMETRY OF VEGETATION: Principles to be observed in the delineation of Plants. 12mo, sewed, 1s.

MARSHALL—
HUMAN BODY. Text and Plates reduced from the large Diagrams. 2 vols., cloth, £1 1s.

NEWTON (E. TULLEY, F.G.S.)—
THE TYPICAL PARTS IN THE SKELETONS OF A CAT, DUCK, AND CODFISH, being a Catalogue with Comparative Descriptions arranged in a Tabular Form. Demy 8vo, 3s.

OLIVER (PROFESSOR)—
ILLUSTRATIONS OF THE VEGETABLE KINGDOM. 109 Plates. Oblong 8vo, cloth. Plain, 16s.; coloured, £1 6s.

PUCKETT (R. CAMPBELL)—
SCIOGRAPHY, OR RADIAL PROJECTION OF SHADOWS. Crown 8vo, cloth, 6s.

REDGRAVE—
MANUAL AND CATECHISM ON COLOUR. Fifth Edition. 24mo, sewed, 9d.

ROBSON (GEORGE)—
ELEMENTARY BUILDING CONSTRUCTION. Oblong folio, sewed, 8s.

WALLIS (GEORGE)—
DRAWING-BOOK. Oblong, sewed, 3s. 6d.; mounted, 8s.

WORNUM (R. N.)—
THE CHARACTERISTICS OF STYLES: An Introduction to the Study of the History of Ornamental Art. Royal 8vo, cloth, 8s.

DIRECTIONS FOR INTRODUCING ELEMENTARY DRAWING IN SCHOOLS AND AMONG WORKMEN. Published at the Request of the Society of Arts. Small 4to, cloth, 4s. 6d.

DRAWING FOR YOUNG CHILDREN. Containing 150 Copies. 16mo, cloth, 3s. 6d.

EDUCATIONAL DIVISION OF SOUTH KENSINGTON MUSEUM: CLASSIFIED CATALOGUE OF. Ninth Edition. 8vo, 7s.

ELEMENTARY DRAWING COPY-BOOKS, for the use of Children from four years old and upwards, in Schools and Families. Compiled by a Student certificated by the Science and Art Department as an Art Teacher. Seven Books in 4to, sewed:

Book I. Letters, 8d.
,, II. Ditto, 8d.
,, III. Geometrical and Ornamental Forms, 8d.

Book IV. Objects, 8d.
,, V. Leaves, 8d.
,, VI. Birds, Animals, &c., 8d.
,, VII. Leaves, Flowers, and Sprays, 8d.

*** Or in Sets of Seven Books, 4s. 6d.

ENGINEER AND MACHINIST DRAWING-BOOK, 16 Parts, 71 Plates. Folio, £1 12s.; mounted, £3 4s.

EXAMINATION PAPERS FOR SCIENCE SCHOOLS AND CLASSES. Published Annually, 6d. (Postage, 2d.)

PRINCIPLES OF DECORATIVE ART. Folio, sewed, 1s.

SCIENCE DIRECTORY. 12mo, sewed, 2s. (Postage, 3d.)

ART DIRECTORY. 12mo, sewed, 8d. (Postage, 3d.)

COPIES FOR OUTLINE DRAWING:

LETTERS A. O. S., Three Sheets, mounted, 3s.

DE LA RUE'S OUTLINES OF ANIMALS, 1s.

DYCE'S ELEMENTARY OUTLIN OF ORNAMENT, 50 Selected Plates, mounted back and front, 18s.; un ed, sewed, 5s.

WEITBRICHT'S OUTLINES OF ORNAMENT, reproduced by Herman, 12 Plates, mounted back and front, 8s. 6d.; unmounted, 2s.

MORGHEN'S OUTLINES OF THE HUMAN FIGURE, reproduced by Herman, 20 Plates, mounted back and front, 15s.; unmounted, 3s. 4d.

ONE SET OF FOUR PLATES, Outlines of Tarsia, from Gruner, mounted, 3s. 6d. unmounted, 7d.

ALBERTOLLI'S FOLIAGE, one set of Four Plates, mounted, 3s. 6d.; unmounted, 5d.

OUTLINE OF TRAJAN FRIEZE, mounted, 1s.

WALLIS' DRAWING-BOOK, mounted, 8s.; unmounted, 3s. 6d.

OUTLINE DRAWINGS OF FLOWERS, Eight Sheets, mounted, 3s. 6d.; unmounted, 8d.

HULME, F. E., Sixty Examples of Freehand Ornament, mounted, 10s. 6d.

COPIES FOR SHADED DRAWING:

COURSE OF DESIGN. By Ch. Bargue (French), 20 Selected Sheets, 11 at 2s., and 9 at 3s. each. £2 9s.

RENAISSANCE ROSETTE, unmounted, 3d.; mounted, 9d.

SHADED ORNAMENT, mounted, 1s. 2d.

ORNAMENT FROM A GREEK FRIEZE, mounted, 9d.; unmounted, 3d.

PART OF A PILASTER FROM THE ALTAR OF ST. BIAGIO AT PISA mounted, 2s.; unmounted, 1s.

COPIES FOR SHADED DRAWING—*Continued*—
    EARLY ENGLISH CAPITAL, mounted, 1s.
    GOTHIC PATERA, unmounted, 4d.; mounted, 1s.
    RENAISSANCE SCROLL, Tomb in S. M. Dei Frari, Venice, unmounted, 6d.; mounted, 1s. 4d.
    MOULDING OF SCULPTURED FOLIAGE, decorated, unmounted, 6d.; mounted, 1s. 4d.
    ARCHITECTURAL STUDIES. By J. B. TRIPON. 20 Plates, £2.
    MECHANICAL STUDIES. By J. B. TRIPON, 15s. per dozen.
    FOLIATED SCROLL FROM THE VATICAN, unmounted, 5d.; mounted, 1s. 3d.
    TWELVE HEADS after Holbein, selected from his drawings in Her Majesty's Collection at Windsor. Reproduced in Autotype. Half-imperial, 36s.
    LESSONS IN SEPIA, 9s. per dozen, or 1s. each.
    SMALL SEPIA DRAWING COPIES, 9s. per dozen, or 1s. each.

COLOURED EXAMPLES:

    A SMALL DIAGRAM OF COLOUR, mounted, 1s. 6d.; unmounted, 9d.
    TWO PLATES OF ELEMENTARY DESIGN, unmounted, 1s.; mounted, 3s. 9d.
    PETUNIA, mounted, 3s. 9d.; unmounted, 2s. 9d.
    PELARGONIUM, mounted, 3s. 9d.; unmounted, 2s. 9d.
    CAMELLIA, mounted, 3s. 9d.; unmounted, 2s. 9d.
    GROUP OF CAMELLIAS, 12s.
    NASTURTIUM, mounted, 3s. 9d.; unmounted, 2s. 9d.
    OLEANDER, mounted, 3s. 9d.; unmounted, 2s. 9d.
    TORRENIA ASIATICA. Mounted, 3s. 9d.; unmounted, 2s. 9d.
    PYNE'S LANDSCAPES IN CHROMO-LITHOGRAPHY (6), each, mounted 7s. 6d.; or the set, £2 5s.
    COTMAN'S PENCIL LANDSCAPES (set of 9), mounted, 15s.
        ,,   SEPIA DRAWINGS (set of 5), mounted, £1.
    ALLONGE'S LANDSCAPES IN CHARCOAL (6), at 4s. each, or the set, £1 4s.
    4012. BUNCH OF FRUIT, PEARS, &c., 4s. 6d.
    4013. ,, ,, APPLES, 4s. 6d.
    4014. ,, ,, WHITE GRAPES AND PLUMS, 4s. 6d.
    4015. ,, ,, BLACK GRAPES AND PEACHES, 4s. 6d.
    4016. ,, ,, PLUMS, MULBERRIES, &c., 4s. 6d.
    4017. BOUQUET OF FLOWERS, LARGE ROSES, &c., 4s. 6d.
    4018. ,, ,, ROSES AND HEARTSEASE, 3s. 6d.
    4019. ,, ,, SMALL CAMELLIAS, 3s. 6d.
    4020. ,, ,, POPPIES, &c., 3s. 6d.
    4039. ,, ,, CHRYSANTHEMUMS, 4s. 6d.
    4040. ,, ,, LARGE CAMELLIAS, 4s. 6d.
    4077. ,, ,, LILAC AND GERANIUM, 3s. 6d.
    4080. ,, ,, CAMELLIA AND ROSE, 3s. 6d.
    4081. ,, ,, SMALL CAMELLIAS AND BLUE BELLS, 3s. 6d.
    4082. ,, ,, LARGE DAHLIAS, 4s. 6d.
    4083. ,, ,, ROSES AND LILIES, 4s. 6d.
    4090. ,, ,, ROSES AND SWEET PEAS, 3s. 6d.
    4094. ,, ,, LARGE ROSES AND HEARTSEASE, 4s.
    4180. ,, ,, LARGE BOUQUET OF LILAC, 6s. 6d.
    4190. ,, ,, DAHLIAS AND FUCHSIAS, 6s. 6d.

SOLID MODELS, &c.:

*Box of Models, £1 4s.
A Stand with a universal joint, to show the solid models, &c., £1 18s.
*One wire quadrangle, with a circle and cross within it, and one straight wire. One solid cube. One skeleton wire cube. One sphere. One cone. One cylinder. One hexagonal prism. £2 2s.
Skeleton cube in wood, 3s. 6d.
18-inch Skeleton cube in wood, 12s.
*Three objects of *form* in Pottery:
    Indian Jar, ⎫
    Celadon Jar, ⎬ 18s. 6d.
    Bottle, ⎭
*Five selected Vases in Majolica Ware, £2 11s.
*Three selected Vases in Earthenware, 18s.
Imperial Deal Frames, glazed, without sunk rings, 10s.
*Davidson's Smaller Solid Models, in Box, £2.
*Davidson's Advanced Drawing Models (10 models), £9.
*Davidson's Apparatus for Teaching Practical Geometry (22 models), £5.
*Binn's Models for illustrating the elementary principles of orthographic projection as applied to mechanical drawing, in box, £1 10s.
Vulcanite set square, 5s.
Large compasses with chalk-holder, 5s.
*Slip, two set squares and T square, 5s.
*Parkes' case of instruments, containing 6-inch compasses with pen and pencil leg, 5s.
*Prize instrument case, with 6-inch compasses, pen and pencil leg, 2 small compasses, pen and scale, 18s.
6-inch compasses with shifting pen and point, 4s. 6d.
Small compass in case, 1s.

      * Models, &c., entered as sets, cannot be supplied singly.

LARGE DIAGRAMS.

ASTRONOMICAL:

TWELVE SHEETS. Prepared for the Committee of Council on Education by JOHN DREW, Ph. Dr., F.R.S.A. £2 8s.; on rollers and varnished, £4 4s.

BOTANICAL:

NINE SHEETS. Illustrating a Practical Method of Teaching Botany. By Professor HENSLOW, F.L.S. £2.; on canvas and rollers, and varnished, £3 3s.

ILLUSTRATIONS OF THE PRINCIPAL NATURAL ORDERS OF THE VEGETABLE KINGDOM. By Professor OLIVER, F.R.S., F.L.S. 70 Imperial sheets, containing examples of dried Plants, representing the different Orders. £5 5s. the set.

      Catalogue and Index to Oliver's Diagrams, 1s.

BUILDING CONSTRUCTION:

TEN SHEETS. By WILLIAM J. GLENNY, Professor of Drawing, King's College. In sets, £1 1s.

LAXTON'S EXAMPLES OF BUILDING CONSTRUCTION IN TWO DIVISIONS:
First Division, containing 16 Imperial Plates, 10s.
Second Division, containing 16 Imperial Plates, 10s.

BUSBRIDGE'S DRAWINGS OF BUILDING CONSTRUCTION. 11 Sheets. Mounted, 5s. 6d.; unmounted, 2s. 9d.

GEOLOGICAL:

DIAGRAM OF BRITISH STRATA. By H. W. BRISTOW, F.R.S., F.G.S. A Sheet, 4s; mounted on roller and varnished, 7s. 6d.

MECHANICAL:

DIAGRAMS OF THE MECHANICAL POWERS, AND THEIR APPLICATIONS IN MACHINERY AND THE ARTS GENERALLY. By Dr. JOHN ANDERSON.

This Series consists of 8 Diagrams, highly coloured on stout paper, 3 feet 6 inches by 2 feet 6 inches, price £1 per set; mounted on common rollers, £2.

DIAGRAMS OF THE STEAM-ENGINE. By Professor GOODEVE and Professor SHELLEY.

These Diagrams are on stout paper, 40 inches by 27 inches, highly coloured. The price per set of 41 Diagrams (52½ Sheets), £6 6s. These Diagrams can be supplied varnished and mounted on rollers at 2s. 6d. extra per Sheet.

EXAMPLES OF MACHINE DETAILS. A Series of 16 Coloured Diagrams. By Professor UNWIN. £2 2s.

SELECTED EXAMPLES OF MACHINES, OF IRON AND WOOD (French). By STANISLAS PETTIT. 60 Sheets, £3 5s.; 13s. per dozen.

BUSBRIDGE'S DRAWINGS OF MACHINE CONSTRUCTION (22). Mounted, 11s.; unmounted, 5s. 6d.

LESSONS IN MECHANICAL DRAWING. By STANISLAS PETTIT, 1s. per dozen; also larger Sheets, being more advanced copies, 2s. per dozen.

LESSONS IN ARCHITECTURAL DRAWING. By STANISLAS PETTIT. 1s. per dozen; also larger Sheets, being more advanced copies, 2s. per dozen.

PHYSIOLOGICAL:

ELEVEN SHEETS. Illustrating Human Physiology, Life size and Coloured from Nature. Prepared under the direction of JOHN MARSHALL, F.R.S., F.R.C.S., &c. Each Sheet, 12s. 6d. On canvas and rollers, varnished, £1 1s.

1. THE SKELETON AND LIGAMENTS.
2. THE MUSCLES, JOINTS, AND ANIMAL MECHANICS.
3. THE VISCERA IN POSITION.—THE STRUCTURE OF THE LUNGS.
4. THE ORGANS OF CIRCULATION.
5. THE LYMPHATICS OR ABSORBENTS.
6. THE ORGANS OF DIGESTION.
7. THE BRAIN AND NERVES.—THE ORGANS OF THE VOICE.
8. THE ORGANS OF THE SENSES, Plate 1.
9. THE ORGANS OF THE SENSES, Plate 2.
10. THE MICROSCOPIC STRUCTURE OF THE TEXTURES AND ORGANS, Plate 1.
11. THE MICROSCOPIC STRUCTURE OF THE TEXTURES AND ORGANS, Plate 2.

HUMAN BODY, LIFE SIZE. By JOHN MARSHALL, F.R.S., F.R.C.S.

1. THE SKELETON, Front View.
2. THE MUSCLES, Front View.
3. THE SKELETON, Back View.
4. THE MUSCLES, Back View.
5. THE SKELETON, Side View.
6. THE MUSCLES, Side View.
7. THE FEMALE SKELETON, Front View.

Each Sheet, 12s. 6d.; on canvas and rollers, varnished, £1 1s.
Explanatory Key, 1s.

ZOOLOGICAL:

TEN SHEETS. Illustrating the Classification of Animals. By ROBERT PATTERSON. £2.; on canvas and rollers, varnished, £3 10s.

The same, reduced in size, on Royal paper, in 9 Sheets, uncoloured, 12s.

THE FORTNIGHTLY REVIEW.

Edited by JOHN MORLEY.

THE FORTNIGHTLY REVIEW is published on the 1st of every month (the issue on the 15th being suspended), and a Volume is completed every Six Months.

The following are among the Contributors :—

SIR RUTHERFORD ALCOCK.
PROFESSOR BAIN.
PROFESSOR BEESLY.
DR. BRIDGES.
HON. GEORGE C. BRODRICK.
SIR GEORGE CAMPBELL, M.P.
J. CHAMBERLAIN, M.P.
PROFESSOR CLIFFORD, F.R.S.
PROFESSOR SIDNEY COLVIN.
MONTAGUE COOKSON, Q.C.
L. H. COURTNEY, M.P.
G. H. DARWIN.
F. W. FARRAR.
PROFESSOR FAWCETT, M.P.
EDWARD A. FREEMAN.
MRS. GARRET-ANDERSON.
M. E. GRANT-DUFF, M.P.
THOMAS HARE.
F. HARRISON.
LORD HOUGHTON.
PROFESSOR HUXLEY.
PROFESSOR JEVONS.
ÉMILE DE LAVELEYE.
T. E. CLIFFE LESLIE.
GEORGE HENRY LEWES.
RIGHT HON. R. LOWE, M.P.

SIR JOHN LUBBOCK, M.P.
LORD LYTTON.
SIR H. S. MAINE.
DR. MAUDSLEY.
PROFESSOR MAX MÜLLER.
PROFESSOR HENRY MORLEY.
G. OSBORNE MORGAN, Q.C., M.P.
WILLIAM MORRIS.
F. W. NEWMAN.
W. G. PALGRAVE.
WALTER H. PATER.
RT. HON. LYON PLAYFAIR, M.P.
DANTE GABRIEL ROSSETTI.
HERBERT SPENCER.
HON. E. L. STANLEY.
SIR J. FITZJAMES STEPHEN, Q.C.
LESLIE STEPHEN.
J. HUTCHISON STIRLING.
A. C. SWINBURNE.
DR. VON SYBEL.
J. A. SYMONDS.
W. T. THORNTON.
HON. LIONEL A. TOLLEMACHE.
ANTHONY TROLLOPE.
PROFESSOR TYNDALL.
THE EDITOR.

&c. &c. &c.

THE FORTNIGHTLY REVIEW *is published at* 2s. 6d.

CHAPMAN & HALL, 193, PICCADILLY.

CHARLES DICKENS AND EVANS,]   [CRYSTAL PALACE PRESS.

www.ingramcontent.com/pod-product-compliance
Lightning Source LLC
Chambersburg PA
CBHW020541300426
44111CB00008B/749